THE LAW OF THE TEMPLE
IN EZEKIEL 40-48

HARVARD SEMITIC MUSEUM

HARVARD SEMITIC MONOGRAPHS

edited by
Frank Moore Cross

Number 49
The Law of the Temple
in Ezekiel 40-48

by
Steven Shawn Tuell

Steven Shawn Tuell

THE LAW OF THE TEMPLE
IN EZEKIEL 40-48

Scholars Press
Atlanta, Georgia

The Law of the Temple in Ezekiel 40-48

by
Steven Shawn Tuell

Library of Congress Cataloging in Publication Data

Tuell, Steven Shawn.
    The law of the temple in Ezekiel 40-48 / Steven Shawn Tuell.
    p. cm. — (Harvard Semitic monographs : no. 49)
    Includes bibliographical references.
    ISBN 1-55540-717-X (alk. paper)
    1. Bible. O.T. Ezekiel XL-XLVIII—Criticism, interpretation,
etc. 2. Law (Theology)—Biblical teaching. 3. Temples—Biblical
teaching. I. Title. II. Series.
BS1545.2.T84 1992
224'.4084—dc20
                                        92-10130
                                        CIP

Printed in the United States of America
on acid-free paper

TABLE OF CONTENTS

vi

ACKNOWLEDGEMENTS

Dr. S. Dean McBride, Jr., has proven a bottomless source of ideas, information and encouragement, first as my dissertation advisor at Union Theological Seminary in Virginia, and then in the editing and revision of this monograph. I have been proud to work with him, and learn from him. Thanks are also due to Dr. Frank Moore Cross, who has made numerous important critical observations and editorial suggestions; Dr. William H. F. Kuykendall of Erskine Theological Seminary, who guided me through the morass of Egyptian religion; and Dr. J. J. M. Roberts, who at Princeton first involved me in the study of Ezekiel's Temple Vision. The library staff at Union has been unfailingly helpful and generous. Erskine College provided financial support for the publication of this monograph, as well as word processing and printing facilities. To all of you, my deepest and most sincere thanks.

Wendy, my beloved wife and my friend, has supported, encouraged, and loved me through this work. Our three boys, Sean, Anthony, and Mark, were born in the midst of this project; they have given more than they will ever know. I dedicate this piece to my father and mother, Bernard and Mary Tuell, my first Bible teachers, whose love and example brought me to faith in Christ.

Steven Shawn Tuell
February 1992

ABBREVIATIONS

AB	Anchor Bible
AGJU	Arbeiten zur Geschichte des antiken Judentums und des Urchristentums
AJBA	The Australian Journal of Biblical Archaeology
AnBib	Analecta Biblica
ANET³	Ancient Near Eastern Texts Relating to the Old Testament, ed. James B. Pritchard (Princeton: Princeton University, ³1969).
AnOr	Analecta Orientalia
AOAT	Alter Orient und Alten Testament
AOS	American Oriental Series
AP	Aramaic Papyri of the Fifth Century B. C., ed. and tr. Arthur Cowley (Oxford: Clarendon, 1923).
AramB	The Aramaic Bible
ASORDS	American Schools of Oriental Research Dissertation Series
ASTI	Annual of the Swedish Theological Institute
AV	Authorized, or King James, version of the Bible.
BA	The Biblical Archaeologist
BASOR	Bulletin of the American Schools of Oriental Research
BHS	Biblia Hebraica Stuttgartensia
BHT	Beiträge zur Historischen Theologie
BJRL	Bulletin of the John Rylands Library
BKAT	Biblische Kommentar Altes Testament
BZAW	Beihefte zur Zeitschrift fur die alttestamentliche Wissenschaft
CBQ	Catholic Biblical Quarterly
CHJ 1	The Cambridge History of Judaism, ed. W. D. Davies and Louis Finkelstein, Vol. 1: Introduction: The Persian Period (Cambridge: Cambridge University, 1984).
CRB	Cahiers de la Revue Biblique
CTA	Corpus des Tablettes en Cuneiformes Alphabetiques Decouvertes à Ras Shamra-Ugarit de 1929 à 1939. 2 Vols. ed. and tr. Andrée Herdner (Mission de Ras Shamra 10; Paris: Imprimerie Nationale, 1963).
EI	Eretz-Israel
FOTL	The Forms of the Old Testament Literature

G	Old Greek text
Gese	*Der Verfassungsentwurf des Ezechiel (Kap. 40-48) traditionsgeschichtlich untersucht,* Hartmut Gese (Beiträge zur historischen Theologie 25; Tübingen: J. C. B. Mohr [Paul Siebeck], 1957).
GHG	*Gesenius' Hebrew Grammar.* Ed. E. Kautzsch, tr. and rev. A. E. Cowley (Oxford: Clarendon, ^{2}1983).
HAT	Handbuch zum Alten Testament
HELOT	*A Hebrew and English Lexicon of the Old Testament,* ed. F. Brown, S. R. Driver, and C. Briggs (Oxford: Clarendon, 1978).
HSM	Harvard Semitic Monographs Series
HUCA	*Hebrew Union College Annual*
IB	*Interpreters's Bible,* ed. George A. Buttrick (Nashville: Abingdon)
ICC	International Critical Commentary
IEJ	*Israel Exploration Journal*
IJH	*Israelite and Judean History,* ed. John H. Hayes and J. Maxwell Miller (Philadelphia: Westminster, 1977).
Int	*Interpretation: A Journal of Bible and Theology*
JAOS	*Journal of the American Oriental Society*
JBL	*Journal of Biblical Literature*
JBLMS	Journal of Biblical Literature Monograph Series
JPS	*Tanakh,* the translation of the Jewish Publication Society
JNES	*Journal of Near Eastern Studies*
JSOT	*Journal for the Study of the Old Testament*
KAT	Kommentar zum Alten Testament
KHC	Kurzer Hand-Commentar zum Alten Testament
KEH	Kurzgefasstes exegetisches Handbuch
KTU	*Die keilalphabetischen Texte aus Ugarit: Einschliesslich der keilalphabetischen Texte ausserhalb Ugarits,* Vol. 1: *Transkription,* M. Dietrich, O. Loretz, and J. Sanmartín, eds. (Alter Orient und Altes Testament 24; Neukirchen-Vluyn: Neukirchener, 1976).
LCL	Loeb Classical Library
M	Masoretic text
NCB	New Century Bible
NEB	The New English Bible
OIC	Oriental Institute Communications

OTL	Old Testament Library
PEGLBS	*Proceedings of the Eastern Great Lakes Biblical Society*
PRU	*Le Palais Royal d'Ugarit*, Charles Virolleaud, ed, Vol. 5: *Textes en Cunéiformes Alphabétiques des Archives Sud, Sud-ouest et du Petit Palais* (Mission de Ras Shamra 11; Paris: Imprimerie Nationale, 1965).
RSV	The Revised Standard Version
SBLDS	Society of Biblical Literature Dissertation Series
UCPNES	University of California Publications, Near Eastern Studies
UF	*Ugarit-Forschungen*
V	Vulgate
VAB	Vorderasiatische Bibliothek
VT	*Vetus Testamentum*
VT Sup	Supplements to Vetus Testamentum
ZDPV	*Zeitschrift des Deutschen Palästina-Vereins*

After the first citation in a footnote, commentaries are cited by the author's last name. Other sources not abbreviated above are cited by short titles after the first reference.

Chapter One

THE UNITY AND THEME OF THE TEMPLE VISION[1]

In the closing chapters of Ezekiel, a great Temple is described, one reminiscent of Solomon's but in fact like none ever built. From that Temple, a river flows through the land, with healing in its wake; within the Temple dwells the divine Glory, depicted here alone in Ezekiel as coming to rest,[2] never again to be removed. All of these features of Ezekiel's grand vision are embedded in the core of Jewish and Christian devotional and mystical practice.

Yet no less intriguing for the exegete is the legislation promulgated in this elaborate vision report. Here is found the only body of law in the Hebrew Scriptures not placed in the mouth of Moses. Laws regarding sacrifices and festivals, the conduct of the prince, the nature of the priesthood, and the division of the land all center upon the Temple, which is the one common reference for this rich, multifaceted material.

Is there, in fact, any order to be found here? Or has Ezekiel's vision, like a magnet, drawn to itself disconnected and disjointed elements, with no overall purpose? Only by seeking out the connections, if indeed such exist, among the Temple Vision's disparate elements may we find the answer.

I. Rabbinic Views Of The Temple Vision

We moderns are not alone in our difficulty. Ancient interpreters, too, struggled with the character and coherence of Ezekiel's

---

[1] Throughout this monograph, I will use the title "Temple Vision" to refer to the final canonical form of Ezekiel 40-48, and "Law of the Temple" to refer to the material inserted by the redactor. When the need arises to distinguish the final form from what I propose to be the prophet's original, core vision, the latter will be referred to as "the Temple vision," without capitalization.

[2] Compare 43:7 with 1:4-28; 9:3; 10:4-22 and 11:22,23.

Temple Vision. Indeed, rabbinical Judaism considered the study of the text dangerous for any but the mature scholar. In a letter to Paulinus, bishop of Nola, Jerome reports a Jewish regulation of his day barring anyone under the age of thirty from reading either the beginning (chapters 1--3, the vision of the chariot throne), or the ending (chapters 40--48), of Ezekiel's book.[3] Still, despite its difficulties, the text was not rejected by the rabbis. Three times Talmud records the story of Hananiah ben Hezekiah, leader of the school of Shammai, who burned three hundred jars of oil laboring over the text until all the contradictions between the Law of the Temple and the תורה of Moses were resolved.[4] Even so, b. Menahot 46a observes that only when Elijah comes in the messianic age will all the discrepancies be explained.

The rabbis were troubled by the contents of the Temple Vision, as these Talmudic references demonstrate. Yet they would not, or could not, reject the text as Scripture. Indeed, b. Baba Bathra 14b, 15a claims the authority of the Great Synagogue for Ezekiel (as well as the Twelve, Daniel, and Esther). For these traditional Jewish exegetes, the Temple Vision belonged, in its entirety, with the book of Ezekiel. Save for an intriguingly vague tradition preserved by Josephus that Ezekiel left behind two books,[5] no evidence exists that anyone in the early Jewish community considered the book of Ezekiel to be anything other than a unit.

II. Early Critical Study Of The Temple Vision And The Unity Of Ezekiel

Even with the beginning of critical historical investigation of the text, most scholars tended to consider Ezekiel a unified work, and to

---

[3] *St. Jerome*, W. H. Freemantle, A Select Library of Nicene and Post-Nicene Fathers of the Christian Church, 2/6 (New York: Christian Literature , 1893) 502.

[4] b. Shabbat 13b; b. Hagigah 13a; and b. Menahot 45a.

[5] Josephus , *Antiquities*, 10. 5. 1.

treat the Temple Vision as a unified, integral part of that whole.[6] Up to and even into the twentieth century, the consensus of biblical scholarship could be said to be the acceptance of the unity of Ezekiel, and hence the authenticity of the Temple Vision. Rudolf Smend was so impressed by the tight structure and unity of vision in Ezekiel as to write "one could not remove any part without destroying the whole structure)."[7] Little wonder, then, that Smend held the entire text to have been set down at once, on the date given in 40:1.[8] So also Johannes Herrmann, though viewing Ezekiel more as a preaching prophet along the lines of Jeremiah, whose brief sermons were secondarily collected and edited by himself and others, nonetheless could still affirm the fundamental unity of the work under one author.[9]

In recent years, arguments for the unity of the Temple Vision under the authorship of Ezekiel have again been advanced. Menahem Haran holds for a unified text with an exilic dating, related to P in style and concerns if divergent in substance.[10] More recently, Moshe Greenberg has presented arguments based on comparison with other legal materials from the ancient Near East. All of these texts, he notes, exhibit shifts of person (particularly regarding the addressee, when both a king and his descendents are addressed)[11] , and the contents are formulated, not topically, but chronologically,

---

[6] A notable exception, cited by H. H. Rowley ("The Book of Ezekiel in Modern Study," *BJRL* 36 [1953] 155), was G. L. Oeder, who in 1756 rejected chapters 40-48 as inauthentic.

[7] Rudolf Smend, *Der Prophet Ezechiel* (KEH; Leipzig: S. Hirzel, 1880) xxi: "*man könnte kein Stück herausnehmen, ohne die ganze Ensemble zu zerstören* ."

[8] Ibid., xxii.

[9] Johannes Herrmann, *Ezechiel übersetzt und eklärt* (KAT 11; Leipzig: A. Deichert, 1924).

[10] Menahem Haran, "The Law-Code of Ezekiel XL-XLVIII and its Relation to the Priestly School," *HUCA* 50 (1979) 45-71. Although Haran's primary interest, as the title of his article indicates, is in the relative dating of Ezekiel and P (he holds P to be pre-exilic), he makes excellent observations about the literary unity of the Temple Vision.

[11] Moshe Greenberg, "The Design and Themes of Ezekiel's Program of Restoration," *Int* 38 (1984) 186-87. Greenberg considers Hittite texts (most notably, a treaty between Ramses II and Hattusilis, "Instructions for Temple Officials,"and "Instructions for the Commander of the Border Guards") and the Aramaic Sefire treaties.

4   The Law of the Temple

thematically, by social standing, by catchwords, or by association of ideas.[12] Greenberg therefore argues that the shifts in number, style, and theme found in Ezekiel 40--48 need not indicate multiple authorship, but are rather indicative of a style and structure no different from that used in other legal materials in the ancient world. Further, in the first volume of his commentary, Greenberg states unequivocally that nothing in the text argues for a date later than the 571 terminus found in 29:17, and that, moreover, the "program of restoration" in these chapters "is entirely out of line with events after 538, when Cyrus allowed the exiles to return home."[13] Therefore, he places the text squarely in the hands of the prophet.

Susan Niditch has taken a different tack, arguing that the closing chapters of Ezekiel follow the form of a liturgy of divine conquest and victory. The liturgy begins, she proposes, with 38:10-13, which presents the challenge of the mythic enemy to the Lord. The battle and victory are then detailed in 39:1-10, followed by the establishment of order (39:11-16), the victory feast (vv. 17-20), the procession (39:25-29) and climaxing with the building of the temple (40--48).[14] Therefore, Niditch argues, chapters 40--48 are an integral part of an organic whole, reflecting the themes of the creation and ordering of the world also found in Genesis 1--11, and hence must be considered as a unit.[15]

Neither these new arguments, nor the classic positions of Smend or Herrmann, can overcome the overwhelming complexity of the Temple Vision. The text contains not only visionary description, but also cultic legislation, land reform, and anti-Levite polemic. The style of presentation is not consistent, but sometimes loses sight of

---

[12] Ibid., 188-89.

[13] Moshe Greenberg, *Ezekiel 1-20* (AB 22; Garden City: Doubleday, 1983) 15.

[14] Susan Niditch, "Ezekiel 40-48 in a Visionary Context," *CBQ* 48 (1986) 221. Niditch draws upon the work of Paul Hanson ("Old Testament Apocalyptic Reexamined," *Int* 25 [1971] 472-73), who identifies this pattern in the Babylonian *Enuma elish* and the Ugaritic cycle of Baal and Yam-Nahar, and suggests it also appears in Zechariah 9.

[15] Niditch, "Context," 222.

the visionary context (note, for example, the contrast between the monotonous sequences of description and measurement in chapter 40 and the language of command in chapter 45). Greenberg's appeal to ancient Near Eastern parallels does not help us, as the texts to which he refers themselves may well have gone through a process of editing, expansion, and revision; indeed, in the case of the legal documents, it would be most surprising were this not the case.

Not only does the form of materials in the Temple Vision vary, but the content is not always self consistent. For instance, in 40:45-46, a division of the priesthood into house clergy and altar clergy is assumed as a given, a simple division of responsibilities; 44:9-14, however, sees the division as a judgement upon the Levites for their unfaithfulness. It is difficult to see how one author could be responsible for these two conflicting perceptions of the divided ministry of Zadokite and Levite. Little wonder, then, that most contemporary scholars have seen and continue to see layers of expansion in the text.

III. Later Criticism: Unity Rejected

After the turn of the century, the tide in Ezekiel scholarship also began to turn. Gustav Hölscher, influenced in particular by Bernhard Duhm, proposed that Ezekiel "is always essentially a poet."[16] The upshot of this analysis was that only 144 of the book's 1273 verses were deemed authentic,[17] with no authentic material found after chapter 32. Hölscher considered the book to be, in large measure, a pseudepigraph, composed by Zadokite clergy in the time of the fifth-century Judean Restoration.[18] This process of editing and expansion was for Hölscher particularly apparent in the Temple Vision, a text

---

[16] Gustav Hölscher, *Hezekiel: der Dichter und das Buch* (BZAW 39; Giessen: Alfred Töpelmann, 1924) 5: Ezekiel "*in allem wesentlichen Dichter ist.*"

[17] According to the reckoning of Walther Zimmerli, *Ezekiel*, Vol. 1 (tr. Ronald E. Clements ; Hermeneia; Philadelphia: Fortress, 1979) 5. Rowley ("Modern Study," 151), by his count of whole and partial verses deemed genuine by Hölscher, comes up with a slightly more generous 170 authentic verses.

[18] Hölscher, 31-34.

which he declared had been worked and reworked, again and again.[19] Even G. A. Cooke, in his on the whole far more balanced commentary, held that these chapters were an incomprehensible mixture of nearly random accretions.[20] However, the most thoroughgoing criticism of these chapters, and indeed of the whole of Ezekiel, began with the work of Torrey, Herntrich, and Irwin.

Torrey, like Hölscher, deemed the book of Ezekiel a pseud-epigraph. However, he denied that any part of the book derived from an exilic prophet named Ezekiel. The book's true setting was clear from its predominate concern with the people and land of Israel,[21] its description of abominable worship practices in the Temple (8-11),[22] and most especially from the date at 1:1 ("In the thirtieth year..."),[23] : it was set in Jerusalem, in the time of Manasseh. Moreover, that setting was itself fictitious, for the language of the text and the customs and events it describes required that it be placed in the Greek period.[24] For Torrey, the Temple Vision became a firm indicator of this late date:

> It has often been remarked as a curious fact that a priest transported to Babylonia and expecting the destruction of Jerusalem should have devoted so much space to the exact measurements (an astonishing list!),specifications, equipment, and even minor details of service of an imaginary temple assigned to the remote future. But for a priest living in Jerusalem in the latter part of the third century, the construction of just such an elaborate plan as this would have been very natural indeed.   Zerubbabel's temple, which never had been a magnificent building (Ezra 3:12), had stood for nearly 300 years and doubtless

[19] Ibid., 190.

[20] G. A. Cooke, Ezekiel (ICC; Edinburgh: T. and T. Clark, 1936). Cooke (426) believes the Temple Vision to be the collected notes of exiled priests in Babylon "engaged in writing down current practice, suggesting plans for future legislation, and handing about drafts. Some of these experiments have been copied into Ezekiel's book and thus preserved; we may regard them as continuing the work Ezekiel has begun." For Cooke, there is no particular pattern or intentionality behind these texts; indeed (427), he "does not venture to go further than to maintain that the additions were made at various times by various hands."

[21] C. C. Torrey, Pseudo-Ezekiel and the Original Prophecy, (New Haven: Yale University Press, 1930; reprint, Library of Biblical Studies [New York: Ktav, 1970]) 29.

[22] Ibid., 50-52; 64-65.

[23] Ibid., 17-18; 64.

[24] Ibid., 71-101, esp. 99.

was in need of considerable repair, even if it was not felt to be out of date and inadequate. It would not be strange if the routine of its service, under changing conditions, should have departed in some respects from the prescriptions of the Pentateuch, with the full approval of its ministers, who felt that new times permitted a certain amount of innovation.[25]

Finally, according to Torrey, this late Greek period pseudepigraph was reworked by anti-Samaritan editors to support the myth of the Babylonian Exile, created by the Chronicler to deny the legitimacy of the Samaritan temple and cult.[26] As transparently absurd as all of this sounds now, Torrey's proposal nevertheless had the virtue of boldness. In a stroke, most of the unsettling qualities of the text, from the obscure double date in 1:1 to Ezekiel's frequently awkward Hebrew to the depiction of a hopelessly corrupt Temple scant years after the Josianic reforms, were solved. Further, this approach supported Torrey's pet project, the demonstration that the "exile" never took place. Others, emboldened by Torrey's example, were quick to follow.

Volkmar Herntrich tackled head-on the aspect of Ezekiel most perplexing to western academics: the frequent occurrence in the book of informational visions, relating to events in Palestine. Like Torrey, he did so by transferring the setting of the prophecy from Babylon to Jerusalem. The exilic setting and the troubling visionary motif (including the entire text of Ezekiel 40--48) were made the work of an exilic redactor.[27] William Irwin, on the other hand, followed not an historical approach, but a literary one analogous to that of Hölscher. Using Ezekiel 15 as the keystone of his study, he believed that he could identify sparse authentic texts of the prophet, which had then been subjected to laborious commentary. The primary mark of authenticity, for Irwin, was the use of certain typical phrases, especially the introductory formula ויהי דבר יהוה אלי לאמר ("And the word of the Lord came to me saying").[28] His unstinting application of

---

25 Ibid., 100.

26 Ibid., 102-6.

27 Volkmar Herntrich, *Ezechielprobleme* (BZAW 61; Giessen: Alfred Töpelmann, 1933) 124-25.

28 William Irwin, *The Problem of Ezekiel: An Inductive Study* (Chicago: University of Chicago, 1943) 269.

these unbending criteria produced nearly as much carnage as
Hölscher's method:

> There are in the entire book of Ezekiel 1,273 verses; of these, 1,013 are in the
> first thirty-nine chapters. Of these again, 251 are genuine in whole or in part,
> the proportion of their originality varying from complete genuineness to a
> bare minimum of not more than a word or two.[29]

Irwin held our present text of Ezekiel to be the result of generation
upon generation of scholarly interpretation and reinterpretation: "That
chapters are commonly made up of comments on comments, all
resting ultimately on a meager nucleus of original has become a
commonplace of our study."[30] It is to this ever-widening circle of
commentary that the Temple Vision belongs; it bears no relationship
to the genuine Ezekiel, and has no inherent pattern or purpose.[31]

IV. The Current State Of Research

In the wake of this early hypercriticism came a more
conservative reaction, led by C. G. Howie, whose work on the
archaeological background and language of Ezekiel re-established the
reliability of the date, setting, and authorship the book claims for
itself.[32] To Howie's mind, that reliability extended to the Temple
Vision as well; though he regarded it as an originally independent
work, joined secondarily by a redactor to the text of Ezekiel, he
nonetheless identified Ezekiel 40--48 as "a well-known vision of the
prophet."[33]

With Howie's monograph, and the consequent publication of
Georg Fohrer and Kurt Galling's archaeologically-minded commentary, the basic reliability of the text of Ezekiel was re-

---

[29] Ibid., 283.

[30] Ibid., 341.

[31] Ibid., 252-59, esp. 256-57.

[32] Carl G. Howie, *The Date and Composition of Ezekiel* (JBLMS 4; Philadelphia:
Society of Biblical Literature, 1950).

[33] Ibid., 102.

established.[34]   Often, however, the Temple Vision has been left out of
this general rehabilitation of both book and prophet. Walther Eichrodt
judged that chapters 40--48 had been shaped and reshaped, with
additions by many hands for many purposes, with the result that "it is
an illusion to think of its having any ultimate unity as a whole."[35]
While arguing for a single editor for the final edition of the entire book
of Ezekiel, including the Temple Vision[36], Wevers nonetheless holds
that the expansions to the authentic Ezekiel core to the vision have no
unified purpose, but are rather scattered attempts to come to terms
with issues raised by the vision proper and its later redaction.[37]
Indeed, Ronald Hals says of Ezekiel 40--48, "Neither in genre nor in
context, neither in literary-critical analysis nor in structural continuity
as literature, does some impression of a positive sense of
completeness emerge."[38]

These views are as unsatisfactory as those that hold the Temple
Vision to be an original unit. The observations of Smend, Greenberg
and, particularly, Niditch, while they cannot demonstrate a compositional unity for these chapters, do demonstrate a final unity, a
purposive construction at odds with the nearly random portrait drawn
of the Temple Vision by much recent scholarship. It is to the nature
of that construction that we now will turn.

---

[34] Georg Fohrer and Kurt Galling. *Ezechiel* (HAT 13; Tübingen: J. C. B. Mohr
[Paul Siebeck], ²1955).

[35] Walther Eichrodt, *Ezekiel* (tr. Cosslett Quin; OTL; Philadelphia: Westminster,
1970) 530-531.

[36] Indeed, John W. Wevers (*Ezekiel* [NCB; Greenwood: Attic, 1969] 29) relies on
the Temple Vision, in a rather left-handed manner, to establish the final dating of the
entire book: "Since there is no evidence that the traditions represented in chapters 33-
48 show any awareness of the post-exilic Temple or of conditions in Judah after the
return, it would seem likely that he did his work before the end of the sixth century."

[37] Ibid., 4. According to Wevers, the original vision consists of chapters 40-42,
43, 44 and 47.

[38] Ronald M. Hals, *Ezekiel* (FOTL 19; Grand Rapids: William B. Eerdmans, 1989)
287. Note that Hals does not deny a final overall effect to this composition. However, in
his estimation, it is an entirely negative effect, ruling out any attempt to reconstruct
positively any particular plan or program (287-89).

10 The Law of the Temple

V. Gese's *Traditionsgeschichte* Of Ezekiel 40--48

Chief among the current interpreters of the Temple Vision is Hartmut Gese,[39] who has sought to determine, not simply the authenticity or inauthenticity of the various texts attributed to Ezekiel in chapters 40--48, but to reconstruct the order and manner of their composition. Gese proposes that the prophet's original vision has been expanded primarily in a series of three discrete levels: a stratum concerned with the נשיא ("prince," or perhaps, "chief"), a stratum involving the division of the land, and a stratum expressing the rights and privileges of the Zadokite priesthood.

The earliest of these discrete strata is the *nasi-Schicht*, found in 44:1-3; 45:21-25; 46:1-10, 12.[40] In these sections, special cult prerogatives are given to the נשיא, particularly relating to the liturgy involving the eastern gate (46:1-10).[41] Indeed, the *nasi-Schicht* apparently assumes the delivery of Temple offerings as a tax to the נשיא.[42] As a chief distinguishing characteristic of the *nasi-Schicht* is the designation of the people as the עם הארץ ("people of the land," 46:3, 9),[43] Gese finds this stratum not only in Ezekiel 40--48 but also in Leviticus 4, a text which details the sin offering of the נשיא (vv 22-26) and of the עם הארץ (vv 27-35). Granting the complexity of the text from Leviticus, Gese still finds, in this conjunction of the two terms in the same context, a parallel to the situation in Ezekiel 40--48.[44]

Entwined about the material of the *nasi-Schicht*, Gese identifies another discrete layer of tradition, sharply contrasting with its

---

[39] Hartmut Gese, *Der Verfassungsentwurf des Ezechiel (Kap. 40-48) traditionsgeschichtlich untersucht* (BHT 25; Tübingen: J. C. B. Mohr [Paul Siebeck], 1957).

[40] Hence, the כבוד vision of 43:1-11 is deemed by Gese (110) as "*Konstitutiv für die nasi-Schicht* (fundamental for the נשיא-stratum)."

[41] Ibid., 110.

[42] Ibid., 112.

[43] Ibid., 110.

[44] Ibid., 111.

princely context in form, vocabulary, and concerns addressed. These texts (44:6-16; 44:17-31 [an insertion]; 44:28-30a; 45:13-15) are characterized by the restriction of priestly rights to Zadokites, and the demotion of Levites to the status of Temple servants: hence, Gese designates this stratum the *Şadoqidenschicht*.[45] Rather than a tax paid to the נשיא, the *Şadoqidenschicht* speaks of offerings delivered to the priests.[46] Gese considers 45:16-17 a redactional suture, attempting to identify the priestly offering with the princely tax and thereby link the *Şadoqidenschicht* and the *nasi-Schicht*. The effort, however, is wasted: between these two strata, according to Gese, "there is no relationship."[47] Even in form, the *Şadoqidenschicht*, characterized by the addressing of the Israelites in the second plural, is distinct from the *nasi-Schicht*.[48] In the relative scheme of 40--48, this material is to be dated late, owing to the the numerous glosses deriving from it in the older material: 40:46b; 43:19; 48:11.[49] The scheme for the division and boundaries of the land (*Landverteilungspläne*) in 48:1-29, which (apart from the gloss at 48:11) reveals no knowledge of the *Şadoqidenschicht*, is to be located between the two, as "a later expansion and supplement of the נשיא-stratum."[50]

In the final form of the text, these three strata have been woven into the core vision and into each other partly by means of the guidance formula, drawn from 40--42.[51] Hence, the *nasi-Schicht* is connected to the Temple description by 44:1, and the *Landverteilungspläne* is connected to the *nasi-Schicht* by 47:1. Other

---

[45] Ibid., 111.

[46] Ibid., 112.

[47] Ibid., 112:"*bestehen keine Beziehungen.*"

[48] Ibid., 111.

[49] Ibid., 112.

[50] Ibid., 113: "*eine spätere Erweiterung und Erganzung der nasi-schicht .*"

[51] Ibid., 114.

12   The Law of the Temple

techniques, such as the oracular formulae and the use of catchwords,[52] also function to bind these materials into a final, formal unity.

By the connections he establishes among the varied materials of Ezekiel 40--48, Gese has effectively rebutted the arguments of those who would view these texts as a randomly assembled hodge-podge. Each of the three major strata identified by Gese brings together a variety of materials, and demonstrates the intentional reshaping and reinterpretation of our base text, the Temple vision of Ezekiel. Yet, the tradition history reconstructed by Gese also has its problems. Walther Zimmerli, who has largely appropriated the work of Gese,[53] is not so certain that a separate Zadokite stratum exists.[54] Rather, he finds 44:6-16 alone a coherent Zadokite section that has prompted later emendations (called, rather ominously, "metastases") elsewhere in the text. Zimmerli's overall thesis for the composition history of Ezekiel is that the text has been redacted within the confines of an Ezekielian school.[55] Hence, he is able to account at once for the remarkable uniformity that is the book's most striking feature, and still allow for the editorial activity evident throughout the text. It is particularly ironic, then, that Zimmerli's rejection of Gese's Ṣadoqidenschicht results in a text nearly as broken as that espoused by those (like Eichrodt) who claim that no connection or overall intention can be found among the expansions of the vision. Even Zimmerli, in the final analysis, fractures the text of the Temple Vision among numerous levels of redaction to the point that any final unity of the text is rejected.[56]

Gese's claim that the Ṣadoqidenschicht and the nasi-Schicht have nothing to do with one another seems strange. They are, after all, closely interwoven in the text we have, and address fundamentally

---

[52] In Ezek 45, the materials of the נשיא and Zadokite strata are combined by use of the catchword תרומה (Gese, 115; see also Zimmerli, 2:467).

[53] In particular, with regard to Gese's nasi-Schicht (Zimmerli, 2:550).

[54] Ibid., 458.

[55] Zimmerli, 1:71-72.

[56] Zimmerli, 2:547-53.

the same issues of cult and calendar. Yet, the position of Haran and Greenberg, who argue for the unity of all of Ezekiel 40--48,[57] is extreme and untenable--though one can understand their palpable frustration. Between the multi-level redaction history of the text proposed by Gese and the simple unity under the authorship of Ezekiel proposed especially by Greenberg lies a middle ground. I propose that while the basic vision of the prophet has been expanded, the expansion is purposive and deliberate, and has taken place virtually in one sitting.

VI. A New Proposal: The Temple Vision As Religious Polity

The proposal that the text of the Temple Vision has a final, purposive unity is similar in many ways to the creative analysis of Jon Levenson.[58] The text is examined, following Levenson, in the light of parallels from Hebrew Scripture and the ancient Near East, which reveal the mythic power and theological profundity of the vision.[59] Particularly significant is Levenson's suggestion that the very high mountain with which our text begins is typologically related to Sinai, so that Ezekiel becomes a new Moses and the text itself the new תורה.[60] I, too, will argue that the legislation in this text is central to its final function. However, this approach differs from Levenson's on two significant points. First, Levenson's analysis assumes a purposive, unified structure. He does not address the potent arguments against this position mustered especially by Gese and Zimmerli. Here, on the other hand, the attempt is made to demonstrate an overall structure, with connections binding materials Gese and Zimmerli consider unrelated. Second, Levenson considers the Temple Vision an attempt to describe the polity of the eschatological kingdom of Israel.[61] I, on

---

[57] Greenberg, "Design and Themes," esp. 184-89; Haran, "Law-code," 47.

[58] Jon Levenson, *Theology of the Program of Restoration of Ezekiel 40-48* (HSM 10; Missoula: Scholars, 1976).

[59] Ibid., e.g. 14 (where the mountain is related to the Ugaritic Ṣpn).

[60] Ibid., 41.

[61] Ibid., 33.

the contrary, will argue that the institutions described in the Temple Vision are actual institutions, which may be dated by comparative means to the Persian period.

Ezekiel 40--48 is the religious polity of the Judean Restoration, a present-tense description of the authors's self-conception and their conception of God. The final form of the text is built on an authentic vision of Ezekiel, chosen by our editors as the perfect statement of their society's foundation and end: right worship in the right Temple. However, the text assumed its present form in the Persian period, probably during the reign of Darius I.

This thesis will be advanced in seven chapters. In the second chapter, the overall structure of the Temple Vision, and the careful fitting and joining of texts which indicates an intentional, purposive structure, will be described. The third chapter will consider the nature of Persian intervention into the religious institutions of subject peoples, with a twofold aim: first, to demonstrate that the interventions of the Persians into the Judean Temple establishment described particularly in Ezra-Nehemiah were typical of Persian conduct throughout the empire; and second, to suggest that the institutions depicted in the Temple Vision are appropriate to the Persian period. The following three chapters will address the three institutions given particular attention in the legal material: the נשיא, the priesthood and cult of the Temple, and the divisions of the land. In chapter four, the proposal that the נשיא of the Temple Vision was the Persian governor of Restoration Judea will be argued. Chapter five will suggest that the exclusive Zadokite priesthood, anti-Levite polemic, and peculiar cultus of these texts can also best be assigned to the early Persian period. Chapter six, then, will address the problem of the land division texts by suggesting that the borders therein described are roughly equivalent to the borders of the Persian province of Abar-Nahara, to which Judah belonged. The concluding chapter will be a brief summary of the arguments and the evidence, with consideration given to some implications of my findings.

VII. Methodology: Geertz's Semiotic Theory Of Culture And Religion

The attempt to identify the community back of the Temple Vision is doubtless a chancy enterprise. However, it is no more chancy than the attempts of archaeologists to identify communities on the basis of their material remains. The analogy is not frivolous; Carol Meyers has observed that the description of a cult object in a text is no less an "artifact" than the same object, found buried in some ancient ruin.[62] However, for our work, the archaeological analogy would be somewhat forced, for our concern is not with objects, but with a culture. True, the opening third of our text is a detailed description of a Temple complex. However, as will be observed, this material belongs to the prophet's original vision, and hence forms but the prologue for the legislative material which is the work of our proposed community, and therefore the legitimate object of our concern. Since this work proposes to describe and interpret that community, the more apt analogy is the field of anthropology.

Particularly evocative for the interpreter of sacred texts is the anthropological work of Clifford Geertz. Geertz holds to a "semiotic" theory of culture:[63] that is, that a culture is made up of sets of symbols, "interworked systems of construable signs,"[64] which provide the context for the ordered life of a people. The object of anthropology is the intelligible explication of these systems, which Geertz (borrowing from Gilbert Ryle) calls "thick description."[65] The interpreter who

---

[62] Carol L. Meyers, *The Tabernacle Menorah* (ASORDS 2; Missoula: Scholars, 1976) 2: "The problems that beset an archaeologist when he unearths a cultic device are of the same order as the problems that must be dealt with in the examination of the textual description of a cultic device. The description of some appurtenance in the tabernacle texts must be considered as belonging to the same order of evidence as the published plate of some such object in an excavation report. We should not be concerned if the visual description found in the biblical account does not always provide us with an accurate mental image or an exactly reproducible object; for the possession of such an image or object in itself would tell us no more than does the possession of an actual artifact."

[63] Clifford Geertz, *The Interpretation of Cultures* (New York: Basic Books, 1973) 5.

[64] Ibid., 14.

[65] Ibid., 6-7.

reports only the observable phenomena, without a sense for the
interconnectedness of the symbol system, will fall far short of this
interpretive task--but so will the one who loses the particularity of the
data, whose interpretation is based on abstract generalities. "Understanding a people's culture," Geertz insists, "exposes their normalness
without reducing their particularity."[66] To attempt to enter the
thought world of another people and understand their symbol systems
from the inside is, of course, an act of the imagination, and the
interpretation resulting from such an attempt is, in the literal sense,
fictional.[67] This does not, however, mean that the interpretation is
imaginary or untrue--at least, not so long as it is based in the public,
observable facts of a particular culture. "Cultural acts," Geertz
observes, "the construction, apprehension, and utilization of symbolic
forms, are social events like any other; they are as public as marriage
and as observable as agriculture."[68]

For Geertz, it is not culture in general (whatever that might
mean), but cultures in particular that are the proper objects of
anthropological investigation:

> . . .the essential task of theory-building here is not to codify abstract
> regularities but to make thick description possible, not to generalize across
> cases but to generalize within them.[69]

Geertz insists upon this same point in the study of religion.[70] As
cultural systems, religions are, like cultures, symbol sets. Religious
symbols in particular, Geertz observes, have a synthesizing function,
serving to unite

> a people's ethos--the tone, character and quality of their life, its moral and
> aesthetic style and mood--and their world view--the picture they have of the

---

66 Ibid., 14.

67 Ibid., 15.

68 Ibid., 91.

69 Ibid., 26.

70 Ibid., 122: "The nature of the bias religion gives to ordinary life varies with
the religion involved, with the particular dispositions induced in the believer by the
specific conceptions of cosmic order he has come to accept."

way things in sheer actuality are, their most comprehensive ideas of order.[71]

The methodology proposed by Geertz for the interpretation of a living, extant culture may also, we propose, be applied to a culture that is no longer extant. "Rather than beginning," Geertz writes, "with a set of observations and attempting to subsume them under a governing law, such inference begins with a set of (presumptive) signifiers and attempts to place them within an intelligible frame."[72]   This is indeed what this work intends, save that the evidence is derived from a text: the Temple Vision. The redactors of the Temple Vision have already selected out "a set of (presumptive) signifiers" in which one can have a fair degree of confidence: after all, the presumption of the text is that of its authors; the principle of selection is theirs, not ours.   Hearing these texts anew, from that distant perspective, we may rediscover their power to shape and challenge life.

---

[71] Ibid., 89.

[72] Ibid., 26.

Chapter Two

THE TEXT AND STRUCTURE OF THE TEMPLE VISION

The text of Ezekiel 40--48 has at its core an original vision of the prophet, which has been subsequently expanded. This study contends that the expansion of the prophet's core vision took place, not by a process of gradual accretion or by the layering of various strata, but in a single, purposive redaction, aimed at producing a religious polity for restoration Judea.

If this hypothesis is to be established, the final, literary unity of the material in Ezekiel 40--48 must first be demonstrated. Where the prophet's original vision has been expanded, it must be shown that the expansion is deliberate and purposive. To this end, this study will first examine the overall shape of the text. Then, the units of the text will be examined one by one. The ways that each unit coheres internally, and how each relates to the materials it follows and precedes, will be considered.[1]

I. Overall Structure

With 40:1, a major new literary unit of the book clearly begins. The preceding verse, 39:29, marks the definite end of a unit, concluding with the oracular formula נאם אדני יהוה ("word of Lord YHWH"). Verse 40:1 opens with an introductory formula common in Ezekiel's prophecy: a date formula specific to the day.[2] The formula

---

[1] In determining the appropriate sub-units of the text, this study will be guided by the division of the traditional Hebrew text into פרשות. This is an ancient, indeed pre-Masoretic, tradition, present in the scrolls from Qumran and represented in some old Greek texts as well. The tradition seems remarkably stable; except for a few variations we will indicate in context, the paragraphing in Codex Leningradensis, as indicated by the editors of the *BHS*, agrees substantially with the paragraphing of the older Aleppo Codex. These ancient scribal divisions provide us an entry into the way the structure of the text was viewed from early on.

[2] Sixteen different occurrences of the date formula can be found in Ezekiel, each time as the heading of an oracle. Of these, eleven are precise to the year, month and day (1:1; 8:1; 20:1; 24:1; 29:1; 29:17; 30:20; 31:1; 32:1; 33:21; and 40:1). Three others (1:2; 26:1;

for expressing prophetic ecstasy (היתה עלי יד יהוה, "the hand of
YHWH was upon me") and the designation במראות אלהים ("in visions
of God") follow the date.[3] These three formulae appear together two
other times in Ezekiel, in 1:1-3 (the call) and 8:1-3 (the vision of the
abominations). Chapters 1--3, 8--11 and 40--48 are also linked by
mutual reference (8:2 recalls the vision by the river Chebar; 43:3
refers to the river and to the vision of Jerusalem's destruction) and by
the image of the כבוד. Chapters 40--48 are further linked to chapters
8--11 in a pattern of departure and return: the כבוד leaves the
corrupted Temple in 11:22, and returns to the pure Temple in 43:4-5.

We have, then, an interconnected network of three visions,
which stand as the milestones of Ezekiel's ministry, and as key points
in the structure of his book. As the inaugural vision initiates the
prophetic work, and the vision of the abominations and the destruction of Jerusalem stands as the grand turning point and climax, so
these concluding chapters, 40--48, represent the end and goal of
Ezekiel's labors.[4]

The major literary segments that comprise 40--48, for all their
ostensibly disparate character, exhibit broad coherence in content and
arrangement. The structure of the whole may be construed as a
chiasm:

---

and 32:17) are precise to the year and day, while two date in reference to some fixed
event (3:16 refers back to the date of the call vision, and sets its vision seven days later,
while a second date in 40:1 specifies the year as the fourteenth after the fall of
Jerusalem). Interestingly, both 1:1,2 and 40:1 are double dates, though, in light of the
troublesome "thirtieth year" of 1:1, not much can be made of this parallel.

[3] This formula occurs seven times in Ezekiel, always in a visionary context: 1:3;
3:14, 22; 8:1; 33:22; 37:1; and 40:1. Zimmerli (1:42) rightly regards the phenomenon of
prophetic ecstasy as a point of continuity between Ezekiel and the pre-classical
prophets. מראה is relatively rare, occurring only eleven times: Gen 46:2; Num 12:6
(both E); 1 Sam 3:15; Dan 10:7 (2 t.), 8, 16; and Ezek 1:1; 8:3; 40:2; and 43:3.

[4] The only later-dated prophecy in the book, 29:17-21, is a definite appendix,
added when it became clear that the Babylonians were not going to be able to despoil
Tyre; no organic extension of the prophet's work or thought is indicated by it. The
Temple Vision was the last great work of the old priest.

40:1-4 Introduction
   40:5-42:20 Survey of the Temple Complex
      43:1-9 Return of the Divine כבוד
         43:10-46:24 The Law of the Temple
      47:1-12 The Course of the River of Life
      47:13-48:29 Survey of Territorial Allotments and Borders
   48:30-35 Conclusion

The text begins with the vision of a "construction like a city" (40:1-4),
and ends with the description of the walled city of the new Jerusalem,
renamed יהוה שמה: "YHWH is there"(48:30-35). The detailed description and measurement of the Temple complex in 40--42 is mirrored
by the boundary-marking, measurement and division of the land in
47:15--48:29. Likewise, the כבוד in 43:1-9 and the life-giving river in
47:1-12 are parallel symbols of the divine Presence, the former
expressing the means of YHWH's presence with YHWH's people, the
latter demonstrating the lifegiving power of that Presence.

In the center, then, is 43:10--46:24, the legislative material
frequently judged as pedantic addenda to the text, corrupting and
concealing the pristine vision of the prophet.[5] Yet, if we are correct in
our evaluation, the overall structure of the text brackets just this
material, commending it to us as of special import. The text as it now
stands is meant to serve as a vehicle for legislation. Far from being
peripheral to the text, the laws contained herein relating to the land,
the priesthood, the נשיא, and the cult are its very heart.

---

[5] So, for example, Eichrodt, 564: "They change the prophet boldly moving
forward to a new future into a petty-minded man who takes refuge in the old-fashioned
forms of the priestly ideal of holiness, who becomes false to his own vocation, and and
uses the prophetic ecstasy in which he felt himself uplifted above all earthly sources of
knowledge as a literary form by means of which he can bestow on his flight the mantle
of divine revelation which may lend it the necessary authority."

The Form of the Temple Vision and the Ancient Near Eastern Law-code

In brief, the Temple Vision in its received form consists of a body of legislation set within a literary frame.[6] Ample precedent can be cited for this pattern in the ancient Near East and in Israel. The ancient cuneiform law-codes of Ur-Nammu, Lipit-Ishtar, and Hammurabi are all, as Shalom Paul observes, "characterized by a clear dichotomy between a prologue-epilogue frame and a juridical corpus."[7] The literary frame places the legislation in a distinctly religious setting, and reveals the function of the text: "Mesopotamian legal corpora, with their personal prologue and epilogue frames, are primarily reports to the gods delivered by the king in order to vindicate his royal office of šar mēšarim."[8]

This pattern of prologue-legal corpus-epilogue can be discerned in biblical collections of law as well. Here, too, the literary frame serves to place the legislation into a religious setting, and to define its function. Paul identifies this structure in the Book of the Covenant (Exod 19--24), with the Decalogue in particular functioning as

---

[6] Greenberg ("Design and Themes," 189-90) also finds a tripartite division in the Temple Vision: 40:1--43:12, "the vision of the future Temple;" 44:1--46:24, called "enterings and exitings" by Greenberg; and 47:13--48:35, "the apportionment of the land among the people." The altar description and consecration in 43:13-27 and the vision of the river in 47:1-11 are transition passages, linking the three parts into a whole. Although his scheme differs somewhat from the one that we propose, he too observes the central position of the legislation. Further, his observation that the legislative section is concerned with "enterings and exitings" is, as will be seen below, the key to understanding the purpose of the Law of the Temple.

[7] Shalom M. Paul, Studies in the Book of the Covenant in the Light of Cuneiform and Biblical Law (VT Sup 18; Leiden: E. J. Brill, 1970) 100. A similar observation is made by Moshe Weinfeld (Deuteronomy and the Deuteronomic School [Oxford: Clarendon, 1972] 148), who notes a commonality in structure between these ancient law-codes and the later treaty-forms of the Hittites and Assyrians: "preamble, historical prologue, laws (the equivalent of the stipulations in the covenantal structure) and blessings and curses." Cf. also Klaus Baltzer, The Covenant Formulary: In Old Testament, Jewish, and Early Christian Writings (tr. David E. Green; Philadelphia: Fortress, 1971), especially 10, and George Mendenhall, "Law and Covenant in Israel and the Ancient Near East," BA 17 (1954): 26-76.

[8] Paul, Studies, 26. Weinfeld (School, 149), who traces the customary pattern of both law-code and treaty back as far as the third millenium reform of Urukagina, observes that that reform "is sanctified by a covenant or agreement with the god Ningirsu."

22   The Law of the Temple

prologue and Exodus 23:20-33 as epilogue.⁹ The function of the law-
code, again, is revealed by the frame: in particular, by the use of the
terms גוי and ממלכה: "Israel is about to become a polity (gwy/mmlkh)
based on law. The future institution of statehood is presently granted
an official charter."¹⁰ The book of Deuteronomy as well gives evidence
of this tripartite structure, with a lengthy prologue (Deut 1--4) and
epilogue (29--32) wrapped about a central law-code.¹¹

   Just such a threefold structure is found in the final form of the
Temple Vision. Once again, the frame expresses the function of the
law-code: we are dealing here with Temple law (as 43:12 states
explicitly). The intra-biblical parallels suggest that here, as well, we
are in the realm of polity. To test this theory of the final, purposive
unity of these chapters, we turn now to a consideration of the several
units of the Temple Vision.

II. The Temple And The כבוד (40:1--43:9)

   Throughout the initial sections of the Temple Vision, an angelic
figure guides the prophet through the Temple complex and selectively
measures its walls, gates and chambers. The guidance is indicated by
the verb בוא in the Hipᶜil preterite, usually with a first person

---

⁹ Paul, *Studies*, 101-102. It must be observed that Paul grants the composite
nature of these texts, insisting only that in the final redaction a purposive structure
must be observed (25- 26). Baltzer (*Formulary*, 27-31) is far more cautious: while he
identifies some parts of his covenant formulary in the Sinai pericope ("antecedent
history" in 19:4 and "statement of substance" in vv 5-6a; the idea of the recitation of the
covenant "by an authorized party" and the consent of the assembly is found in 19:7-8,
and again in 24:3-4a and 24:7), he resists positing some final formal unity (28): "the text
itself presents so many difficulties, which must complicate any results...we are dealing
literarily with a series of independent texts deriving from different sources, which have
been brought together in the present recension under the rubric 'revelation at Sinai.'"

¹⁰ Ibid., 31.

¹¹ As Paul (*Studies*, 27), Baltzer (*Formulary*, 31) and Weinfeld (*School*, 150) all
observe. Note however the subtle distinction made by von Rad, who regards the
Deuteronomy text as preaching based upon a law-code, rather than a law-code *per se*
(*Studies in Deuteronomy* [tr. David Stalker; London: SCM, 1953] 15-24). S. Dean
McBride, Jr. has proposed that Deuteronomy functions as a polity, providing a
constitutional framework for the Israelite state ("Polity of the Covenant People: The
Book of Deuteronomy," *Int* 41 [1987] 229-255). Von Rad's proposal (*Deuteronomy*, 70-
73) of a more theological purpose (the affirmation that the Israel of the late monarchy
is still the elect people of God) cannot adequately come to terms with the specificity of
the text, especially on matters of politics (Deut 17:14-20).

ot ze??.. ry

singular suffix; the measurement by מדד[12] Nothing is said of the purpose of the chambers marked off by the guide, and little is said of their appearance; they are measured in outline, as if on a blueprint. This has often prompted scholars to propose that Ezekiel based this vision on a temple plan he had preserved himself, or found in the archives.[13] This, however, is unlikely. The massive, fortified gates of the complex, for example, are all out of proportion to its relatively scant walls.[14] The tripartite structure of the Temple itself is reminiscent of the Solomonic Temple, but the Temple complex Ezekiel describes is decidedly not Solomon's. In fact, nothing like Ezekiel's Temple ever existed. Ezekiel's Temple plan is a hybrid, combining different sorts of structures remembered by the prophet into a wholly unique form. Its pattern came to him, as he tells us, in vision.

The basic structure of the Temple description seems to involve elements of guidance and measurement in two dimensions. Critics have often considered breaks from this pattern to indicate insertions into the original text. Since this text is a visionary description, however, one ought not expect strictly logical sequences. To conclude that 40:5 is secondary because the wall is measured before the gates,[15]

---

[12] See Table 1, "The Distribution of the Guidance Formula."

[13] For instance, Cooke, 425; Zimmerli, 2:412; Shemaryahu Talmon and Michael Fishbane, "The Structuring of Biblical Books: Studies in the Book of Ezekiel," *ASTI* 10 (1975/76) 139.

[14] The study of Carl Gordon Howie ("The East Gate of Ezekiel's Temple Enclosure and the Solomonic Gateway of Megiddo," *BASOR* 117 [1950] 13-18) was seminal in this regard. He himself was inclined to view the structure as a memory of the First Temple's eastern gate. Zimmerli (2:352, illus. 2:353) has a neat, brief summary of the more recent work and conclusions drawn from similar gateways uncovered at Hazor and Gezer, leading to the conclusion that the gateways described in 40--42 are Solomonic city gates, not temple structures. Frank Moore Cross (private communication), however, finds this a false distinction. He writes, "The temple area of Solomon was an 'independent' citadel, a fortified bastion, and probably even on the south where it joined the City of David was independently fortified... the entrances to the temple are in fact city gates, gates to citadel." Still, as Cross observes, the Temple vision applies this fortified gate plan to inner as well as outer gate structures, which seems unlikely--as does the pairing of a fortified gate with what seems (for defense purposes) a token wall. The possible theological significance of these outsized gates will be discussed below, pp. 59-61.

[15] Fohrer-Galling, 423-24.

TABLE 1: "THE DISTRIBUTION OF GUIDANCE
AND MEASUREMENT FORMULAE"

40:	2	הביאני	
	3	ויביא אותי	
	5		וימד
	6		וימד
	8		וימד
	11		וימד
	13		וימד
	17	ויביאני	
	19		וימד
	20		מדד
	23		וימד
	24	ויולבני	ומדד
	27		וימד
	28	ויביאני	וימד
	32	ויביאני	וימד
	35	ויביאני	ומדד
	47		וימד
	48	ויביאני	וימד
41:	1	ויביאני	וימד
	2		וימד
	3		וימד
	4		וימד
	5		וימד
	13		ומדד
	15		ומדד
42:	1	ויוצאני	
		ויביאני	
	15		וכלה את מדות
			ומדדו
	16		מדד
	17		מדד
	18		מדד
	19		מדד
	20		מדדו

TABLE 1 (cont.)

43:   1 ויולכני

44:   1 וישב אתי
      4 ויביאני

45:   3   תמד

46:   19 ויביאני
      21 ויוצאני

47:   1 וישני
      2 ויוצאני
      3   וימד
      4   וימד
                                                     וימד
      5   וימד

or that 41:5-15a must be secondary because the prophet could not witness the measuring of the side galleries from the most holy place, his last stated location,[16] is inappropriate. The vision opened with the miraculous transport of the prophet in vision from Babylon to the Zion of mythical reality; a sudden shift from the interior of the Temple to its exterior is mild by comparison!

Nor can we rule out 40:5, 41:5-15a or 42:1-12 on the grounds that they are complex, three-dimensional descriptions.[17] Ezekiel's visionary experience was three-dimensional. In the eastern gate he describes the palm trees carved on the pilasters and the windows set in the walls of the gate chambers, and observes (40:13) that the width of the eastern gate was measured מגג התא לגגו ("from the roof of the chamber to its roof," that is, across the ceiling of the gateway).[18] We are dealing here with a complex, three-dimensional structure, even if it is generally measured only in two dimensions.[19] When the height of structures is not given, we can only conclude that that information was not commended to the prophet's attention.

Finally, as Greenberg in particular has observed, ancient scribes were far less bound by notions of style than we tend to think.[20] Hence, while the element of guidance is lacking in 41:5-15a, and

---

[16] So Gese, 25; Wevers, 208; and Zimmerli, 2:374. Zimmerli and Wevers both suggest that the text has been expanded in light of 1 Kgs 6:5-10, though Zimmerli at least proposes that Ezekiel himself may have been responsible for the expansion.

[17] 40:5 is held suspect by Wevers (209). While Eichrodt holds 41:13-14 to be original, with the guidance element lost in the text's redaction (547), he otherwise considers all of 41:5-42:14 as secondary (546-48), as they run counter to the "purely two-dimensional geometric arrangement which, without a word about the elevation of the buildings, produces its effect solely through the symmetry of the plan" (549). Hals (298), while considering it generally impossible "to get behind the present text to some reconstructed, trouble-free original," notes that in 41:5-12, 15b-26, and 42:1-14 "a decided difference in style appears."

[18] No such emendation as מגו התא לגוו ("from back to back," suggested by the BHS on the basis of the G απο του τοιχου του θεε επι τον τοιχον του θεε, "from the wall of the chamber [Greek here a transliteration of the Hebrew תא] to the wall of the chamber," and followed by the RSV) is necessary: given the barriers across the front of the side chambers (40:12), the easiest way for the guide to measure the breadth of the gateway was to measure along the ceiling.

[19] As Hals (299) also observes.

[20] Greenberg, "Design and Themes," 185-86.

measurement is absent in 42:1-12, both are in style and content in perfect continuity with the remainder of the vision, which in a sparse and laconic fashion sketches the outline of the Temple complex. To rule them secondary because of a fluctuation in form would be rather extreme.[21]

Possible Expansions to the Text of 40:1–42:20.

Five textual segments from this opening descriptive section are, however, worthy of further consideration as regards the possible expansion of 40:1--42:20. These are the curious phrase וטפח באמה from 40:5; 40:38-43 and 41:5-15a, the only mentions of furnishings or materials in the vision; and 40:44-46 and 42:13-14, the only mentions of the priesthood. Here, legitimate differences from the rest of the vision are readily apparent. It remains to be seen which, if any, are different enough to be warranted secondary accretions or expansions.

40:5: The Length of the Reed. In 40:5, we are told that the angelic guide has in his hand a measuring reed of שש אמות באמה וטפח ("six cubits with a cubit and a handsbreadth[?]"). The function of the ב here is difficult to discern; the best option seems to be the ב of specification, as followed by the RSV: "each being a cubit and a handsbreadth in length."[22] Still, the unevenness of the phrasing suggests that expansion may have occurred.[23] We must wonder, at any

---

[21] Gese (24-25) argues in his rejection of 41:5-15a that it is in fact stylistically as well as formally distinct, being a mere *Katalog* lacking narrative flow--an argument with which Zimmerli (2:374) concurs. However, this argument really only establishes that the style of 41:5-15a is inferior to the remainder of the work, not that it is secondary. Zimmerli (2:397) likewise asserts that the guidance formula in 42:1-14 is used differently than in the unquestionably authentic sections, here merely introducing this section rather than illustrating the guidance of the prophet from place to place. Here, too, I would propose that too much rigor is being demanded of a text which, in form as well as substance, fits the rest of the vision quite well. One wonders if perhaps, in 41:5-15a as in 42:1-12, it is not the irritating presence of the unexplained בנין, rather than any solid disjunction from the context, which has prompted rejection by scholars.

[22] Cf. Ronald Williams, *Hebrew Syntax: An Outline.* (Toronto: University of Toronto , [2]1976) 45.

[23] So Fohrer-Galling, 224. Gese (13) rightly asserts that the verse cannot be secondary, as the length of the reed is necessary for the understanding of all the measurements that follow. Still, one wonders why it should be necessary to define the

rate, at the significance of this "long" cubit. It is possible that a long, "royal" cubit, analogous to the larger royal talent of weight, was used for royal projects such as Temple building, and that this is the reference in 40:5.[24] But we have no evidence that such was the case.

If, in the interim between the composition of this text and its redaction, a new standard of measurement was imposed upon Israel from without, the insertion of the long cubit at 40:5 would make sense. The measures detailed in the vision would need to be brought into conformity with the new standard, especially if the redacted vision was an official document. We have indirect evidence that such a shift did take place in the Persian period. 2 Chronicles 3:3, which describes the building of the Solomonic Temple, states that that structure was built במדה הראשונה ("by the former measure"). If a new measure had been introduced by the Chronicler's day, he would have needed to explain to his audience that a different system had been used for the First Temple's dimensions. This could suggest that the longer cubit of 40:5 became the standard under Persian rule, and that the definition of the cubit in that verse is therefore an addition from the period of the restoration.

Zimmerli, on the contrary, argues that the "former measure" of 2 Chronicles 3:3 was just another way of indicating the long cubit. In support, he cites an old temple inscription of Esarhaddon, which details the erection of a temple "with the long cubit... in accordance with its old plan."[25]   However, one cannot compare the inscription of Esarhaddon, relating to the rebuilding or repair of an old temple, to the text in Chronicles, which describes the erection and measurement of a brand new structure. The plain sense of the Chronicles text is that the measurements used by the First Temple's builders were not the measurements of the Chronicler's audience. Given the proclivity

---

length of the *cubit* here, and particularly, why that definition is given in terms of some other, assumedly more familiar, unit of measure.

[24] Cooke (431) notes the existence of a longer as well as a shorter cubit among the Babylonians and the Egyptians (the long cubit being a handsbreadth longer than the short cubit); he further observes that though "traces of the longer Babylonian cubit have been discovered at Palestine and Taanach... at all periods the shorter Egyptian scale was the one commonly used by the Israelites."

[25] Zimmerli, 2:349.

of the Persians for order, and especially the strong interest of Darius
in standard measures,[26] it makes sense that that different system of
measurement was a standard system, enforced by the Persian
government. This, of course, is far from conclusive. However, in
conjunction with other evidence to be presented, this little bit of
evidence for a Persian-period redaction is enticing.

40:38-43 and 41:15b-26: Materials and Furnishings. 40:38-43
and 41:15b-26 alike depart significantly from the pattern of the
Temple description, and are frequently regarded as secondary.[27]
Neither segment contains the guidance formula, and in both
measurements are stated as mere fact, without description of the act
of measuring by the guide. Most significantly, these two passages
contain the only mention of furnishings or materials to be found in this
opening section: the hewn stone tables of 40:38-43, with their hooks
and instruments for the preparation of sacrifices, and the carved
wooden panelling, table and doorways of 41:15b-26. Apart from these
sections, one would think the Temple of Ezekiel's vision entirely
empty and unadorned. Eichrodt has proposed that it was deliberately
so:

> The sober unembellished portrayal of this miracle of the divine presence,
> pervaded once again by an implicit criticism of the old temple, appears
> altogether in keeping with Ezekiel's whole method of describing man's
> relationship with God and concentrating entirely on the cleansing power of
> God's action on his people.[28]

---

[26] More will be said of this in Chapter Four, in the discussion of 45:12.

[27] Eichrodt (550) holds that 40:38-46 and 41:15b-26 are made up of expansions,
added at various times, to accomodate the concerns of those who "could not envisage a
new sanctuary without associating it with the performance of a cult pleasing to God. "
Such additions were necessary, as (551) "Ezekiel's vision of the future had a character
all its own, and was wholly unsatisfactory to the priestly interest." Zimmerli, too,
(2:365) considers 40:38-46 an expansion, and on similar grounds. He makes a much
stronger case for the secondary character of 41:15b- 26 (2:386), observing the sharp
transition at 41:15b from the בנין behind the Temple to the Temple nave, the abrupt,
and doubtless corrupt, conclusion in mid-phrase at 41:26, and the shift in terminology:
דבר instead of אמר for the guide's speaking, confused usage of הבית הפנימי as well as
ההיכל הפנימי for the inner room of the Temple, and הקדש instead of קדש הקדשים
for the most holy place. Gese (32), Wevers (207-8), and Hals (298) similarly regard these
texts as expansions, perhaps reflecting later Temple-building concerns.

[28] Eichrodt, 550.

This argument from silence holds only if we consider these descriptive sections to be later additions--and even then, only if we can somehow hold that their addition is antithetical to the intent of the original visionary. We lack the evidence to do either. Although formally distinct from the rest of 40--42, 40:38-43 and 41:15b-26 are in keeping with the spirit and mood of the text. Descriptions and explanations are kept sparse and succinct. The materials mentioned are ordinary: dressed stone and wood (not even cedar!). This is in sharp contrast with other Temple description texts from Israel and the Near East, which emphasize the precious materials of the building. The fine stuff used in the Tabernacle and its accoutrements (Exod 25-28) and in the First Temple (1 Kgs 6) is paralleled by the lengthy tale of precious stones, woods and metals in Gudea Cylinder A[29] , and by the Ugaritic litany of CTA 4.5.74-81; 91-97 (98-102):

lyrgm . l'aliyn . b[c]l	Let it be told to Victorious Ba[c]l:
ṣḥ . ḥrn . bbht!k	'Summon a caravan[30] into your house,
c̣dbt . bqrb . hklk	Furnishings[31] into the midst of your palace.
tblk . g̀rm . mid . ksp	The mountains will provide you with much silver,

---

[29] Gudea Cylinder A, especially 15.1-17.1. English translation: Thorkild Jacobsen, *The Harps That Once... : Sumerian Poetry in Translation* (New Haven and London: Yale University 1987) 406-8. Cf. also George A. Barton, *The Royal Inscriptions of Sumer and Akkad* (New Haven: Yale University, 1929) 219-21.

[30] Reading the Ugaritic *ḥrn* as a cognate of the Akkadian *harrānu*, "caravan,"

with André Caquot, Maurice Sznycer, and Andrée Herdner, *Textes Ougaritiques*, Vol. 1, *Mythes et Légendes: Introduction, Traduction, Commentaire* (Paris: Cerf, 1974) 208. Joseph Aisleitner's proposal (*Wörterbuch der ugaritischen Sprache* [Berlin: Akademie-Verlag, 1963] 116) *Erdarbeiter* ("digger, laborer"), from the Akkadian *ḥerū* ("dig") and

ḥurru ("hole") and the Hebrew חר ("hollow"), is strained; H. L. Ginsberg's reading

(*ANET*[3], 133), "Summon *weeds* into thy house," is incomprehensible.

[31] Again, following *Textes Ougaritiques*, 208, which renders c̣dbt as "fourniture," relating the Ugaritic to the Hebrew עזבונים ("wares," found only in Ezek 27, and only in the plural, as a description of imported manufactured goods) and the Akkadian c̣uzubbu ("payment"). Aisleitner (*Die mythologischen und kultischen Texte aus Ras Schamra*, Bibliotheca Orientalis Hungarica 8 [Budapest: Akadémiai Kiadó, 1959] 42) reads *Bauleute* ("builders"), in parallel with his rendering of *ḥrn* in the previous line

and in comparison with the Old South Arabic c̣db, "to make." The reading followed here provides a better fit phonetically and better sense contextually, and is bolstered by the Ezek 27 citations.

gb^cm . mḥmd . ḫrṣ	The hills with the finest gold;
yblk . 'udr . 'ilqṣm	Camels[32] will bring you precious stones.[33]
wbn . bht . ksp . wḫrṣ	Now, build a house of silver and gold,
bht . ṯhrm . 'iqnim	A house of pure lapis lazuli.'

40:38-43 and 41:15b-26, then, stand in contrast to the expected ancient Near Eastern pattern for Temple texts, and in continuity with the remainder of 40--42. For all their distinctiveness, they share the same thought world as the undoubtedly authentic portions of the Temple description.[34]

40:44-46: the Chambers of the Priests. The two chambers[35] that are the subject of these verses are neither measured or described. We are only told that the south-facing chamber is לכהנים שמרי משמרת הבית ("for the priests who have charge over the service of the Temple"), while the north-facing chamber is לכהנים שמרי משמרת המזבח ("for the priests who have charge over the service of the altar"). These latter priests are further defined: המה בני צדוק הקרבים מבני

---

[32] Reading the Ugaritic *udr*, with Aisleitner (*Wörterbuch*, 9), as "camel," in comparison with the Akkadian *'udru*. Cyrus H. Gordon (*Ugaritic Textbook* [AnOr 38; Rome: Pontifical Biblical Institute, 1965] 353), providing no evidence but context, reads "quarry;" while Ginsberg (*ANET*[3], 133) and G. R. Driver (*Canaanite Myths and Legends*, Old Testament Studies 3 [Edinburgh: T. and T. Clark, 1956] 97), influenced by the Hebrew אדר ("be great, noble") understand this as the object of the verb in construct with the following *ilqṣm* and read, respectively, "god's glory aplenty" and "noblest of gems." No such contortions are necessary: this is a perfectly natural parallel to the mention of the caravan in l. 75.

[33] No cognate evidence is available for the enigmatic *ilqṣm* . With the majority of scholars, I have understood it as a reference to some sort of precious stone, paralleling the later mention of lapis lazuli.

[34] The mere absence of guidance or measurement motifs alone, as we have seen, is not sufficiently strong to weigh against the striking similarity in tone and theme to found in these texts. Given the visionary character of the material, abrupt transitions should not surprise us; neither should textual corruptions and copyists's errors. The terminological evidence cited by Zimmerli for the secondary character of 41:15b-26 in particular is strong, but not finally compelling; such shifts may be for stylistic effect, to break up the monotony of the interminable rounds of measurement and description.

[35] *M* has לשכות שרים, "to the chambers of the singers," an odd designation for chambers that, as the context indicates, were rather intended for the priests. Targum Jonathan reads *lskt lyw'y*, "to the chambers of the Levites," which clearly presupposes the *M* and is an attempt to explain the reference. We do best to emend the text to לשכות שתים,"to the two chambers," following *G* (δυο εξεδραι).

לוי אל יהוה לשרתו ("They are the Zadokites, those from among the Levites who draw near to YHWH to serve him"). Those who, following Wellhausen, place the two-stage clergy in the post-exilic period must as a matter of course deem this passage an expansion.[36] The mention of Zadok, moreover, has prompted many to connect at least 40:46b to 44:6-16, which rejects the priesthood of the Levites and affirms that only the Zadokites are to present offerings to YHWH.[37]

The relationship of these texts to the history of the priesthood cannot be resolved here. However, the content of 40:44-46 stands in marked contrast to the anti-Levitical polemic of 44:6-16.[38] The two priestly classes are treated with virtual equality: some favoritism may be implied in the placing of the altar clergy in a chamber situated on

---

[36] Julius Wellhausen, *Prolegomena to the History of Ancient Israel* (New York: Meridian, 1957), especially 123-24. Scholars who regard 40:44-46 as secondary, or at least suspect, include Eichrodt (545), Herbert May (*IB* 6: 54), Wevers (208), Gese (32), Zimmerli (2: 366), and Hals, 298.

[37] So Hölscher, 192 and Cooke, 439-40. Eichrodt, 545; Gese, 32; and Zimmerli, 2:368 consider 40:44-46a secondary, with v 46b coming later still. In contrast, Rodney Duke ("Punishment or Restoration? Another Look at the Levites of Ezekiel 44.6-16," *JSOT* 40 [1988]74-75) argues that both groups in 40:44-46 are Zadokites. The Temple clergy could not be Levites, he argues, as Levites were not permitted in the inner court. Rather, the designation in v 46b is to be taken as applying to both groups, Num 18:5 having given responsibility for Temple and altar service to the sons of Aaron. Duke's reading of 40:44-46 seems strained , however. The most natural referrent for the phrase in v 46b is the group described in v 46a, especially given the reference to sacrificial service (הקרבים...לשרתו: "those who draw near... to serve him"). Moreover, by stating that the Levites could not enter the inner court, Duke assumes what the sets out to demonstrate: that the Levites were not regarded as priests. Finally, the use of the Num18 reference indicates a facile and unwarranted identification of the Zadokites and the Aaronids: as will be seen in Chapter 5, while Zadokites appear to be Aaronids, not all Aaronids are Zadokites.

[38] Zimmerli (2:458) sees here a development in the attitude of Ezekiel's school toward the priesthood, reflected first in an addition merely denying altar rights to the Levites (40:44-46a), then in the utter rejection of priestly status, with the Levites becoming Temple servants (44:6-16, with a later expansion at 40:6b to bring that text in line). On this point, Zimmerli follows A. H. J. Gunneweg (*Leviten und Priester* [Göttingen: Vandenhoeck & Ruprecht, 1965] 195), who proposes that a similar gradual devaluation of the Levites can be found in the additions to P: particularly Num 18, with its increasingly stringent rules for keeping the Levites from contact with the holy (cf. especially 198-200). Neither Zimmerli nor Gunneweg, however, deals with the explicit designation of the Levites as כהנים in 40:45. The difference between this text and the polemic in Ezek 44 is more than a matter of degree: in 40:45, as everywhere in the pre-exilic materials, Levites are priests; in 44:1-14, and elsewhere in the Law of the Temple, they are not.

the eastern gate,[39] but this is questionable. Both groups are called
כהנים, and their tasks are described in identical fashion. Not even in
v 46b can any trace of polemic be found. The text exalts the Zadokite
altar clergy, but does not in any way belittle the other priestly class,
the Temple clergy. We have no reason to regard this text, or any part
of it, as belonging to a later tradition, identified with 44:6-16.[40]

Zimmerli proposes another reason for rejection. Arguing that
the description of the most holy place in 41:4 is the climax of the
narrative, he holds this text, with its mention of service before YHWH,
to be premature, and hence inappropriate.[41] Zimmerli, however, has
misplaced the climax--of a necessity, as his opinion that the vision of
the כבוד is a later expansion[42] has truncated the narrative. When the
Temple description and the return of the כבוד are viewed (in
accordance with the ancient scribal divisions) as an organic unity, the
true climax becomes clear: it is 43:7a, in which YHWH, having taken
possession of the Temple, declares: בן אדם את מקום כסאי ואת מקום
כפות רגלי אשר אשכן שם בתוך בני ישראל לעולם ("O human, this is
the place of my throne and my footstool, where I will dwell in the
midst of the people Israel forever"). Texts such as 40:46, 41:4 and
41:22 (and, indeed, 42:14) all foreshadow this event, the actual
indwelling of the divine Presence, and the kingly declaration of YHWH
that the Presence will never be removed. There is no need to deny
40:44-46 a place in Ezekiel's original vision.

---

[39] Usually the הקדים ("east") of *M* is emended to הדרון ("south"), on the basis of
G (προς νοτον, "to the south"). However, it is not clear how a confusion between south
(had that been the intention) and east could have taken place. On the other hand, for
purposes of symmetry and balance, the alteration from east to south is perfectly
understandable. Perhaps, then, we should stay with *M* at this point, and picture the two
structures as being part of the northern and eastern inner gate complexes (so JPS).

[40] Cooke (445) suggests that the use of an explanatory pronoun, and the absence
of a conjunction, points to a gloss. It may rather, however, indicate a vigorous, albeit
laconic, style. The result is a special emphasis on the identity of the altar clergy as
Zadokites, but such is scarcely surprising from the pen of a Jerusalemite priest such as
Ezekiel.

[41] Zimmerli, 2:366.

[42] Ibid., 2:412-13.

34   The Law of the Temple

42:13-14: The Temple Sacristy. A different situation faces us in
42:13-14. These verses are markedly different in character from
anything else in these first two chapters. They are not description at
all, but legislation, reminiscent of the priestly legislation regarding
sancta contagion in Leviticus 2:1-10; 7:7-10, and later in the Temple
Vision (44:28-31). It is, of course, not impossible that the prophet
could have written legislative material into his vision, but it is unlikely.
Throughout these opening chapters, we are admitted to the
experience of the prophet: we see what he sees, hear what he hears,
from his miraculous transport to the high mountain in 40:1, through
the tedious measurements and descriptions of 40--42, to the
triumphal return of the כבוד in 43:1-7a. Only here is that sense of
participation, of immediacy, broken. On the other hand, in the
sections ahead, legislation in the second and third persons will
entirely supercede first-person experience. The central concern of
that legislation is access to the Divine: who may enter, how may they
enter, how then shall they exit? This, also, is the concern of 42:13-14.

We suggest, therefore, that 42:13-14 is a later addition, in
deliberate imitation of 40:44-46. There, two chambers (שבות) are in
view; here, two groups of chambers (again, שבות). The chambers are
identified, in each case, by their north-south orientation. The altar
clergy are identified as those who draw near (קרב) to YHWH. Now,
however, there is no provision made at all for Temple clergy: no
parallel place is mentioned where they may eat the sacred meal, or
change their vestments preparatory to leaving the Temple precincts.
Here, the interests of the priestly redactors of Ezekiel's vision are in
view, and their desire to enforce holy conduct upon their successors
by means of legislation is in force. As the redactor has shown
considerable reticence in breaking into this opening section, we must
conclude that this was a matter of considerable urgency, which could
not be postponed. Before the Temple description was completed, it
was necessary that this injunction against the communication of
holiness was heard. In 42:20, the function of the *temenos* wall is
given: להבדיל בין הקדש לחל ("to separate the holy from the
common"). The redactors needed it to be understood by their priestly
successors that they must not transgress that barrier. The sacred

offerings were to be consumed in a holy place, and the priestly vestments, charged with holiness, were also to be kept within. As a piece of legislation, then, 42:13-14 does not belong to the original vision of the prophet, but to the redaction which has transformed that vision into the work we now have.[43]

The Vision of the כבוד (43:1-9)

With 43:1, a striking new element is introduced. In language reminiscent of the storm theophany, the prophet describes the approach of YHWH's כבוד from the east. The divine Presence enters by the east gate, and then the prophet, miraculously transported to the inner court, sees that the Temple is filled with YHWH's כבוד. A voice speaks: definitely not the voice of the guide, who stands beside Ezekiel, but rather the voice of YHWH enthroned, who declares, in the climax to the vision, that the Presence will never again depart from Israel.

The vision of the כבוד has frequently been rejected as an expansion of the Temple description. Hölscher believed there to be a contradiction between 42:15-20 and 43:1, since both present the guidance of the prophet to the east gate, and therefore rejected 43:1-9 as secondary.[44] Even Howie considered the כבוד vision inauthentic, holding it to be "little more than a literary device used to tie this section to the rest of the book."[45] Gese notes that the vision of the כבוד belongs far more clearly to what follows than to what precedes; indeed that it is central to all the material that follows, opening as it does a new section where YHWH speaks.[46]

---

[43] Scholars who deem this text secondary generally also reject 42:1-12: e.g., Eichrodt, 548; Gese, 32; Wevers, 208; and Hals, 286, 292. Zimmerli (2:403), while holding that the text is an insertion, believes it to be, like 41:5-15a, from the hand of Ezekiel. May (54), while considering the first twelve verses of the chapter genuine, holds vv 13-14 suspect.

[44] Hölscher, 193.

[45] Carl G. Howie, "Ezekiel," *IDB* 2:208.

[46] Gese, 114.

36   The Law of the Temple

Other scholars propose that while this segment is an expansion, it may be nonetheless the authentic work of the prophet.[47] A particularly intriguing approach is taken by Shemaryahu Talmon and Michael Fishbane, based on the idea that 43:12 is the original summary notation for the unit 40:1-43:12.[48] The connecting ideas, the mountain and the wall, are found together in 40:1-5, yet severed in 42:20, which speaks of the wall, and 43:12, the summary notation which speaks of the mountain.   Hence, Talmon and Fishbane determine that the two were originally consecutive verses, and that the prophet inserted the כבוד vision later. "If the כבוד unit were integral to the architectural plan," they argue, "we would have expected some reference to this important event in the summary notation."[49]

None of these arguments is finally convincing. No contradiction need be seen between 42:15-20 and 43:1, since the first text involves the guidance of the prophet *through* the east gate, presumably to follow the guide in his measuring of the outer wall, while in the second text, he is guided specifically *to* the gate.[50]   The parallels which prompt Howie to conclude that this text is a redactional suture are, as we have seen, due to the close relationship of the vision of chapters 40--48 with those in chapters 1--3 and 8--11, the other two texts designated מראות in Ezekiel. Far from arguing for the rejection of 43:1-7a, this similarity urges the unit's authenticity, for both of these preceding visions incorporate the image of the כבוד. Nor has Gese demonstrated a break between 40--42 and 43:1 so much as the dependence of the legislative material on the כבוד-vision; with this observation we have no argument.

---

[47] A position taken by Cooke (427), Zimmerli (2:412-13, though in his judgement chapter 43 stands "closer to the real core of prophetic experience" than its parent material), and Talmon and Fishbane, "Structuring," 148. Hals (298), on the other hand, finds "no sharp break" at 43:1.

[48] Talmon and Fishbane, "Structuring," 139-48.

[49] Ibid.,143.

[50] As Zimmerli, 2:413, has noted.

The proposals that grant the authorship of the vision of the כבוד
to the prophet while still seeing it as a later expansion are no more
convincing, for the vision of the כבוד is a necessary part of the
Temple vision. Having demonstrated in chapters 8--11 that, with the
presence of God withdrawn, the Temple is but a place, the prophet
must now demonstrate the reality of the divine Presence in this
glorified Temple, else it, too, is devoid of transcendent significance.
The parallel is quite deliberate and specific: as the כבוד had departed
the Temple by means of the eastern gate (11:1, 22-23), so now, by
means of the eastern gate, the כבוד returns (43:1).[51]

The Occupation of the Temple by the Divine in Israel and the Ancient Near East

The Temple Vision fits the model of other Temple texts in
Israel and the Near East. Following the construction of the
Tabernacle, the cloud of the כבוד filled it (Exod 40:34-38). Similarly,
Solomon's Temple was inhabited by the divine Presence when the Ark
was carried in procession into the holy place (1 Kgs 8:1-11, esp. 10,
11). In both contexts, as in Ezekiel 43:5, the Divine Presence is said
to fill (מלא) the sanctuary.

A similar pattern can be seen in the Ugaritic myth of the
building of Ba°l's temple. As soon as the structure is completed, Ba°l,
rejoicing, moves in and summons all the gods and goddesses for a
magnificent feast (CTA 4. 6. 44-59). The Gudea cylinders illustrate the
antiquity of this conception. After the detailed description in Cylinder
A of the building of the temple and the opulence of its materials and
furnishings, Cylinder B details the coming of the god to inhabit the
newly-built structure. Gudea prays:

Ningirsu, my master,
lord, semen reddened in the deflowering,
lord, whose word takes precedence,
heir of Enlil, warrior! You commanded me,
and I've set hand to it for your right.
Ningirsu, I have built here your house for you,
May you enter it in joy![52]

---

[51] As Hals (305) also observes, though he holds 43:1-12 to be "more a parallel to
40:1-5 than a continuation."

[52] 2.16-23; Jacobsen, Harps, 427. Cf. Barton, Inscriptions, 239.

38   The Law of the Temple

The following lines detail the preparations that follow: sacrifices,
special offerings and libations are made, the path of the processional is
prepared and purified, the people bow down. Then, the coming of the
god is described:

> The warrior Ningirsu entered the house,
> the owner of the house had come,
> a very eagle catching sight of a wild bull!
> The warrior's entering his house
> was a storm roaring into battle.
> Ningirsu roamed through his house,
> it was (the sound of) the Apsu temple precincts
> when festivals are celebrated.
> The owner was ready to come out from his house--
> it was like the sun rising over Lagash land![53]

Only when the image of the god in procession had entered the temple
and the deity had taken possession of it could the temple be truly said
to be finished.

The return of YHWH's כבוד in Ezekiel 43:1-9 is an organic and
essential part of Ezekiel's original vision, and ought not be severed
from it. Those who would regard the vision of the כבוד as a later
expansion or, worse, as an intrusion, violate the integral unity of the
prophet's vision.[54]   The vision of the כבוד begins in 43:1, and
extends to v 9.[55]   However, with v 7b, the character of the text

---

[53] Cylinder B, 5.1-9; Jacobsen, *Harps*, 429. Cf. Barton, *Inscriptions*, 241.

[54] The arguments of Talmon and Fishbane will be addressed in more detail
when we analyse 43:12; for now it is sufficient to note, as we have done above, the
ancient pattern in Israel and the Near East of temple description followed by the
entrance of the god.

[55] Zimmerli, who holds that the motif of YHWH's כבוד coming to the Temple in
judgement is secondary in 8:4 and 9:3a (1:232), naturally regards 43:3, which makes
reference to that manifestation, as being itself secondary--belonging, indeed, to the
final editing of the book (2:414). This conclusion is based upon Zimmerli's distinction
between two portrayals of the Divine Glory in 8-11: a simple, and authentic one, which
uses the title כבוד יהוה and assumes the כבוד to move of its own accord, and another,
belonging to Ezekiel's school, which uses the more fulsome title כבוד אלהי ישראל,
and in which the Presence moves about in a chariot-throne. I would propose that, by
insisting upon consistency in the portrayal of the כבוד in this vision account,
Zimmerli has forgotten the very character of the text he is interpreting: this is, after all,
a vision, a dreamlike experience. As Robert Wilson has observed concerning the vision
of the כבוד in Ezekiel's call, "some of the so-called inconsistencies in Ezekiel's
description actually underlie the supernatural aspects of the vision. By using extraordinary images, the prophet seeks to describe the divine world, which is ultimately

changes.   The divine speech shifts from words of assurance to a pronouncement of judgement.   The holy Name had been profaned in times past by the proximity of the royal palace, and especially by the erection of memorial stelae to departed kings (פגרי מלכיהם).[56] Because of this harlotry and adultery, the wrath of YHWH had been poured out, but now, if memorial stelae are no more established and this idolatry is forgotten, "I will dwell in their midst forever." What is stated in v 7a as a sovereign act of unconditional promise has in v 9 been predicated on the removal of memorial stelae to dead kings from the Temple precincts.

---

indescribable.   As is frequently the case in dreams and visions, objects begin to blur, and events no longer conform to logic or to the laws of common experience." ("Prophecy in Crisis: The Call of Ezekiel," Int 38 (1984) 124)   I would suggest that we have no reason to regard the motif of the כבוד's appearing as secondary in 8--11, and hence need not regard the reference to that event in our text as secondary.

[56] The M of v 7 reads ובפגרי מלכיהם במותם, rendered literally in the AV as "by the carcasses of their kings in their high places;" Samson Levey, in his translation of the Targum Jonathan of Ezekiel, similarly renders this phrase as "the shrines of the corpses of their kings" (Targum of Ezekiel, [AramB 13; Wilmington Michael Glazier, 1987] 116).   The first problem with this text is the translation of פגר.   The usual interpretation, "body" or "corpse," suggests that the offense in this passage is the profanation of the Temple by royal graves (so especially Cooke, 464).   However, evidence for royal graves in the Temple precincts is lacking: of those kings whose burial places we know, all but Manasseh and Amon, who were buried in the palace gardens (2 Kgs 21:18, 26) were laid to rest in "the city of David," a necropolis outside the Temple area.   Fohrer-Galling suggest that it is the graves of Manasseh and Amon that are referred to here (243).   However, David Neiman ("PGR: A Canaanite Cult-Object in the Old Testament," JBL 67 [1948] 55-60) proposed another possibility.   He identified in two Ugaritic memorial inscriptions and comparative inscriptions in Phoenician a term pgr which, in the context, must mean "stele."   Neiman suggested therefore that Ezek 40:7 refers to the erection of royal funerary stelae in the high places (58-59): an interpretation also favored by Albright ("The High Place in Ancient Palestine," Volume du Congrès, Strasborg 1956, VT Sup 4 [Leiden: E. J. Brill, 1957] 247-48).   However, twenty Hebrew manuscripts have a different pointing for the final word of this verse: bĕmôtām in their deaths," a pointing also assumed by the Second Rabbinic Bible (bmwthwn) and Theodotian.   As Zimmerli in particular (2:417) has argued, the context of the term pgr in the texts cited by Neiman--specifically, memorial inscriptions--argues in favor of this pointing.   This reading also makes best sense in the context: the problem is the pollution of the Temple complex by the proximity of the royals.   The mention of the erection of stelae in the high places, while an idolatrous act condemned by YHWH, is really not so directly to the point of contention here as would be the erection of memorial stelae in the Temple precincts.   Kurt Galling ("Erwagungen zum Stelenheiligtum von Hazor," ZDPV 75 [1959] 11-12) thought to find in the stelae-sanctuary at Hazor an example of the practice here described.   However, given the unprecedented placement of the stelae at that site in the most holy place, it is perhaps best to conclude, with G. W. Ahlström ("Heaven on Earth--at Hazor and Arad," Religious Syncretism in Antiquity: Essays in Conversation with Geo Widengrin, ed. Birger A. Pearson. Formative Contemporary Thinkers 1 [Missoula: Scholar's Press, 1975] 79), that the stelae here are cult images, representative of the divine assembly.

Still, the authenticity of this text has been ably championed by Zimmerli. He observes that the language is typical of that used elsewhere by the prophet: in particular, the profaning of קדשי שם ("my holy Name," 20:39; 36:20, 23; 39:7) and the description of the people's infidelity as זנותם ("their harlotries," 23:27).[57] Moreover, Zimmerli suggests that the very theme of this text, the exclusion of the palace complex and indeed of the royal influence from the Temple grounds, is also a remarkable characteristic of the Temple description. Unlike the first Temple, which was indeed part of the palace complex, the Temple of Ezekiel's vision is freestanding and independent. Zimmerli writes:

> The most revolutionary element of the temple description in the great guidance vision consists precisely in the clear separation of the temple from the palace complex. What was expressed there in the cryptic language of a building plan is here translated into a concrete demand: Separate cleanly the sacred from the profane, separate clearly God's sphere of ownership from the sphere of human, even royal, claims.[58]

Although intriguing, Zimmerli's arguments are not finally convincing. To conclude from a failure to mention the royal presence in the Temple description that there is, in fact, no such presence is to go further than the facts warrant. The visionary description is, as we have seen, remarkably laconic. To argue from Ezekiel's silence concerning a royal presence on the Temple mount for some sort of anti-royal polemic is inappropriate. Moreover, the specific agent of defilement in this text, the erection of memorial stelae to Israel's defunct kings, is never mentioned in Ezekiel's prophecy (or, indeed, anywhere else).

The similarities cited by Zimmerli between the language of 43:7b-9 and that of the body of Ezekiel's prophecy are scarcely surprising, given the redactor's evident respect and affection for, if not veneration of, his source. Still, important differences can be noted. In the occasions cited by Zimmerli from the body of the prophecy, the profanation of the divine Name is expressed by the verb

---

57 Zimmerli, 2:417-18.

58 Ibid., 418. So also Hals, 306-7.

חלל. Here, the verb טמא ("make unclean") is used. Most glaring, however, is the use of the word מלך to describe Israel's kings. Ezekiel's standard term for the kings of Israel is נסיא. מלך is used only twice in the body of the book to designate a king of Israel (7:27 and 17:12); yet, this designation occurs three times in 43:7b-9. Zimmerli's suggestion, that the use of מלך here is meant to intensify the break with the past,[59] does not follow: it is נסיא which, in the bulk of Ezekiel's prophecy, is applied to the monarchs of Israel's sinful past. We cannot, then, attribute this text to Ezekiel.[60]

It does, however, fit quite nicely into the proposed Persian setting of our redactor. It was certainly no secret in the Near East that Israel had, in the glory days of David and Solomon, possessed a considerable little empire. As the Aramaic document preserved in Ezra 4:8-24 shows, enemies of Israel were able to use this memory of former greatness to shut down the rebuilding of Jerusalem. If the redactor was indeed engaged in the establishment of a religious polity for the restoration state, he would have had to demonstrate to the Persians that all dynastic pretentions, all aspirations for empire, had been relinquished by the leadership he represented. The polemic against the old monarchy, and specifically against the sacral memorializing of the old monarchy, in 43:7b-9 would have accomplished this purpose decidedly.

The redactor has neatly woven this affirmation into Ezekiel's original oracle by means of a scribal technique which Talmon and Fishbane call "repetitive resumption."[61] In this technique, a

---

[59] Zimmerli, 2:418.

[60] Cooke (427) and May (54) consider the entire speech of YHWH, vv 6-9, as secondary: an extreme, and unnecessary, conclusion that robs the opening section 40:1-43:9 of its climax. Eichrodt (553) selectively excises v 7b from המה ומלכיהם ("they and their kings..."), all of v 8, and the mention of the פגר in v 9, on the grounds that the further definition of the people's abominations is not necessary at this point. The justification for this excision is slim, however, and the contradiction between the unconditional statement of presence in v 7a and the conditions of 7b-9 is not resolved. Wevers (215), who sees all of vv 7b-12 as "a series of accretions," comes closest to what we are doing here, save that we are proposing, not a gradual process of accretion, but a single, purposive redactional expansion of the text.

[61] Talmon and Fishbane, "Structuring," 144.

redactional insertion is followed by a resumption of the wording preceding the insertion. The comparison of v 7a with v 9b shows how this has been accomplished here: אשכן שם בתוך בני ישראל לעולם (Qal imperfect first person singular of שכן) in v 7 is paralleled by ושכנתי בתוכם לעולם (Qal perfect/waw consecutive first person singular of שכן, the object expressed by third plural suffix) in v 9. Artfully bracketed in this manner, the redactional insertion subtly alters the shape of YHWH's proclamation, from unconditional promise to word of command. In the material that follows, this shift will become more pronounced, as Ezekiel's grand vision of the divine Presence is made over as a vehicle of law.

III. The Law Of The Temple (43:10-46:18)

The Introduction to תורת הבית: *(43:10-27)*

The next section, 43:10-27, introduces three themes unconnected with the previous section: the idea of Temple ordinances, the description of the altar, and the ritual for the altar's dedication.[62] Throughout this section, and indeed throughout the next several sections, the mood has shifted from the indicative to the imperative, from description to legislation, from first-person report of the prophet's visionary experience to second- and third-person commands of YHWH. The perception of the ancient scribes that a break occurs between vv 9 and 10 could lend support to the view that with v. 10 we leave the original prophecy behind, and enter into its secondary expansion.

Some commentators, however, have doubted that 43:10 begins a new unit. This does seems an odd place to begin a literary division-- smack in the middle of a divine speech. Hence, a number of contemporary scholars have tended to view 43:1-12 as a unit.[63] The

---

[62] Fohrer-Galling, 238. Earlier, Hölscher (194) had also placed a break here, dismissing vv 10-11 as "*eine ungeschickte Naht*" ("a clumsy suture"). They have been followed by Eichrodt (555-56) and Wevers (215), among others. Talmon and Fishbane ("Structuring," 142) consider 43:10-11, 12b as part of the editorial expansion involved in combining the vision of the כבוד (43:1-9) with the architectural plan in 40--42.

[63] Gese (41-43), who regards 43:1-11 as an unbroken, albeit secondary, unit, is followed in this analysis by Zimmerli (2:411), save that Zimmerli also defends the

strongest case for the unity of 43:1-11 has been made by Gese,[64] who observes a formal connection between v 11 and v 8a, both of which (following the reconstruction of v 11) are structured with a series of

---

authenticity of v 12 and, as we have seen, regards the whole as the work of the prophet. Cooke (427) and May (54) consider the divine speech in 43:6-12 a secondary expansion. Hals (306-7), who sees here a combination of numerous strands of tradition, nonetheless regards vv 1-12 as a unit.

[64] Gese, 40-41 n. Verse 11 is awkward and repetitious, with numerous textual problems. In place of the opening conditional phrase in M (אשר מכל נכלמו ואם עשו), G and V read a simple third plural pronoun with the verb, assuming the reading יכלמו והם ("and they will be ashamed..."). Cooke (465; 474), Gese (40), Zimmerli (2:410), and Hals (304) emend the text accordingly, and read this as the concluding clause of v 10. Fohrer-Galling (237), Eichrodt (553) and Wevers (216) strike the entire clause as an insertion. I would propose (with May, 303, and the RSV) that the M reading be preserved here, as in keeping with the conditionality expressed earlier in vv 7b-9. Here, as there, the very possibility of experiencing reconciliation with the divine is predicated on the repudiation of past sins. The other difficulties in v 11 all owe themselves primarily to the fourfold repetition of צורה ("form"). G renders the first instance verbally, as διαγραφεις ("draw out"), apparently for the Hebrew וצרת (from צור "fashion, delineate"). This reading, adopted by the RSV, is again inferior to M. The Greek translator, troubled by the lengthy object clause prior to the verb הודע, has resolved the awkwardness by reading the first noun as a verb. Hence, most commentators accept the first צורה as genuine: so Fohrer-Galling (237), Cooke (465, on the grounds that "the word is repeated erroneously no less than three times, and the repetitions must have some starting-point"), Gese (40), Wevers (216), Eichrodt (551) and Zimmerli (2:410). Like Cooke, most contemporary scholars consider the other three occurrences of צורה in this verse to be erroneous. Support for this belief comes from G, which recognizes only the second occurrence (translated by υποστασιν αυτου, "its substance"), rendering the first verbally, lacking the third, and apparently understanding the fourth as תורה (translated δικαιωματα μου, "my commandments"). Cooke (474-475), proposing that the second incidence of צורהwas an error for תורה, suggests that a marginal note to that effect has itself been mistakenly incorporated into the text. Hence, he emends the second incidence to תורתו, strikes the old marginal note תורתו וכל צורתי וכל, and reads תורתו for the fourth incidence, following G. This procedure, also followed by Gese (40), yields a series of three word pairs as the object of הודע ("make known"): ותבונתו... צורת ("form ...and its arrangements"), ומובאיו ומוצאיו ("its entrances and its exits"), and חקתיו כל ואת תורתו כל ("all its laws and all its ordinances"). This very attractive resolution to an awkward situation is also followed by Eichrodt (552), Wevers (216), May (303), Zimmerli (2:410-11), and Hals (304); Fohrer-Galling (237) simply excise צורה in all but the first instance. A question about this solution, however, is raised by the reading of Targum Jonathan, which not only preserves צורה in all the places it is preserved in M, but fails to read תורה in the one place it is found, having instead wkl dhzy lyh, rendered by Levey (117) as "everything to which it is entitled." This suggests that תורה, not צורה, may be the misplaced element here. With Cooke, I would propose that a marginal note has been erroneously copied into the text; unlike Cooke, I suggest that the note itself was erroneous: the second incident of צורה, following G, is to be preserved. The phrase חקתיו כל ואת צורתו כל is authentic in both its occurrences; the shift in G is a misreading, prompted by 44:5, where the order is "law" and "ordinances." Note, however, that in this reconstruction, Gese's tripartite structure still holds.

three word pairs as the object. An even closer parallel, he observes,
can be seen in the the structure and terminology of v 8 and vv 10-11:

v 8   וטמאו...בתועבותם אשר עשו
v 10   ויכלמו מעונותיהם
v 11   אשר עשו   מכל   יכלמו [65]והם

Thus, he argues, vv 10-11 cannot be separated from vv 1-9.[66]

However, the connections Gese establishes between vv 10-11
and 1-9 are with that section we have already described as expansion:
vv 7b-9, which also manifests a continuity with the earlier prophecies
of 1--39. Hence, what Gese has established is not the continuity of vv
10-11 with the vision of the כבוד in vv 1-9, but their commonality
with the earlier insertion at vv 7b-9. The same redactor who inserted
the anti-royal polemic of vv 7b-9, transforming a word of promise into
a word of command, here continues in that same legislative vein.

43:10-12: The Title "תורת הבית". Verse 12 is an interpretive
crux. Suggested emendations to the text are entirely without
foundation: the verse has an elegant structure, the repeated
declaration זאת תורת הבית ("this is the law of the Temple") forming
an *inclusio* about the assertion על ראש ההר כל גבלו סביב סביב קדש
קדשים ("the entire mountaintop will be most holy")[67] The question is,
what precisely is the "this" of the reference? Zimmerli proposes that
the verse is self-referential: the holiness of the mountaintop is itself
the content of the תורת הבית.[68] This, however, seems unlikely. As

---

[65] Gese, 42.

[66] Zimmerli, too, (2:418-19) argues for the authenticity of these verses, on the
basis of continuity in theme and vocabulary between 43:10-11 and the chapters before
the Temple Vision.

[67] Gese (44), Wevers (216) and Elliger in his notes to Ezekiel in the *BHS*
recommend that the repetition of the phrase at the end of the verse be deleted, following
G and the Syriac. However, the translator of G has clearly not understood the verse at
all, reading ואת for זאת and צורת for תורת. Moreover, Alexandrinus and
Marchalianus restore the concluding phrase, which Origen had placed under the
asterisk. A strong case, then, can be made for the originality of this repetition,
expunged from the text by translators who deemed it a meaningless repetition.

[68] Zimmerli, 2:419.

has often been observed, the form of this text is very like the form
used elsewhere in priestly legislation to designate a particular ritual
ordinance; it never refers to a general quality (such as holiness).[69]
One must then ask, does the verse refer backwards, as a summary of
what has gone before, or forwards, as a heading to the material that
will follow?

Talmon and Fishbane argue that this formula is to be seen as the
conclusion of the Temple blueprint.[70] In support for this conclusion,
they cite Leviticus 14:54-47, where an inclusio with תורה serves as a
concluding summary of the body of legislation regarding leprosy.[71]
Three objections to their argument can be raised. First, unlike the
proposed parallel in Leviticus 14:54-57, Ezekiel 43:12 is not preceded
by a body of legislation, but rather by descriptive material.[72] Second, a
number of cases can be cited where the formula זאת תורת... is used to
introduce a body of legislation (cf. Lev 6:2, 7, 18; Num 19:2, 31:21).
Third, explicit mention is made again of the תורה of the Temple in
Ezekiel 44:5, which resumes, after the necessary description of the
altar and its purification ritual, the detailing of the Temple's sacrificial
cult.   The concept is nowhere raised prior to 43:12.[73] The likely
reference, then, is not back to the Temple description of 40--42, but
forward, to the ritual laws regulating access to the Divine Presence
(entrances and exits) which are to come.   These are introduced by a

---

[69] An observation made especially by Cooke, 466; cf. also Eichrodt, 556; and
Talmon and Fishbane, "Structuring," 140-42.

[70] Talmon and Fishbane, "Structuring," 140-42. Note that they translate תורה
here as "Instruction-plan" (140). Cf. also Hals, 306.

[71] Cooke (466) also regards 43:12 as a concluding summary. Zimmerli (2:420),
for all that he considers the תורת הבית to consist of the verse itself, views 43:12 as the
formal close of the vision's first section, returning us to the motif of the mountaintop.

[72] So Herrmann (53); and Hölscher (195), who regards the verse as a secondary
transition between the Temple description of 40:5--42:20 and the legislation that
follows. Gese (45), too, sees v 12 in disjunction from the verses preceding: "Es handelt
sich daher entweder um ein stehengebliebenes Fragment oder aber um ein
Vermittlungsstuck zwischen 43, 1-11 und der Altarbeschriebung in 43, 13ff "(One deals
here either with a freestanding fragment or with a transition verse between 43:1-11 and
the altar description in 43:13ff). Eichrodt (556) declares that the description of 40--42
as תורה is an "impossibility."

[73] See above, n. 64.

typical priestly legislative heading, which also summarizes their
content: they are the law of the Temple, concerning the holiness of
the sanctuary and its environs.[74] תורת הבית ("The Law of the
Temple") is the title of this legal corpus.

   43:13-17: The Altar Description. May has proposed that 43:13-
17 is an original composition of the prophet, being a descriptive
elaboration which originally followed the mention of the altar in
40:47.[75] This is unlikely, though not primarily because of the absence
of guidance and measurement motifs.[76] The contrast between the
description of the altar and Ezekiel's description of the Temple comes
rather in the mythic designations given to the parts of the altar in
43:13-17.

   In this text, the base of the altar is called חק הארץ ("the bosom
of the earth," 43:14), the hearth ההראל ("the mountain of God,"
43:15). Albright proposes that the altar was something of a Babylonian
ziggurat in miniature, חק הארץ being the literal translation of *irat
kigalli* ("bosom of *kigallu*"), the formal designation of the foundation of
the ziggurat, and הראל a parallel to the Akkadian *ziqqurratu* (also
"mountain peak," and referring properly only to the uppermost stage
of the pyramid, not the entire temple tower).[77] This proposal is
rejected by Zimmerli, who sees these expressions rather as mundane
architectural terms: the חק is a drain alongside the altar to accom-
modate the flow of blood and water, while הראל or אריאל means
simply "altar hearth."[78]

---

[74] So also Eichrodt (556): "The declaration that the whole of the Temple area is
most holy is therefore put at the beginning as the presupposition of all the laws that are
to follow: their aim is to preserve and assert the special character of the area."

[75] May, 54.

[76] So Zimmerli, 2:425; Eichrodt, 557; and Wevers, 216. But the motifs are also
lacking in some sections one ought to consider original (i.e., 41:5-15a or 42:1-12).

[77] W. F. Albright ("The Babylonian Temple-tower and the Altar of Burnt-
Offering," *JBL* 39 [1920] 140-41) relates the spelling אראל used in vv 15b and 16 to the
Akkadian *arallu*, a word which he claims designates the underworld, yet also means
mountain of God (137-39).

[78] Zimmerli (2:425-26) observes that the Hebrew חק ordinarily refers to a
hollow or indentation (the lap, or the fold of a garment above the belt, or even the

It must be granted that Albright's parallel between the altar and the ziggurat is somewhat forced. However, against Zimmerli, it is also clear that the rendering of חק as "bosom" is a cogent opinion.[79] Further, the description in v 13 can be applied far more naturally to a square, solid object than to a trench about the altar's perimeter. Albright proposes that the הארץ חק may have been the altar's foundation, sunk to a cubit's depth into the earth so that its surface was level with the ground.[80]   The contrast between the sunken foundation and the lofty hearth would then be heightened by the designation of the altar's topmost portion as הראל in 43:15.

The term אריאל is difficult. That אריאל/אראל is an ancient designation for the altar hearth is made clear by its use in the Moabite Stone inscription and in Isaiah 29. In the latter context, it is the altar hearth, and not the Akkadian *arallu*, that is in view in the designation of the city as Ariel. This is clear from Isaiah 29:1, which emphasizes

---

interior of a chariot [1 Kgs 22:35]). A similar proposal was made by Fohrer-Galling (238, see fig.). Support for this approach is lent by G, which reads in 43:13 κολπωμα βαθος επι πηχυν ("the depth of the hollow was about a cubit"). Zimmerli (2:426-27) also demythologizes הראל. He sees the spelling אריאל used for this feature in vv 15-16 as linking unquestionably to Isa 29, where the name Ariel is used five times for Jerusalem. Further, he observes that the Akkadian *arallu* always means "underworld" (never "mountain") and that indeed even for *ziqqurratu* the meaning "mountain peak" is uncertain, its usage generally being restricted to the temple-tower. Cooke (467) also interprets these terms in a mundane fashion. He proposes that חק is used as a description of "a platform or base, into which the square above appeared to sink, as into a bosom." In similar fashion, Cooke suggests that הראל and אריאל (which he renders "lion of God") are but two "popular explanations" of the word for altar-hearth, *'ar'al* or *'ar'el*, derived from a root meaning "to burn." As evidence, Cooke recalls l. 12 of the Moabite Stone, where Mesha describes how he carried off from Daudoh the *'ar'al*: presumably, altar-hearth (468). However, Samuel Feigin ("The Meaning of Ariel," *JBL* 39 [1920] 134) argues that אראל cannot refer to an altar-hearth, "since an altar-hearth cannot be carried captive"; he prefers therefore to understand the אראל here as a stele representing a deity. As he gives no other evidence than the Mesha stele for this interpretation, however, it seems best to stay with an otherwise-attested meaning. Further, it is difficult to see why, despite Feigin's assertion, an altar hearth could not be taken into captivity. If one can drag off a stele, one presumably could also drag off an altar hearth.

[79] Cf. Qoh 7:9; Job 19:27; 23:12, in which the translation "bosom" or "breast" is the only natural rendering.

[80] Albright, "Tower," 139: an interpretation not inimical to the reading of G. Targum Jonathan reads *tswyt'* ("the base" or "the pavement") for חק in 43:13, which could support this interpretation.

the cultic character of Jerusalem as the site of the pilgrim feasts with
their sacrifices, and the loftiness of Jerusalem as a fortified acropolis
(קרית חנה דויד, "city of David's encampment").[81]   It is also supported
by the reading *mdbh'* ("the altar") in Targum Jonathan. From the
positive designation of Jerusalem as Ariel in 29:1, the prophet moves
naturally to its negative consequence: Jerusalem as a place of sacrifice,
of death and burning. For Isaiah of Jerusalem, then, as for Mesha the
Moabite and in our context, the uppermost level of the altar where the
sacrifices are burned is called אריאל.

Whatever the original derivation of the name אריאל, the gloss in
Ezekiel 43:15 relates its significance for the redactor: it is the
mountain of God. This juxtaposition of the depths and the heights, of
the mountain of God and the bosom of the earth, is common in ancient
Near Eastern Temple imagery. The ancient temple at Nippur was
called Dur-an-ki, "the bond of heaven and earth."[82] Similarly, in the
Enuma elish, Marduk founded his temple on Apsu (the fresh-water
abyss), "And its 'horns' were gazing at the foundations of Esharra."[83]
In the Ugaritic literature as well the temple can span the cosmos: in
CTA 3.3.19-20 we find this hauntingly beautiful description of the
temple of Ba[cl]:[84]

rigmu	...the speech
^c*issi wa-l-h-satu 'abnil*	Of wood and the whisper of stone,
t'anatu samīma ^c*imma 'arsi*	The converse of heaven with the earth,
tihāmatu ^c*imma-n-kabkabima*	Of the deeps with the stars.

---

81 With, especially, Hans Wildberger, *Jesaja* (BKAT 10; Neukirchen-Vluyn:
Neukirchener, 1982) 3:1098, 1104 and R. B. Y. Scott, "Isaiah, 1-39," *IB* 5: 323; *contra*
Feigin, "Ariel," 132-33; Albright, "Tower," 138. To be sure, v. 4 reads like a description
of the underworld. This may be because, following the destruction threatened in vv 2-3,
the population of the city is to be found in the underworld; more likely, the depiction of
the city as *arrallu* is in mind. However, the Akkadian background to the designation is
nonetheless secondary; the primary referent in the analogy of Jerusalem as Ariel is the
altar hearth.

82 Richard J. Clifford, *The Cosmic Mountain in Canaan and the Old Testament.*
(HSM 4; Cambridge: Harvard University, 1972) 15.

83 As Clifford (*Mountain*, 20) observes, "The temple appears therefore to be a
part of the structure of the universe. Its base reaches into the underworld and its top to
the heavens.".

84 As pointed and translated by Clifford, *Mountain*, 73.

So also the temple at Lagash could be described, in language to us
conflicting and contradictory, as at once mountain and abyss:

> They made the house grow
>   (high) as the foothills,
> had it float in heaven's midst
>   like a cloud,
> they had it, like a bull,
>   slowly lift its horns,
> had it raise the head over all mountains,
>   like the *kishkanu* tree of the Apsu.
> The house lifted, like the (horizon's) foothills,
>   the head 'tween heaven and earth,
> a sappy cedar, grown among (low) weeds,
> Allure decked Eninnu abundantly
>   among Sumer's brick structures.
>
> They were setting up
>   the wood (scaffolding) in the house,
> it was like the basilisks of the Apsu
>   coming out all together.[85]

The juxtaposition of mountain and abyss, heaven and earth, is a
common element of temple language in the ancient Near East. When
the parts of the altar are designated חק הארץ and הראל, then, they
are addressed by names with profound mythological resonance: the
altar is the meeting-place of heaven and earth, the *axis mundi*.[86]
Such language is out of place in the Temple description, with its stark
prose. There, Jachin and Boaz are simply עמדים אל האילים ("pillars
before the doorposts," 40:49); the table of shewbread המראה כמראה
המזבח עץ ("something resembling a wooden altar," 41:21-22). It is
also intriguing that we are given, in 43:13, another description of the
length of the cubit.[87] If that measurement was part of the redactional
expansion of the vision in 40:5, it is certainly so here as well.

---

[85] Cylinder A 21.19-28; Jacobsen, *Harps*, 414-15. Cf. Barton, *Inscriptions*, 227.

[86] So Mircae Eliade, *The Myth of the Eternal Return, or, Cosmos and History* (tr.
William Trask; Princeton: Princeton University, 1965) 12. Usually, as we have seen,
this language is used of a temple or temple city. That it is here used of the altar shows
the extremely high regard in which the community which preserved and interpreted
this text--doubtless Zadokite altar clergy--held the sacrificial cultus.

[87] Also observed by Fohrer-Galling, 239; and Zimmerli, 2:425.

While the altar description does not belong in 40--42, it does not seem to belong in its present context either. Many scholars separate 43:13-17 both from the material that precedes it and the legislative material regarding the altar consecration that follows, as an oddly placed appendix.[88] Yet biblical precedent exists for placing the laws regarding the altar at the opening of a law-code. Shalom Paul has observed that the Book of the Covenant, the Holiness Code in Leviticus and the Deuteronomic Code all begin with laws regarding the place of sacrifice: the law of the altar and sacrifices in Exodus 20:22-26, the stipulation that sacrifice was to be performed only before the Tent in Leviticus 17:1-9, and the laws regarding the centralization of the cult in Deuteronomy 12:1-27.[89]   This pattern is continued in the Law of the Temple.

Moreover, the placement of the altar description at just this point can be seen to be essential. In 44:5, which resumes the תורת הבית motif, consideration of the laws regarding sacrifice begins. Before the sacrificial personnel and cultus can be described, however, it is necessary that the altar be described and consecrated. The differences in style between the altar description and the ritual of consecration need not point to two separate redactions. They may rather indicate two distinct sources, combined purposively in a single redaction to supply the preconditions necessary for the description of the sacrificial cultus. If the חק הארץ was a sunken foundation, the height of the altar described in Ezekiel 43 is the same as the height given in 2 Chronicles 4:1 for the Solomonic altar. The altar description, then, could derive from an ancient document or tradition describing the pre-exilic altar.[90]

Further evidence that the altar description is an older document reworked by the redactor can be found in the insertion regarding the length of the cubit, and in the explanatory gloss הראל for אריאל in 43:15. This gloss accomplishes two purposes. First, it explains the

---

[88] So Wevers, 216; Eichrodt, 557; Gese, 45; Zimmerli, 2:422; and Hals, 308-9.

[89] Paul, Studies, 34.

[90] With Albright ("Tower," 139); contra Hals (309), who denies any connection between our text and ancient tradition.

ancient name for the altar hearth in a way that complements and contrasts with the designation of the foundation as חק הארץ, thereby making a profound statement in mythic terms about the altar's significance. Second, however, it ties the altar description firmly into its literary context. The designation of the altar hearth as הראל ("mountain of God") recalls the הר גבה מאד ("very high mountain") of 40:2, as well as the ראש ההר ("mountaintop") of 43:12. The connection observed by the scribes between 43:10-12 and 13-17 is thus formally established,[91] as is the intersection of the Law of the Temple with the old prophet's original vision.

43:18-27: The Consecration of the Altar. The ritual for the consecration of the altar, for all that it is thematically connected with the preceding altar description, is generally considered a separate work. 43:18-27 manifests considerable formal integrity. The ritual is at least outwardly structured as a prophetic oracle, beginning with כה אמר יהוה and concluding with נאם אדני יהוה. These formulae have not appeared in Ezekiel 40--48 prior to this point; they are, however, characteristic of the material in 44:6--46:18; 47:13--48:29.[92]

Due to the mention of the Zadokites in 43:19, Gese finds here a portion of his *Sadoqidenschicht*.[93] He proposes that the altar description and consecration were placed here late in the redaction history of these chapters, as by that time 40--42 were well established as a unit and hence closed to further insertions. The oracular setting[94] and the divine speech in first person in v 24[95] derive from the later redaction of the consecration ritual. Though the text has been reworked in the second-person style of 45:18-20 and 46:13-15,

---

[91] The altar description is joined in a single paragraph with the introductory heading in vv 10-12\and the cultic legislation of vv 18-26.

[92] כה אמר יהוה occurs at 44:6, 9; 45:9, 18; 46:1,16; 47:13; נאם אדני יהוה is found at 44:12, 15, 27; 45:9, 15; 47:23; 48:29.

[93] Gese, 115.

[94] Gese, 46, 49.

[95] Ibid., 48.

its original third-person plural formulation is still distinguishable.[96]
With the addition of v 19, the ritual finds its proper context in
conjunction with the later priestly legislation.[97]

Zimmerli, on the contrary, considers the altar consecration of
43:18-26 to be a substantial unit. The shifts in person indicate a
plurality of agents: second singular for the prophet, third plural for the
priests and people.[98] However, Zimmerli finds in vv 24-27 evidence
of the later expansion of the text, on grounds of both form (v 24, with
its "twofold formulaic reference to Yahweh," should mark the end of
the unit) and content (seven days of consecration rather than the two
days of vv 18-24, and no mention of the bull for the sin offering).
Zimmerli concludes that these three verses are a later expansion,
harmonizing with later regulations in P regarding a seven-day
purification period (Exod 29:37; Lev 8:33, 35).[99]

The careful work of Gese and Zimmerli has identified probable
layering in the text. However, this layering can be understoood as the
result, not of multiple redactions, but rather of multiple sources and
documents, joined in a single redaction with a single purpose. Thus,
in vv 13-17, an old altar description from the First Temple period was
joined to the vision and the legislation by the designation of the altar
hearth אריאל as הראל. The cultic legislation regarding the altar's
consecration also has been transformed by its context: whoever the
second singular verbs may originally have addressed (perhaps the high
priest?), in our setting they address the visionary, and so tie the

_____

[96] Gese, 48, 115. Others, while not so systematic as Gese, have also found in the
shifts from second to third person evidence for the text's redaction. Eichrodt (558)
agrees that the original text must have been in third-person plural. The readings of G
may support this interpretation, as G consistently has third plural verbs for M's second
singular through v 23. Note, however, that the G of vv 24 and 25 has, like M, the second
singular, and further that G[967] has second rather than third plurals in vv 22 and 23.
Still, the expected form for a ritual would be the impersonal third person plural (as in
Lev 1-3). Wevers, oddly, holds that it is the second singular verbs that are original, the
third plural being secondary (217). Cooke (469) and May (305), while recognizing signs
of redaction in the shifts in person, do not form a judgement as to what the original
form may have been, and keep M

[97] Ibid., 112.

[98] Zimmerli, 2:431.

[99] Ibid., 435.

legislation to the vision. Further indication that vv 18-27 have been picked up by the redactors and adapted to their present context can be found in vv 25-27. While Zimmerli has discovered a second tradition regarding the consecration ritual in vv 25-27, he has not necessarily identified thereby a distinct redactional layer. Instead, the text confronts us with the harmonization of two authoritative traditions, performed by one redactor at one sitting.[100]

In sum, the altar description and the regulations for the altar's consecration fit quite nicely into their present setting. Though the texts have separate histories, they have been joined in their present context as the necessary prerequisite for the cultic legislation of the Law of the Temple which follows.[101]

---

[100] Michael Fishbane (*Biblical Interpretation in Ancient Israel* [Oxford: Clarendon, 1985] 134) identifies a similar process at work in the Chronicler's text regarding the preparation of the Passover. Confronted with conflicting authoritative traditions in Exod 12:9 (which directs that the Passover must not be boiled [בשל] in water, but is rather to be roasted [צלה] in fire) and Deut 16:7 (which directs that the Passover is to be boiled [בשל]), the Chronicler describes the Passover of Josiah thusly: ויבשלו הפסח באש ("Then they boiled the Passover in fire," 2 Chr 35:13)! He further affirms that this was done כבתוב בספר משה ("as it was written in the book of Moses," 35:12). As Fishbane rightly observes, "Evidently the Chronicler knew two distinct sets of ritual norms, and, regarding both as authoritative traditions, preserved them by an artificial, exegetical harmonization." A similar process is at work here in Ezek 43:18-27, and indeed throughout these chapters. Varying old traditions and current practices and norms are being carefully culled and reworked and harmonized wherever possible, so as to produce a single authoritative statement of the ancient traditions. Seams and contradictions will remain evident, some perhaps as glaring as the impossible "boiling in fire" of 2 Chr 35:13. Yet always, we have to do, demonstrably, with a unified vision of right service to YHWH.

[101] The scribes concluded this section oddly, with a double marking in v 27: a break סתומה following the אתנח, and another at the close of the verse. Perhaps this has been done to emphasize the break between the conduct of the normal sacrificial cultus described in v 27b, and the completion of the altar consecration described in v 27a (curiously, missing in G): only after the seven days of consecration are entirely past can sacrifices be performed. If this was the scribes's intent, they have accurately reflected the vital concern for the altar's holiness found in the text itself.

54   The Law of the Temple

The Law of the Temple Proper: 44:1--46:18[102]

With the exception of 44:1-4, this section contains nothing at all
like the first person visionary account of the Temple description in
40:1--43:9. Rather, these text segments continue, by and large, the
prescriptive style of the altar consecration. The legislation in this
section deals with the cultic personnel (particularly the Zadokite altar
clergy and the נשיא as patron of the Temple liturgy), the daily cultic
life of the Temple, and the major festivals. Though the section opens
with the guidance formula (vv 1 and 4), that formula then disappears,
and does not recur until 46:19. 44:1-5 introduces this entire legal
corpus as divine speech (44:2, 5) which the prophet is instructed to
heed carefully (44:5). It is little wonder, then, that 44:1-46:18 is
characterized by the use of the oracular formulae כה אמר יהוה and
נאם אדני יהוה.[103]

44:1-14: A Judgement Oracle Against the Levites. Though many
modern interpreters propose that the text should not break until after
v 16,[104] formal analysis demonstrates that 44:1-14 is an oracle of
judgement.[105] Although 44:1-2 are probably authentic words of the

_____

[102] While the scribes have subdivided this material into several sections, 44:1-
46:18 has its own internal unity, and may with some justification be considered as a
block. The פרשות, however, provide important insights into the tight structure of this
law-code, and will continue to guide our discussion. Intriguingly, the Aleppo Codex and
Codex Leningradensis differ in their paragraphing through this section, though
generally along understandable lines. The Aleppo Codex tends to subdivide the longer
sections of Codex Leningradensis, usually breaking at the opening of a divine speech.

[103] Zimmerli (2:443) observes that on this basis alone "the complex 44:4--46:18,
for all the variety of its contents, acquires a certain self-contained character as to
form."

[104] Gese, 111. Cf. also Wevers, 220-221; Eichrodt, 566; Zimmerli, 2:453. Hals
breaks this material into three parts: 44:1-3, 4-5, and 6-31 (312-18). The scribal
paragraphing, on the other hand, sets 44:1-14 apart: both Codex Leningradensis and
the Aleppo Codex have a break פתוחה following 44:14; Aleppo also has a break סתומה
following v 8, in keeping with the identified pattern of breaks at markers indicating
divine speech. Intriguingly, May (310) breaks after v 14, and the RSV has a paragraph
break there.

[105] Though directed against the Levites, this oracle is formulated in the classic
style of the judgement speech against the individual identified by Claus Westermann
(*Basic Forms of Prophetic Speech* [tr. Hugh Clayton White; Philadelphia: Westminster,

prophet, and vv 4 and 5 act as redactional sutures, the final unity of this section is not thereby impeded. 44:1-5 function in context as the necessary background and setting for the judgement oracle that follows. 44:6-8 describe the reason for the judgement: the בני נכר ("foreigners; aliens") have been permitted to perform altar service. Following the messenger formula in 44:9, the judgement is delivered: because they permitted this abomination, Levites are barred from altar service (vv 9-14).[106]

44:1-3: The Eastern Gate. Chapter 44 opens with the recurrence of something like the guidance formula, save that שוב rather than בוא is used: the prophet is brought *back* to the eastern gate, so that he may see that the gate is closed. In the strong words of absolute prohibition, YHWH commands Ezekiel,[107] השער הזה סגור יהיה לא יפתח ואיש לא יבא בו כי יהוה אלהי ישריל בא בו והיה סגור") "This gate shall remain closed; it shall never be opened, and no one shall enter it, for YHWH God of Israel entered by it. It shall remain closed"). Yet these words of prohibition are immediately compromised in v 3:

1967] 128): 1) the commissioning of the messenger (vv 1-5), 2) summons to hear (v 6a), 3) accusation (vv 6b-8, introduced with the messenger formula--a variation in the expected pattern), 4) messenger formula (v 9a), 5) announcement of judgement (vv 9-14).

[106]The more precise analysis of this accusation, and its probable setting in the early days of the Judean Restoration, will be the business of Chapter Five.

[107] In the *M* of 44:2, YHWH is identified as the speaker. The editors of *BHS*, however (noting that the divine name is absent in *G*[239]), propose that it be stricken. Indeed, it does seem odd for YHWH to speak at this point. In the Temple description, the guidance formula is usually followed by the speech of the guide, identifying what the prophet sees. Moreover, later in this very verse, the divine Name recurs, so that YHWH ends up referring to self in the third person. Hence, most scholars (cf. Cooke, 477; May, 308; Wevers, 218; Eichrodt, 557; Gese, 50-51; Zimmerli, 2:437) strike the divine Name, and understand the guide to be the speaker. However, other than the single Greek witness cited by the editors of *BHS*, the ancient versions all have the divine Name in this context: indeed, as Zimmerli (2:437) has demonstrated, even the odd word order (ויאמר אלי יהוה) is preserved. Moreover, divine self-reference in the third person is not without precedent. Zimmerli (2:432) observes that, in 6:11 as in 43:18, the messenger formula itself is enclosed in divine speech. Further, Greenberg ("Design and Themes," 186) has observed that in ancient treaties, the shift from "I" to the speaker's name is commonly found. The odd shift in 44:1-2 between divine speech and the speech of the angelic guide ought not surprise us. In theophanic literature, the voice of YHWH's messenger can abruptly become the voice of YHWH himself; indeed, the very identity of the messenger can suddenly become lost in the personal manifestation of YHWH (so Gen 18:1-33; 22:10-19; Ex 3:2-6). Hence, I would argue, the divine Name should be preserved in v 2 (which, incidently, makes all of the legal material that follows one complex divine speech).

the prince, we are told, is permitted to eat the sacred meal in the
vestibule of the gate, though the gate itself remains closed. The
structure of v 3 as well is worthy of comment: oddly, the verse begins
with the direct object marker, joined to הנשיא. Next comes a
repetition of נשיא, followed by the pronoun הוא, and only then do we
at last come to the verb. This curious structure, together with the
repetition of נשיא, rouses suspicion as to the state of the text.

Most scholars have attempted to reconstruct the text by striking
the second נשיא as dittography (following G and the Syriac) and
reading אב for the initial את (hence, "only the prince").[108] Zimmerli,
on the other hand, stresses that the reading of אב for את is without
support, and prefers either to regard the initial את as an error for אל,
so that the verse is introduced by a "prefatory note," or to leave the
text as is, reading the initial את as for emphasis, assuming an
understood *verbum regens*.[109] The use of את with the nominative is
common in later Mishnaic Hebrew, and hence may be evidence for the
later dating of this text.[110]   In any case, the verse is clearly
parenthetical, and hence could be regarded as a later addition to its
context.[111] Gese has mounted its major defense. Observing the
connections between the נשיא and the inner eastern gate in 46:1-10,
and the fact that there, as well as here, the outer eastern gate is
presumed closed, Gese concludes that 44:1-3 forms the necessary

---

[108] This route, proposed by the editors of *BHS*, has been followed by Cooke (478),
Eichrodt (559), May (308), Gese (50) and the translators of the RSV. Hals (312) deletes the
את , but does not read אב in its place. Wevers (218) merely rejects this verse as a
secondary expansion based on 46:2, 8. Fohrer-Galling (243), while giving consideration
to the reconstruction of the text in a footnote, also strike the verse entirely in their
exegesis of the section.

[109] Zimmerli, 438. This procedure is also preferred by Fohrer-Galling, 243.

[110] So *GHG* 117i.

[111] Cf. Fohrer-Galling, 243; Wevers, 218. On the contrary, Eichrodt (559) holds
for the unity of these three verses as a secondary link connecting the Temple
measurements to the legislation following, while Cooke (476) attributes all three verses,
and indeed much of the remainder of chapter 44, to Ezekiel.

Text and Structure   57

prerequisite for the later material,[112] and is therefore the opening of the interpretive layer regarding the נשיא, the *nasi-Schicht*.[113]

It is clear that, particularly in 46:1-10, the holiness of the eastern gate and the role of the נשיא in the liturgy regarding the gates are closely linked. However, against Gese, it seems unlikely that 44:1-2 have the נשיא in mind. The verses are rather concerned with the irrevocable pronouncement of YHWH: the gate by which the כבוד has entered is to remain forever closed. Their natural referent is not forward to v 3 (which qualifies and compromises the command of v 2) but rather back to 43:7a. The closing of the eastern gate for all time is a concrete symbolization of the promise there made: YHWH's presence will never be withdrawn again.[114] In the original vision report of the prophet, 44:1 may well have followed immediately upon 43:7a. In 44:1-2, we have once more to do with the words of the prophet Ezekiel.[115]

The Redactional Function of 44:4-5. The guidance formula, this time with the expected בוא Hip^cil, is repeated in v 4, seeming to introduce yet another section. But instead we are given a brief reprise of the vision of the כבוד: again the prophet stands before the Temple, again the כבוד fills the sanctuary, again the prophet falls prostrate. Then, in v 5, we find a virtual recapitulation of the introduction to the entire vision in 40:4, and the resumption of the motif of Temple תורות from 43:12. It is not surprising that these two verses are widely regarded as a secondary construct, part of the editorial frame of Ezekiel 40--48.[116]

---

[112] Gese, 86.

[113] Ibid., 110.

[114] So also Hals (313), though he does not regard the use of the gate by the נשיא as secondary.

[115] So also Cooke (476), though as we have see, he also regards v 3 as authentic, and Fohrer-Galling (241-42), who suggest that 43:1-9, 44:1-2 and 47:1-12 belong together as a second vision of the prophet, to be placed alongside the Temple description of 40--42. Zimmerli, too, holds 44:1-2 to be authentic Ezekielian material, though added later (2:549).

[116] Cf. Wevers, 218; Eichrodt, 562; Gese, 52-53; Zimmerli, 2:444; Hals, 313-315.

To regard vv 4-5 as a redactional suture is not to devalue or
disregard them. On the contrary, these two verses give ample witness
to the ways the redactor has combined his materials into a final,
coherent unit. By recalling the vision of the כבוד, v 4 brings us back
from the necessary excursus regarding the altar to the business of the
holiness of YHWH in the Temple, and hence to Temple service.
However, more precise connections are also afoot. The use of בוא in
the Hip^cil not only recalls the guidance formula as generally found in
the Temple description, but also makes explicit contact with 46:19,
where once again בוא in the Hip^cil is used. The movement of the
prophet from the outer gate to the front of the Temple in the inner
court in 44:4-5 prepares the reader for the resumed description in
46:19-20, as the structures described there are found in the inner
court. In this way, the materials in 44:4--46:19 are both bracketed by
guidance formulae, and joined by them to the Temple description
preceding (with the vision of the כבוד as an integral part) and to the
vision of the River which follows. Similarly, v 5, by recapitulating the
commission to the prophet to see and hear in 40:4, draws the focus of
the text from the earlier Temple description to the legislation
regarding the Temple personnel and cult. Finally, the mention of
Temple תורות makes explicit connection back to the title at 43:12.
The necessary preliminaries regarding the altar and its consecration
are completed; the Law of the Temple proper can now be presented.
In 44:5 as in 43:11, we have to do with "entrances and exits."[117] Here

---

[117] M reads למבוא הבית בכל מוצאי המקדש ("concerning the entrance to the
Temple with all the exits of the sanctuary"). Targum Jonathan has lm^clny for the
singular למבוא, which need not indicate an emendation, or even a separate tradition.
Zimmerli (1:227) notes the confusion of א for ו(י) in the word בוא "no less than eight
times in the book of Ezekiel (10:3; 14:1; 20:38; 22:24; 23:44; 33:22; 36:20; 44:25)." We are,
then, justified in regarding the consonantal text of M, למבוא, as a scribal error for
למבאי. Zimmerli's further proposal (2:443), that בכל be emended to וכל , provides a
smoother reading, and has the support of G. However, as Zimmerli himself observes, it
is just as likely that G has altered the text to provide a smoother reading as it is that the
Greek represents a different text; we do better to keep M. The reading of the RSV ("mark
well those who may be admitted to the temple and all those who are to be excluded from
the sanctuary") is based on a distinguished, but wrong, scholarly tradition (Fohrer-
Galling, 247; May, 308; Eichrodt, 561; and even HELOT, 99). Even the usually
hypercritical Wevers concludes that "there is no evidence to warrant" such an
emendation (219). Moreover, this reading loses the connection back to 43:11, and so
misses a major element in the careful structure of our document.

lies the most intimate point of contact with Ezekiel's original vision, and also that vision's most significant transformation.

We have already noted the massive, fortified gate complexes in 40--42. These are built, it appears, not for access but for defense: to protect the sacred from contaminating contact with the profane. 44:2 makes this point quite explicit: the כבוד having returned to fill the sanctuary, the gate by which the divine Presence had entered--and by which, before, the Presence had departed--is closed forever. This same theme, of doors and gateways, of entrances and exits, is worked out in 44:4--46:18. However, note the subtle transformation, already hinted at in the qualification of the divine prohibition against the use of the eastern gate (44:2-3). 44:6-31 bars the Levites from access to the Presence via the altar, but it also describes the mode of life the Zadokites must follow, that they may gain access. Chapter 45 hedges the נשיא about with regulations regarding his lands and responsibilities; but in 46:1-10, his leadership in the cult, worshipping by the *open* eastern gate, is set forth. Similarly, in the land division and allocation of 47:13-48:29, tribal boundaries are closed off. But the stranger is not closed out; an inheritance in the land is assured (47:22,23).

In brief, the doors of Ezekiel's original vision are *closed* doors. Though the River of life flows out of the Temple into the land, carrying the blessings of the divine Presence to all, it flows beneath closed doors (47:1-2). Perhaps with greater optimism regarding human value and ability than that harbored by the old priest, the redactors of his vision have opened the doors: not indiscriminately, not without great care and caution, but open them they have. The sacrificial liturgy described in the Law of the Temple is, for its practitioners, a legitimate means of access to the Divine. Properly performed by the proper persons, the liturgy is a means of discovering and celebrating (though never of coercing) YHWH's presence in Judah's midst.

44:15-31: The Law Regarding the Zadokites. 44:15-31 are likewise functionally distinct. As a unit, these verses contrast the Zadokites with the castoff Levites. Initial emphasis on Zadokite faithfulness over against the Levites' faithlessness (44:15a) is followed by an account of the responsibilities that fall to the Zadokites (vv 15b-16, 23-24, 28-31) and the strictures which act to preserve Zadokite purity (vv 17-22, 25-27). Gese and Zimmerli both regard vv 15-16 as belonging with vv 6-14, this being, together with vv 28-30a, the original Zadokite material; vv 17-27 and 30b-31 came later.[118] While vv 6-16, 28-30a reflect the same, intensely partisan viewpoint regarding the Zadokite priesthood, the materials in vv 17-27 and 30b-31 are far more sedate, and seem drawn from legislation regarding the priesthood preserved elsewhere in the Scriptures, particularly Leviticus.[119]

However, this need not mean that we are concerned with two (or more) redactional layers. Although vv 15 and 16 are unquestionably from the same pen that produced vv 6-14, they do not belong with that material *functionally*. 44:1-14 is a judgement oracle against the Levites, and a coherent unit: words concerning the Zadokites have no place here. 44:15-16, then, must have another function. In the context, they introduce the following complex, vv 17-31, which deals with the conduct and responsibilities of the Zadokite priests. This section has its own organizing principles. The statement that the Zadokites may enter (יקרבו) the sanctuary leads to a consideration of the vestments to be worn when they enter (בבואם, v 17) the inner court to serve (vv 17-19). This leads naturally to other matters of dress, and hence to matters of conduct appropriate to priestly office, culminating in marriage regulations for clergy (vv 20-22). Having opened thereby the issue of the priest's relationship with and responsibilities to the people, the writer turns to the priest's

---

[118] Gese, 111; Zimmerli, 2:551. Although he divides the text differently, and prefers not to attempt to sort out earlier and later materials, Hals also sees vv 15-16 as belonging with the material preceding, rather than the cultic ordinances which follow (316).

[119] Linen vestments (Lev 6:10), care of the hair (Lev 21:5; Deut 14:1, 2), drinking of wine (Lev 10:9), marriage (Lev 21:7, 13-15), the priest as teacher (Lev 10:11) and as judge (Deut 21:1-5), defilement by corpses (Lev 21:1-3), an inheritance not given the priest (Jos 13:14; Num 18:20-32), the priest's eating of sacrifices and first fruits (Lev 2:3-10; 6:14-18; Deut 18:3-5) and abstention from unslaughtered meat (Lev 7:24)--all are traditions attested elsewhere in the Scriptures. The significance of these attestations for the dating of this material and for the development of the priesthood will be considered in Chapter Five.

responsibilities and conduct outside the Temple, and introduces the mechanism whereby defilement taking place in that context may be remedied, that he may again enter (בָאו, v. 27) the holy place. The motif of entrance, indicated by the verb בוא, characterizes and unites all this material, drawn from various old texts and traditions--a motif which also characterizes 44:15-16.

With 44:28, a definite shift takes place. It is not possible to find an easy or clear connection between the following consideration of Zadokite property rights and the preceding prescription for cleansing from ritual defilement. This does not, however, damage the thesis, for it is also difficult to find such a connection between this material and the cultic context of 44:15-16. A continuity is evident, particularly between the sacrificial concerns of vv 15-16 and the regulation regarding such sacrifices in vv 29-30a. However, the intervening verse is a puzzler. Why should the issue of priestly inheritance be introduced here? Vv 28-31 are concerned with the property rights, or more broadly, the livelihood of the priests. Perhaps they have been composed (again, making use of older traditional materials) as a transition to the land division material in 45:1-8. Zimmerli has noted the connection between the אחזה ("possession") denied the Zadokites in 44:28, and the אחזה given the Levites in 45:5.[120] It is also important to note that נחלה ("property"), another key concept in

_____

[120] Zimmerli, 2:467. Partly on this basis, he develops an argument that 45:1-8 is a later, even more firmly anti-Levitical, expansion to the complex concerning priests and Levites. Zimmerli observes that the M of 45:1, as well as 48:9, has the breadth of the holy portion set not as twenty (עשרים) thousand cubits, but as ten (עשרה here, עשרת at 48:9). With virtually everyone, he agrees that the original reading must have been "twenty," as witnessed in G and demanded by the next two verses. However, Zimmerli suggests that the problem does not derive, as commonly thought, from a scribal confusion of ה or ת for מ, but rather is a "tendentious alteration" (2:465), designed to deny the Levitical lands any place in the holy portion (2:468). The designation of the Levitical lands as אחזה (a "possession") is the final straw: while the possession of the priest is YHWH alone, the Levite is given land: "Even in their 'possession' the Levites are no longer as close to God as the priests in their right to sole use of what is most holy. While the Levites appear to be given more in tangible property, they become poorer in actual sacred 'possession.'" Intriguing as this argument is, it is not finally convincing. Zimmerli has placed too much weight on an easily explained scribal error and a single term for property. Although unquestionably the redactor intends by the use of אחזה to contrast priest and Levite as well as to link 44:28-31 to 45:1-8, what is said here does not in any substantial way go beyond what is said either in the anti-Levite polemic of chapter 44 or the land division scheme of 47:13--48:29.

45:28, is found in 45:1 as a designation for the entire land, a portion of which is then allocated to Temple, priest, Levite, city and נשיא. Generally, it has been held that the inclusion of 45:1-8 has been prompted by 44:28.[121]   However, 44:28 cannot be understood as the continuance, either of the legislation in 44:17-27, or of the Zadokite affirmation in vv 15-16. It makes sense only as a foreshadowing of 45:1-8, to which it is connected by theme and by vocabulary. We do not, then, have to do here with an original text 44:6-16, 28-30a, divided by interpolations, expanded by additions, which called up an abbreviated form of the land division scheme at a later date. Rather, we have two deliberate redactional units, 44:1-14 and 15-31, each incorporating older material, in which we can plainly discern the pen of the redactor as author at three junctures: vv 3-14, the actual judgement oracle against the Levites; vv 15-16, which introduce the following section regarding the Zadokites; and vv 28-30a (itself based on older materials, though composed by the redactor), which effects the transition between the legislation regarding the Zadokites and that regarding the division of the land.

   45:1-8: The Land Division Foreshadowed. The relationship between these verses and the much fuller account of territorial boundaries in 47:13--48:29 has occasioned considerable debate. Obviously, the two texts are connected. The size of the parcels allotted is in each case the same. The allotments are presented in the same sequence (sanctuary, priest, Levite, city, נשיא). Even certain key terms are shared.[122]   However, 45:1-8 is not a misplaced fragment from 47:13--48:29, but rather a summary of it.[123]

---

[121] E.g., Cooke, 493; Wevers, 223; Eichrodt, 569; Zimmerli, 2:467; Hals, 322.

[122]   I.e., the use of the root נחל in reference to the land (the noun נחלה, "inheritance," in 45:1; the verb נחל in the Hithpaᶜel, "divide for an inheritance," in 47:13) and the description of the Temple lands as תרומה קדש (45:1, 6; 48:10)

[123] So especially Eichrodt, 569, *contra* Fohrer-Galling, 258-59. As Eichrodt observes, we have here not a section from the longer work, but rather a terse summary. Gese indeed has proposed that 45:1-8a is rather the first draft of 47:13-48:29 (115). A similar proposal is made by May (314), though he attributes both to one author, "here concerned only with the heart of the allotment; he later repeats and elaborates when giving the total allotment of the land, including tribal territories." This is possible

As the land division scheme begins with the holy portion as
divided among sanctuary, priests and Levites and ends with the
portion given to the נשיא, these summary verses provide a smooth
transition from the legislation regarding the priests to that regarding
the נשיא.[124] By placing this abridged portion of the territorial
allotments here between laws regarding the Zadokite priest and his
patron, the נשיא, the redactor foreshadows the centrality of these
figures in the grand scheme of 47:13--48:29.

The transition between land division and the legislation
regarding the נשיא, which opens with a prophetic critique (45:9), is
neatly effected by yet another critique in v 8. This first critique refers
to the scheme for land division, and stresses that the נשיא shall not
violate the land rights of the people. Since the parcels accorded to
the tribes are not mentioned in 45:1-8, the grand scheme is already in
view. The principle at work here is made explicit in the closing
verses of the Law of the Temple, 46:16-18: the continued wealth of
the נשיא is insured for the Temple's sake, and as a bar against
temptation to greater gains by the oppression of the people.
Apparently, at the time of the redactor's work, a history of oppression
at the hands of the נשיאים could already be cited; future נשיאים are
enjoined against repeating past offenses. The negative tone of v 8 does
not disqualify it from inclusion in the prior section;[125] its content
makes clear reference to the land division, and its tone serves as an
appropriate transition to the forceful critique of v 9.

45:9-17: The נשיא. As 44:15-31 defined the role of the
Zadokite priest, so 45:9-17 defines the role of the נשיא. 45:9, as we

---

from a strictly formal perspective: the connections cited above as signs of dependency
can run either way. However, as will be discussed below, the significance of the Temple
as center of the land, and of priest and נשיא as the dual center of the community,
cannot be seen apart from the context in the larger land division scheme. Since these
concerns are back of the placement of 45:1-8 here, the longer work must be in view.

[124] Hals, too, describes this as a transition text, noting connections in
vocabulary backwards to material preceding, and connections forward in theme in the
"admonitory instruction" aimed at the נשיאים (322). Note, however, that Hals
considers vv 8-9 as a unit.

[125] *Contra* Wevers, 223; and Eichrodt, 571.

64   The Law of the Temple

have seen, opens the section with a critique: evictions are to cease (a
reference back to v 8), משפט וצדקה ("justice and righteousness") are
to be established. A quite precise definition is then given of the nature
of this righteousness: the נשיא is given responsibility for maintaining
proper (צדק) weights and measures--essential, if the sacrificial cultus
is to function properly. This just system having been defined (vv 10-
12, the plural "you" in v 10 referring to the plural נשיאים in v 9), it is
immediately given application: the amounts of the תרומה ("offering;
portion") to be given to the נשיא for the support of the sacrificial
cultus are established. Hence, the two chief responsibilities of the
נשיא, as far as the Law of the Temple is concerned, are established: he
is to guarantee just measures, and to collect the תרומה by which the
Temple cultus is maintained.

The redactor is probably making use of multiple sources in this
section. He opens with his own prophetic critique of the נשיאים in
direct address (vv 9-10). Then follows the authoritative table of
weights and measures to be instituted and guaranteed by the נשיא (vv
11-12), drawn, as was the long cubit of 40:5 and 43:13, from the
Persian standard.126 The תרומה-table in 45:13-15 may well date from
the First Temple--or, it may be an exilic proposal for the support of
the restored cult, preserved in the redactor's community. In either
case, it has been instituted, here, as the means for the Temple's
support. The concluding two verses, again by the redactor, clarify that
the נשיא is responsible for the collection.127

45:18-25: The Cultic Calendar. The cultic calendar which
concludes this chapter (vv 18-25) is similarly assembled from the

---

126 See Chapter Four, pp. 118-121, below.

127 Gese (111-12) deems vv 13-15 a part of the *Sadoqidenschicht*, and vv 16-17 a
redactional suture. It is in any case clear that these are two independent units. 45:13-15
addresses the people directly in the second person and has a clearly marked beginning
(זאת התרומה אשר תרימו), "This is the offering which you shall present;" analogous to
the זאת תורת הבית of 43:12) and end (the oracular formula נאם יהוה). 45:16-17
shifts to third person, addressing the people as עם הארץ. However, we need not
postulate a second redactional layer here. 45:13-15, which is plainly a compositional
unit, may well have its own history, but a separate history does not indicate a separate
redactional layer in the text.

tradition of the redactor, though recast in such a way as to stress the role of the נשיא as patron. It therefore is most appropriate in the context, following naturally on the designation of the נשיא as provider in vv 9-17. These three units follow upon one another quite naturally. The divisions are thematic, vv 1-8 dealing with the division of the land, vv 9-17 with the general responsibilities of the נשיא, and vv 18-25 presenting the cultic calendar of the Temple community. Yet, the three segments are also bound together, and to the previous section regarding the priest, by the use of the word תרומה (in 44:30; 45:1, 6, 7, 13, 16) This is not, as Gese and Zimmerli in particular have proposed, an instance of organization by catchword.[128]   Rather, it is an intentional redactional device, used to stress the final unity of these many and various parts.

46:1-11 and 12-15: Temple Service. [129]   The compositional unity of vv 1-10 is unquestionable. The use of the expression עם הארץ, the concern for the נשיא and the connection of the נשיא with the gates have all been encountered before, in passages we have attributed to the redactor. Here, too, the redactor is at work as an author. While connections with earlier traditions are certainly possible, the liturgy of the eastern gate found here is entirely the work of the priestly redactor, and probably describes a current practice in his community. 46:11 sounds much like the תרומה-table in 45:13-15, although it is not in the second person; it may well derive from the redactor's tradition and hence have its own separate history.[130]   Here, however, it functions as the conclusion to the prescription for the liturgy of the

---

[128] Gese, 115; Zimmerli, 2:467.

[129] The next פרשה, 46:1-11, is subdivided in the Aleppo Codex by a break סתומה following v 5, between the prescription for the sabbath and new moon offerings of the נשיא. It may seem that v 12 ought to be included, as it too deals with the liturgy involving the eastern gate. The scribes, however, chose to place v 12, with its instructions regarding the נדבה ("free-will offering") of the נשיא together with the instructions regarding the daily sacrifices (תמיד) and separate from the instructions regarding the major feasts. This scribal section is virtually identical with the main body of Gese's *nasi-Schicht*, the only difference being that Gese considered v 10 a later insertion and concluded the section with v 12 (110).

[130] As Gese (ibid.) observed.

66   The Law of the Temple

appointed feasts. As the ancient scribes sensed, a new section begins
at v 12, though tied to v 1-11 by the motif of the eastern gate. Having
described the liturgy of the gate connected with the major feasts,
sabbaths and new moons, the priestly redactor turns now to the נדבה
and the תמיד, described in vv 12-15.

46:16-18: A Final Critique of the נשיא. It was earlier proposed
that the Law of the Temple proper is bracketed by the guidance
formulae in 44:4 and 46:19. Although neither scribal tradition breaks
following 46:18, such a break is consonant with their evident
intention.[131] 46:16-18, moreover, is plainly a compositional unit, with
a definite beginning (כה אמר יהוה) and end (as the guidance formula
in 46:19 begins a new unit) and a consistent theme: the insurance that
the estate of the נשיא remains in his family, joined to an injunction to
deprive none of his people of their property.

These themes have been sounded before. Remember that the
section regarding the נשיא was introduced at 45:9 with a prophetic
oracle calling for evictions to cease, and that that oracle itself followed
on a denouncement of the greed of the נשיאים, in connection with the
land grant to the נשיא and his family. The material between 45:9-10
and 46:16-18, moreover, is all concerned, in one way or another, with
the נשיא. Here again, then, we see the redactor at work, setting off
the laws related to the נשיא with prophetic critiques of the misuse of

---

[131] At this point, the Masoretic traditions of the Aleppo Codex and Codex
Leningradensis go their separate ways. In the Aleppo Codex, a break סתומה is made
after v 16, and then no breaks are found until a break פתוחה following 47:12. In Codex
Leningradensis, the break (סתומה) follows v 19, with the following section
incorporating 46:20-47:12 (as in the Aleppo Codex, a break פתוחה). The disagreement
appears to come from the attempt to determine where the divine speech begun in 43:7
(and explicitly continued in 44:2) is to be concluded. Since the speaker in 47:1-12 is
explicitly the guide, and since by analogy with earlier material the speaker in 46:20, 24
is also the guide, the divine speech must close prior to these texts. The scribes who
copied the Aleppo Codex apparently took the messenger formula in 46:16 as the
indicator of the last unit of divine speech, and lacking an explicit marker of closure
such as נאם יהוה, concluded conservatively that only v 16 itself was to be included.
This, as we have seen at other points of variance between the paragraphing of the
Aleppo Codex and Codex Leningradensis in the Law of the Temple, is in keeping with the
tendency of the Aleppo Codex to break at markers indicative of divine speech. The
Masoretic tradition of Codex Leningradensis, on the other hand, does not break until
the beginning of the guide's first speech in v 20.

that office through greed. Finally, this concluding section regarding
the land grant of the נשיא functions as a transition into the material
concerning the land which will follow.

46:19-24: The Temple Kitchens

This section recalls the opening Temple description in several
striking ways. Here, again, we find the familiar guidance formula (vv
19, 21), the figure of the guide, and first-person description of
Temple structures: here, kitchens in the inner court for the priests to
prepare the sacred meal, and corresponding kitchens in the outer
court, where the Levites may prepare the sacred meal for the people.

However, 46:19-24 cannot be a misplaced portion of Ezekiel's
original vision.[132] 46:19-20 in particular is strongly reminiscent of
42:13-14, already identified as a composition of our redactor. Both are
set in the inner court, both are concerned with the priesthood in
particular, and both deal with the problem of the communication of
holiness (42:14; 46:20). 46:19-20 presupposes the existence of the
לשכות ("cells, chambers") described in 42:13-14, since it is there that
the sacred meal, prepared in these kitchens, is to be eaten. 46:21-24
similarly is dependent on 46:19-20. The repetition of the guidance
formula in v 21 presupposes that the prophet had gone into the inner
court, since he must be led back into the outer court. The kitchens in
vv 23-24 are in clear parallel to the kitchens in v 20. Most striking of
all, however, is the mention of משרתי הבית ("those who serve in the
Temple"). These, set in explicit contrast to the כהנים of the previous
section, are evidently Levites (44:14). The point of view in evidence is
not that of the prophet, who identified both altar and Temple clergy as
כהנים, but that of the redactor. Here, as in 42:13-14, the redactor is
functioning as author.[133]

---

[132] With Eichrodt, 578; Wevers, 227; Fohrer-Galling, 256; Gese, 89; Zimmerli,
2:500; and Hals, 336; *contra* Cooke, 425-26; and May, 54.

[133] Zimmerli (2:500) also associates 46:19-24 with 42:1-14, and argues against
attributing it to Ezekiel. However, he argues that it is a *far* later addition, placed here
because the preceding materials were already closed (a similar argument is advanced by
Hals, 336). He argues further that as the Levites are not even called "Levites" here, this
text represents an even more extreme devaluation of their role than chapter 44. But, as
is argued below, a motivation for the placement of the text here by our single redactor

These bits of description seem oddly placed, disrupting the
natural connection between 46:16-18 and 47:1-12, but they could not
have have been conveniently introduced earlier. Our redactor was
reluctant to tamper with the original Temple description in 40:1--
43:7a. The two insertions identified there (באמה וטפח in 40:5 and
42:13-14) involved elements essential to his enterprise; these
addenda to the Temple description do not.   46:19-24 answers a
question implicit in the description of the sacrificial cultus (45:13-
46:15): where will the sacred meal after the offerings be prepared and
eaten? However, a description of the Temple kitchens could not have
been placed prior to 46:16-18 without interrupting the unity of the
text involving the נשיא. By placing 46:19-24 just prior to the
prophet's vision of the River, the redactor counterbalances 44:4 by
another descriptive section with the guidance formula, reintroduces
the guide, and so nicely concludes the Law of the Temple.

IV. The River and the Land (47:1-48:35)

47:1-12: The River

The prophet Ezekiel's vision report resumes in 47:1. While the
original continuity between 44:1-2 and 47:1 was broken by the
insertion of material belonging to Law of the Temple, the connection
is still signalled by the technique of repetitive resumption: וישב אתי
("Then he brought me back") in 44:1, וישבני ("Then he brought me
back") in 47:1.

These twelve verses read naturally as a continuous narrative,
describing the river which flows out from the Temple, bringing life to
the land. Zimmerli, however, proposes that an original unit, vv 1-8,
has been expanded by a series of four separate additions: v 9 fills out
the originally succinct statement of the life-giving waters, and is
written in "the language of P"; v 10 elaborates on the boon the waters
will provide for fishermen; v 11 is an even later supplement, which

can be found. Moreover, the title "Levite" is not found in 40:45, either--yet that text
represents the most positive evaluation of the Levites to be found in the Temple Vision.
Hence we need not postulate a further redactional layer to account for either the
location or the content of this passage.

declares that the marshes, with their life-preserving salt, will not be lost; and the material following the אתנה in v 12, which gives the purposes of the fruit (for food) and the leaves (for healing) of the trees that thrive alongside the waters.[134] The laconic phrasing of the earlier Temple description would seem to support Zimmerli's analysis. However, the supposed addenda are not mere descriptive detail. They are essential to the depiction of the river as the means by which the blessings of the divine Presence are mediated to the land.

The river of Ezekiel's vision, with its life-giving waters and miraculous trees, is a river of paradise: a return to the well-watered garden of Eden (Gen 2:8-14).[135] However, the blessings wrought in the land by the Divine presence are not to be limited to paradisial trees and fresh water. Economic benefits are reaped as well: abundant blessings of material wealth, represented by the abundant supply of fish for fishermen, and of salt. Parallels with the Gudea cylinders are particularly interesting. Cylinder B, 14.19-24 describes the preparation of a royal bedchamber in the temple for the god and his consort. That accomplished, the material benefits which the temple will bring to the land are recorded:

> With the river filled with flowing waters,
> the marshes stocked
>   with marsh carp and giant carp,
> Their inspector of fisheries,
>   the one stocking (them with) fish,
>   guiding them;
> with the grain laden
>   for (transport on) the great waters,
> with the storage piles and heaps
> of Lagash piled up,
> with the cowpens built,
>   the sheepfolds built,
>   the lambs placed with good ewes,
>   the ram released unto its good ewes,
>   with the calves placed with good cows,
>   and the bull bellowing loudly among them,
>   with the oxen properly in their yokes,
>   and their oxdriver standing by their side,
>   with the asses saddled with their packsaddles,
>   and their drivers who feed them
>   following after them,

---

[134] Zimmerli, 2:513-14.

[135] So Levenson, *Program*, 27.

with huge copper ingots
strapped on the jackasses,
with the huge millhouse supported[136]

Sure enough, once mother Baba and lord Ningirsu had made themselves at home in the bedroom, the jars and goblets of the temple
became "(like) the Tigris and Euphrates rivers continually carrying
abundance."[137] Although the sexual imagery of the Gudea Cylinders is
absent from the Temple Vision, the connection made between the
construction of the temple and an abundant supply of pure water gives
support to the original linkage of Temple and river in our text as well.
Moreover, the explicit mention of fish, and of other material blessings
brought by the temple to the city and its people, provides precedent
for the use of these motifs in Ezekiel's vision report.

Fertility in nature and material prosperity are also linked to
temple-building in Ugaritic mythology. When 'El decrees that a house
be built for Ba^{c}l (CTA 4.5.68-73), Lady 'Atirat jubilantly responds,

wn'ap . ^{c}dn . mtrh   Now, indeed, his rainy season[138]
B^{cl} . y^{c}dn . ^{c}dn . ṯkt . bglṯ   Ba^{cl} will appoint; the season of ships[139]

---

[136] Cylinder B, 14. 25-15. 15; Jacobsen, Harps, 438. Cf. Barton, Inscriptions,
249-51.

[137] Cylinder B, 17. 10-11; Jacobsen, Harps, 440. Cf. Barton, Inscriptions, 251-
53.

[138] F. M. Cross (private communication) suggests interpreting ^{c}dn here and in
the following line as referring to "fertility and the giving of fertility," based on this use
of Aramaic ^{c}dn in the Tell Fekhariyeh inscription, lines 4-5: m^{c}dn mt kln, translated
"he who makes all lands luxuriant" by Stephen Kaufman ("Reflections on the Assyrian-
Aramaic Bilingual From Tell Fakhariyeh," Maarav 3/2 (1982) 169) and "who enriches
all lands" by A. R. Millard and P. Bordreuil ("A Statue from Syria with Assyrian and
Aramaic Inscriptions," BA 45 (1982) 137). Millard and Bordreuil, indeed, suggest a
possible parallel between this Aramaic term and the biblical Eden ("Statue," 140).
Based on this usage, Cross translates CTA 4. 5. 68-69 as,
          "Now, behold, let Ba^{cl} make fertile with his rains,
          Let him make luxuriant with flowage and torrents."
This rendering, however, depends also on reading ṯrt instead of ṯkt (see following note).
If ṯkt is indeed the reading, we do best to see ^{c}dn as cognate to Aramaic ^{c}iddān, Arabic
^{c}adān, and Akkadian adānu, and translate as "time" or "season."

[139] Textes Ougaritiques (207) proposes reading ṯrt here, explained by the Arabic
ṯarra ("to make water spout"), and translates "l'heure du jaillissment des flots" (the time
of gushing floods). Given the close similarity of the cuneiform signs r and k, this
rendering is of course possible. However, I propose that this reading is prompted as
much by translation difficulties as by morphological concerns. With Aistleitner

upon the waves.[140]

w<y>tn . qlh . b^crpt	Now he will give his voice in the clouds;

w<y>tn . qlh . b^crpt   Now he will give his voice in the clouds;
srh . l'arṣ . brqm   He will loose lightnings upon the earth.
bt . 'arzm . ykllnh   The house of cedar, he may build it;
hm . bt . lbnt . y^cmsnh   Even the house of brick, he may raise it![141]

If the translation here proposed for the difficult *ṯkt bglṯ* is correct, the temple of Ba^cl at Ugarit was a blessing to merchant as well as farmer, bringing material as well as natural abundance.[142] In 47:1-12, as in the temple texts from Lagash and Ugarit, the temple brings blessings of fertility and material prosperity. There is, then, no reason to consider vv 9-11 and 12b secondary.

(*Wörterbuch*, 334), Gordon (*Textbook*, 502), Manfried Dietrich and Oswald Loretz ("Zur ugaritischen Lexikographie I," *Bibliotheca Orientalis* 23 [1966] 129), and E. Lipinski ("Epiphanie de Baal-Haddu RS 24.245," *UF* 3 [1971] 86), among others, I have read *ṯkt* here, which must be understood as an ancient word of indeterminate origin meaning "ship" (note the Egyptian *ṯkti* and the Phoenician city of Shigata). When the context is properly understood, this yields a perfectly natural reading, as the next note reveals.

[140] *Glṯ* may be cognate to the enigmatic Hebrew גלש, used twice in the Song of Songs (4:1; 6:5). In each instance, גלש is used in a simile comparing a woman's hair to the movement of a flock of goats. In the Song, the apparent meaning is "wave." A flock of sheep or goats, observed from a distance as they move down a hillside, appear to flow in a wavelike motion: hence, the point of the obscure simile in the Song would be that the woman's hair is wavy. The reading "wave" for the Ugaritic *glṯ* is further supported by *PRU* 5.1.5, where *glṯ* parallels *thmt* ("the watery abyss"). In light of this parallel, Dietrich and Loretz ("Lexikographie I," 129) also propose the translation *"die Zeit für das Schiff auf den Wogen"* (The time of the ship on the waves), while Lipinski ("Epiphanie," 86) renders the phrase as *'l'heure ou les bateaux seront dans la tempête"* (The time when the ships are caught in a storm). Another, more puzzling use of *glṯ* comes from *KTU* 1.101.7, in a hymn to Ba^cl: *rišh bglṯ bšm[m]* ("his head in/with *glṯ* in the heavens"). The proposed translation in *Ugaritica 5* (ed. Charles Virolleaud [Mission de Ras Shamra 16; Paris: Imprimerie Nationale, 1968] 558), *"Sa tête est en mouvement dans les cie[ux],"* (His head is in motion in the heavens?) seems strange. Given the parallel with Cant 4:1; 6:5, which describes the beloved's hair, a more likely translation may be "his hair in waves in the heavens."

[141] Instead of "build" and "raise," Ginsberg (*ANET*³, 133) reads "destroy" and "remove." The Ugaritic *ykllnh* is from *kll* or *kly*, which, like the Hebrew כלה, means "finish, complete" in both the positive and the negative sense. Similarly, *y^cmsnh*, from *^cms* (cf. Hebrew עמס), means literally "load up," for which both positive and negative readings are possible. Ginsberg chose to see these texts as descriptive of the destructive power of Ba^cl's lightning. However, in their context, they are more likely to refer to the building of Ba^cl's temple. Hence, the positive rendering is to be preferred.

[142] The association of Ba^cl with merchant fleets is also supported by this ritual curse, from a treaty between Esarhaddon and Baal, king of Tyre (ca. 677 BCE): "May Baal-sameme, Baal-malage, and Baal-saphon raise an evil wind against your ships, to undo their moorings, tear out their mooring pole, may a strong wave sink them in the sea, a violent tide [...] against you" (Erica Reiner, tr.,*ANET*³, 534).

47:13-23: The Borders

This section, which describes the borders of the land, is cast as a prophetic oracle, introduced by כה אמר אדני יהוה and concluding with נאם יהוה. Since these formulae never occur in the original vision, but are characteristic of the legislative expansion, we have here to do with the work of our redactor. From the description of the river, which brings new life to the land, he moves naturally to the depiction of the borders of that land. Then, before relating the division of the land among the tribes, he pauses to insure the land rights of הגרים בתוככם ("the aliens in your midst"). The sense of this provision is extraordinary: the alien is made co-inheritor of the land with the ethnic Israelite.

48:1-29: The Division of the Land

The following section, 48:1-29, describes the borders of the land and its division among the tribes. The center of this unit is the allocation of land to the Temple and its personnel (48:8-22), summarized and foreshadowed at 45:1-8. By their identification with the Temple, the Zadokite priest and the נשיא his patron are affirmed as central figures for the believing communuity.

In 48:11, a sharp hierarchical distinction is made between the Zadokite priest and the Levite. Both Zimmerli and Gese consider this verse a later expansion of the text, based upon the anti-Levite polemic of 44:6-14.[143] This, however, is only necessary if we assume that the land division text as a whole does not know of the polemic. Yet a clear division is made throughout the text between the allotment for the כהנים and the allotment for the Levites, who are thus most evidently *not* considered כהנים. Since the reason for their no longer being called כהנים is given in 44:6-14, (as contrasted with 40:45-46, which observes a two-stage clergy but refers to both as כהנים) that distinction must already be presupposed by the land division itself; excising v 11 removes the explicit polemic, but does not affect the underlying assumption evident in the land division itself: that the

---

[143] Gese, 112; and Zimmerli, 2:458. Codex Leningradensis breaks following v 11, a division which has the effect of separating the land provisions of the priests and the Levites, and indicates scribal sensitivity to the the polemic expressed in this verse.

Levites are not priests. More will be said concerning the doctrinal function of the program for land division in a later chapter.

The City: 48:30-35

With this brief description of the walls and gates of restored Jerusalem, our text, and the entire book of Ezekiel, concludes. The twelve gates of the city, three to each side, are designated with the names of the twelve tribes. The order, however, bears no relation to the order of the tribes in the land allotment,[144] and the tribal designations themselves differ. The land allotment does not mention Levi (though the Levitical inheritance is located within the sacred precinct) or Joseph, but fills out the twelve with the Joseph tribes Manasseh and Ephraim. The city description, on the other hand, mentions neither Manassah nor Ephraim, filling out the twelve with Levi and Joseph.

Zimmerli and others have proposed that this section be dated later than the land division text.[145] However, there is an intriguing parallel here between the city description of the Temple Vision's

---

[144] Levenson (*Program*, 116-21) observes a similar principle at work, based upon the birth-order and mother of each tribe's eponymous ancestor. Hence, in the land allotment, those descended from the handmaids Bilhah and Zilpah are placed furthest from the Temple, Gad (Zilpah's firstborn) being the southernmost, and Dan (Bilhah's firstborn) being the northernmost, with Asher (Zilpah's second) and Naphtali (Bilhah's second) next in line. Similarly, the western city gates are designated with the names of Gad, Asher and Naphtali, east being the direction of honor (as the Temple faces east). Preference is shown, generally, to the Rachel tribes: in the land allotment, the sacred precinct is adjoined to the north (!) by Judah (a Leah tribe, but also the tribe of royalty) and to the south by Benjamin; the eastern city gates are designated Joseph, Benjamin and Dan (firstborn of Rachel's maid Bilhah). Levenson does not, however, suggest a common authorship for the two (127). He sees the same principle at work in the battle camp of the priestly work (Num 2; 3:21-28), where the north is the direction of least honor; perhaps this tradition is back of both land division and city description texts.

[145] Zimmerli (2:547), observes that the "last sentence of the book of Ezekiel shows how the old tradition of the city of God has forcefully obtained justice for itself against the priestly reform project, which, through the separation of city and temple, has robbed the city of much of its dignity." He therefore classes the text with the similar exaltations of the city in Deutero- or even Trito-Isaiah (2:545). Cooke (536), Wevers (233), Eichrodt (593), Gese (107), and Hals (347) similarly attribute these verses to another, later, hand. May, however (337), defends the text as the work of the same redactor, suggesting that Joseph has been used to designate both Ephraim and Manasseh and so make room for Levi in the naming of the twelve gates. Similarly Fohrer-Galling (262), while denying the Ezekielian authorship of the text, do not propose an additional redactional layer here.

74   The Law of the Temple

closing words and the "construction like a city" with which the vision
opened. The literature gives no satisfactory explanation for the phrase
כמבנה עיר ("construction like a city"). The usual explanation, that the
large complex of Temple buildings, walls and gates looked like a
city,[146] is unconvincing: Ezekiel clearly knew what a temple looked
like, and his negative evaluation of the city of Jerusalem makes the
choice of this simile anything but natural. In its immediate context,
כמבנה עיר creates tension and suspense. The reader, from the clues
ארץ ישראל and הר גבה מאד, already knows that the prophet has
been transported to Zion. One's expectations, however, are initially
thwarted: instead of moving immediately to a description of the city-
palace-Temple complex associated with the mountain, the text tells
only that atop the mountain is a "construction like a city." Only with
the word בית in v 5 is the tension resolved: it is the *Temple* the
prophet has seen. Yet, this function could have been served simply by
indicating that the summit of the mountain was occupied by a
"structure," or by remaining silent. The explicit designation of the
structure as being like a *city* makes best sense in parallel to 48:30-35,
where the city is laid forth. The two mentions of עיר then function as
brackets about the entire Temple vision. If this is so, then 48:30-35
cannot be even an early addition to the text. It must be part of the
original compositional unit, and hence must derive from Ezekiel
himself.[147]

V. Summary And Conclusions

The final form of the Temple Vision is a purposefully
constructed, unified document, possessing an overall chiastic
structure. This form can also be described as a juridical corpus
embedded in a literary frame (prologue 40:1--43:9; legislation
43:10--46:24; epilogue 47:1--48:35). However, it is clear that our text
is a redactional creation. The overall shift in mood from the
descriptive sections to the legislative, and the grammatical shift from

---

[146] Cf. Cooke, 429; May, 284; Eichrodt, 541; Gese, 10-11.

[147] Alfred Bertholet (*Das Buch Hesekiel eklärt* [KHC 12; Freiburg: Mohr, 1897]
168) also judged this text part of the original prophecy.

first to second person, suggest that an earlier Temple vision has
undergone expansion; qualifications of statements from material
deriving from Ezekiel (compare 43:7a with vv 7b-9; 44:2 with 44:3)
and outright contradictions (compare 40:44-46 with 44:6-14) further
support this conclusion.

Based on this analysis, the original vision consisted of 40:1--
43:7a (with minor insertions at 40:5 and 42:13-14); 44:1-2; 47:1-12;
and 48:30-35. This material, as might be expected, evidences its own
structure, also construable as a chiasm:

    40:1-4 construction like a city (כמבנה עיר)
       40:5-42:20 Temple measured (מדד)
          43:1-4 כבוד enters the eastern gate
          43:5-7a: YHWH speaks
          44:1-2: eastern gate closed forever
       47:1-12 the river measured (מדד)
    48:30-35 city (עיר) called יהוה שמה ("YHWH is there")

The expansion of this core vision has been accomplished with great
artistry, by three major insertions: at 43:7b-27, 44:3-46:24, and 47:13-
48:29. These insertions transform the original chiasm, centering on
the divine promise of eternal presence, into a new chiastic structure,
centering on the divine word as legislation. The prophet's original
concern for the divine Presence has been preserved. However, the
function of the text has been redirected. Ezekiel's visionary
experience of YHWH's presence has become a law, describing the
means by which the divine Presence may legitimately be
approached.[148] The following chapters explore what this transformed
document can tell us about the community that produced and revered
this law.

---

[148] See Table 2: "The Structure and Coherence of Ezekiel 40--48."

TABLE 2: THE STRUCTURE AND COHERENCE OF EZEKIEL 40-48

I. 40:1-43:9 (סתומה): The Temple of YHWH
    A. 40:1-42:20*: Temple description (בוא Hip^cil; מדד)
       [1. minor insertion at 40:5: באמה וטפח
       2. minor insertion at 42:13-14: Temple sacristy]
    B. 43:1-7a*: the כבוד fills the Temple
    [C. 43:7b-9: redactional expansion; transition to תורה]

II. 43:10-46:24: The Law of the Temple
    A. 43:10-27 (double סתומה): first major insertion--the
        introduction to תורת הבית
       1. 43:10-12 command to write; the title זאת תורת הבית
       2. 43:13-17: the altar (הראל [43:15] recalls הר גבה מאד
          [40:2] and ראש ההר [43:12])
       3. 43:18-27: altar consecration (messenger formulae
          appear)
    B. 44:1-46:18: תורת הבית proper
       1. 44:1-14 (סתומה; פתוחה after v 8 in the Aleppo Codex
         [AC]): judgement oracle against the Levites
         a. 44:1-2*: the closed eastern gate (שוב Hip^cil)
         b. 44:3: the second insertion begins (absolute
           prohibition of v. 2 qualified; נשיא introduced)
         c. 44:4-5: redactional suture (בוא Hip^cil recalls
           40:1-42:20; brackets legislation with שוב
           Hip^cil at 46:19. כבוד recalled [43:1-7a].
           Commission in 40:4 recalled. תורת signals
           resumption of Law after necessary excursus on
           the altar)
         d. 44:6-14 accusation and announcement of
           judgement
       2. 44:15-31 (פתוחה): the Zadokites (organized by idea of
         entrance [בוא]; connected to following section by
         אחזה [44:28; 45:5], נחלה [44:28; 45:1], and תרומה
         [44:30; 45:1, 6-7, 13-15]).

3. 45:1-8 (פתוחה in AC, סתומה in Leningrad Codex [LC]):
   the land division foreshadowed; first prophetic
   critique of the נשיא (45:8)

4. 45:9-17 (סתומה): the נשיא

    a. 45:9: the second prophetic critique--call for
   וצדקה משפט

    b. 45:10-12: just (צדק) weights and measures

    c. 45:13-15: תרומה-table (break פתוחה , AC)

    d. 45:16-17: redactional suture

5. 45:18-25 (סתומה): cultic calendar

6. 46:1-11 (פתוחה AC, סתומה LC): major feasts, sabbaths
   and new moons (AC divides at v 5, between sabbath
   and new moon regulations), particularly as related to
   the eastern gate.

7. 46:12-15 (סתומה AC, פתוחה LC): freewill and daily
   offerings; eastern gate motif continued.

[AC: פתוחה at 46:16; LC: סתומה at 46:19. The problem: where to
 conclude the Divine speech, begun in 43:7 and explicitly continued at
44:2?]

    8. 46:16-18: the third prophetic critique of the נשיא.

   [C. 46:19-24: the Temple kitchens (שוב Hip^c^il)]

III. 47:1-48:35: River, Land and City

    A. 47:1-12* (פתוחה AC, סתומה LC): the River (שוב Hip^c^il; מדד)

    B. 47:13-48:29: the third major insertion--the land

       1. 47:13-23 (פתוחה AC, סתומה LC): the borders

       2. 48:1-29 (סתומה AC, פתוחה LC): the division of the land
   (subdivided at v. 11 [סתומה] in the Leningrad Codex,
   dividing the land appropriated to the Levites from
   land given to the priests)

    C. 48:30-35*: the city יהוה שמה

* Starred sections belong to the original vision.

Chapter Three

THE NATURE OF PERSIAN INVOLVEMENT IN THE RELIGIOUS INSTITUTIONS OF SUBJECT PEOPLES

The clear and unified witness of Scripture is that Judean exiles began to return to their homeland during the reign of Cyrus, first of the Persian empire's great kings. According to the Aramaic documents in Ezra 5:1--6:18 and 7:12-26, this return, the subsequent rebuilding of the Temple, and the ordering of its cultus were carried out at Persian behest. If the scriptural testimony is accurate, Restoration Judah was in large measure a Persian creation--or, at least, it was organized and established under express Persian authority.

Relatively little critical attention has been given to the character and significance of Persian involvement in Judean affairs. The evidence of a deliberate Persian role in the Judean reconstruction has often been downplayed and even denied, or at best viewed as the accidental benefit of Persian political interests in the broader region of Syria-Palestine. Indeed, it has been argued that the Persians would have had scant interest in Judean religious traditions and aspirations, and hence any apparent support given to the small Restoration community by the crown must have been the result of political machinations by Judeans in the Persian court.[1]

A very different conclusion is reached if we consider the Persian role in Judah's revitalization against the backdrop provided by extrabiblical evidence of Persia's involvement in the religious affairs of its empire. A pattern quickly emerges of deliberate, intentional intervention, not just in Judah but across the expanse of the empire.

---

[1] Martin Noth went so far as to suggest that "perhaps the whole text of Ezra's official instructions was drafted by exiles" (*The History of Israel* [tr. R. Ackroyd; London: Adam and Charles Black, 2 1960] 333), a possibility also, in more limited form, entertained by George Widengren ("The Persian Period," in *IJH*, 497). Shemaryahu Talmon ("The Cult and Calendar Reform of Jeroboam I," in *King, Cult and Calendar in Ancient Israel* [Jerusalem: Magnes, 1986] 136) has attributed the proclamations of Cyrus and Darius I found in Ezra, as well as the Passover Proclamation of Darius II from the Elephantine Papyri, to the activities of "Jewish agents."

Viewed in broader perspective, the biblical evidence takes on sharper, more vivid hues. Far from being merely incidental, the role of Persia in Israel's religious life is seen to have a direction and an intentionality that have played a large part in the formation of the faith of Israel. This is particularly important for the proper dating and interpretation of the Law of the Temple in Ezekiel 40--48. If the pattern of a state-supported cult and priesthood presented there can be correlated with a pattern of Persian intervention in the religious affairs of subject peoples, the argument that the elaborated Temple Vision is to be read as programmatic for the reconstruction of the society and cult of the Judean restoration is strengthened considerably.

I. The Sources For The Early Persian Period

The Cyrus Cylinder and the monumental inscriptions of Darius I, which date to the final decades of the sixth century BCE, provide primary insight into the Persian perspective on the religious and political currents in the empire. Viewed together with other sources for the period, they enable us to form a fairly coherent picture of the nature and extent of Persian interventions into religious affairs.

The Hebrew Bible gives a fair accounting of attitudes and institutions in Palestine for the first years after the return, both from the perspective of the returning establishment of the exiles (Haggai/Zechariah; the Chronicler) and from the perspective of more critical, fringe elements, perhaps reflecting the concerns of the people in the land (Third Isaiah; Malachi). Further, the text of Ezra preserves versions of an edict of Cyrus in both Hebrew (1:2-4) and Aramaic (6:3-5), a correspondence in Aramaic between the satrapal administration of Abar-Nahara (the Persian satrapy in which Judah, or Yehud, was located) and the imperial courts of Darius (5:6-17; 6:6-12) and of Artaxerxes (4:8-22), and an Aramaic document commissioning Ezra the scribe for his special task (7:12-26). Though their order has been somewhat confused, we have no reason to doubt the authenticity of any of these documents.[2] Still, the policy goals of the Persian

---

[2] Roland de Vaux (*The Bible and the Ancient Near East* [tr. Damian McHugh; London: Darton, Longman and Todd, 1972] 93), for reasons similar to those given

government are not expressly stated, and must be inferred from the evidence at hand.

The Greek historians who wrote concerning this period must also be read carefully and critically, as they tend to ascribe to the Persians the worst possible behavior and motivation.[3] For the purposes of this study, the history of Herodotus of Halicarnassus (ca. 490-420 BCE) is the most useful. The very incredulity of Herodotus can be an asset to us, for he tells us consistently what he has heard, both credible and incredible, without prejudging to any marked degree. Diodorus Siculus (1st century BCE) wrote concerning our period in his world history; however, he did so from a distance of nearly four centuries. Moreover, the works of Diodorus, and of Strabo, the geographer, are clearly dependent upon the work of Herodotus. Josephus is largely dependent upon the biblical sources for his account of the Persian period.[4] Hence, he is of little or no use as an independent source for Persian religious policy. Again, we must make logical inferences from the evidence at hand.

Perhaps our best evidence for the religious climate of the early Persian period is the miscellany of texts and inscriptional material from across the ancient Near East, including Egypt (notably the Udjahoresne inscription, the Elephantine papyri, and the so-called Demotic Chronicle), Syria (the Aramaic funerary inscriptions), Asia Minor (the Magnesia inscription), and Babylon (the Nabonidus Chronicle and related texts). This scattered material, for all its disparate character, does seem to support a general picture of the religious world of the Persian period, and the Persian role in the production of that world.

---

below, argues that the Temple-building decrees of Cyrus and Darius in Ezra are at least historically plausible, and literarily acceptable: in brief, that "there is no valid objection whatsoever against the two edicts."

[3] Note, for instance, the "madness" of Cambyses, cited by Herodotus (3.25) and Diodorus Siculus (10.13.3), and the attribution of almost all temple destructions in Egypt to this one figure in Strabo (17.1.16, 27; 10.3.21). In fact, as will be noted below, Cambyses's program of the selective support and rejection of native cults is in keeping with Persian policy as practiced throughout the period.

[4] Though Josephus does offer some interesting differences from the biblical witness on points of chronology and historical detail (cf. Widengren, *IJH*, 493-494).

From these sources, a pattern of involvement and direct intervention by the Persians into the religious affairs of their subjects can be reconstructed. As will be seen, the pattern of Persian involvement reflected in the biblical texts (including, I propose, the Law of the Temple) is in evidence throughout the history of the empire, and everywhere within its borders. Judah is not an anomaly, but the norm. To assemble this reconstruction, the evidence from the reigns of Cyrus, Cambyses, and Darius will be considered in chronological order (with some mention, where appropriate, of how policies begun in this time were continued by later rulers, in particular Xerxes and Artaxerxes). For each of these three periods, the extrabiblical evidence will be considered first, and then the conclusions drawn from this material will be correlated with the witness of the biblical materials.

II. Religious Involvement Under Cyrus

The Cyrus Cylinder and Related Cuneiform Texts

Involvement in the religious life of subject peoples was Persian policy from the time of Cyrus, the founder of the Achaemenid dynasty. Upon conquering Babylon, Cyrus quickly reinstated the Marduk cult, long neglected by Nabonidus, the last Baylonian ruler and a devotee of the moon god Sin. That Nabonidus's neglect was keenly felt in Babylon is seen in the cuneiform text of the Nabonidus Chronicle, which in mournful monotony repeats year after year, "The king did not come to Babylon for the ceremony of the month Nisanu; the god Nebo did not come to Babylon, the god Bel did not go out of Esagila in procession, the festival of the New Year was omitted."[5] Indeed, one fragmentary text says of Nabonidus, "With evil intentions against Babylon he let its sanctuaries fall into disrepair, disturbed the(ir) foundation lines and let the cultic rites fall into oblivion."[6] According to the Chronicle, Cyrus came into Babylon as a liberator. We are told that Cyrus entered the city without a struggle; indeed, that he was welcomed with

---

[5] A. Leo Oppenheim (tr.) *ANET*[3], 306.

[6] Ibid., 309.

celebration.[7] In his own account of the conquest, the Cyrus Cylinder, the great king claims the patronage of Marduk, and asserts that Marduk had chosen him, out of all the world, as the righteous ruler fit to lead the god in the annual processional.[8] A poem from the period affirms:

> [. . . for] the inhabitants of Babylon he (i.e. Cyrus)
>   declared the state of "peace,"
> [. . .] . . . (the troops) he kept away from Ekur.
> [Big cattle he slaughtered with the a]xe, he slaughtered
>   many aslu-sheep
> [Incense he put] on the censer, the regular offerings
>   for the Lord of Lords he ordered increased.[9]

Cyrus not only re-established the Marduk cult, but continued to be concerned with its proper conduct. Texts from this period witness to the trial of Gimillu, a temple official charged with theft and graft, in the satrapal court.[10]

Cyrus's religious involvement was not limited to the Marduk cultus. On his cylinder he claims:

> (As to the region) from ...as far as Ashur and Susa, Agade, Eshunna, the towns Zamban, Me-Turnu, Der as well as the region of the Gutians, I returned to (these) sacred cities on the other side of the Tigris, the sanctuaries of which have been in ruins for a long time, the images which (used) to live therein and established for them permanent sanctuaries. I (also) gathered all their (former) inhabitants and returned (to them) their habitations. Furthermore, I resettled upon the command of Marduk, the great lord, all the gods of Sumer and Akkad whom Nabonidus has brought into Babylon ...to the anger of the lord of the gods, unharmed, in their (former) chapels, the places which make them happy.[11]

---

[7] Ibid., 306.

[8] Ibid., 315.

[9] Ibid., 314-15.

[10] A. T. Olmstead, *History of the Persian Empire* (Chicago: University of Chicago, 1959), 71-73.

[11] A. Leo Oppenheim (tr.) *ANET*[3], 316. Note, however, Amélie Kuhrt's objection to using this text for the reconstruction of general Persian policy ("The Cyrus Cylinder and Achaemenid Imperial Policy," *JSOT* 25 [1983] 83-97). Observing that only specified localities, all near Babylon, are mentioned in the Cylinder, and further observing the general Babylonian focus of the text (the specific relation of Cyrus to Marduk, the similarity of the text in form to other Mesopotamian building texts, and especially the mention in a new fragment of Assurbanipal as a predecessor of Cyrus), Kuhrt concludes that the text says nothing of Persian imperial policy, but is rather a propaganda text

The Biblical Witness

It is in this light that the biblical witness of Ezra 1 and 5:1--6:18 must be seen. What is said of Cyrus in these texts--that he ordered the return of the exiles and provided for the rebuilding of the Temple--is entirely in keeping with his practice elsewhere. Indeed, one is immediately stricken by the parallel between the words of Cyrus in Ezra 1:2b ("YHWH the God of heaven has given to me all the kingdoms of the earth, and has appointed me to build for him a temple in Jerusalem, which is in Judah") and the claim on the Cyrus Cylinder that Marduk had chosen Cyrus to become "the ruler of all the world."[12] In each case, direct divine patronage is claimed by Cyrus, and the re-establishment of the patron god's cult is attributed to him.

That the restored cult of the rebuilt Temple in Jerusalem was state-supported may be implied already in the edict of Cyrus recorded in Ezra 1:2-4. This document not only permits the return of the exiles מִכָּל הַמְּקֹמוֹת אֲשֶׁר הוּא גָר שָׁם ("each from wherever he sojourns") but also commands that יְנַשְּׂאוּהוּ אַנְשֵׁי מְקֹמוֹ: the "men of his place" give as offerings (taking נָשָׂא in a cultic sense) money, materials and animals. Later, in the Aramaic section of Ezra, another form of this proclamation (or another, related edict)[13] states explicitly that the royal treasury is to absorb the cost of the Temple's construction (6:4). This is also in keeping with Cyrus's close involvement with and direct support of the Babylonian Marduk cult, in particular. Certainly the evidence for deliberate intervention in religious affairs by the first of the Achaemenids is clear.

---

establishing Cyrus's right to rule in Babylon. The focus upon Babylon in the Cylinder is undeniable. Indeed, it would be surprising in a text with a Babylonian audience if such was not the case. Kuhrt's reservations would be legitimate if the Cyrus Cylinder was the only indication we had of Persian policy. However, in the context of the actions of his successors, one can legitimately generalize from Cyrus's conduct in Babylon to his conduct throughout the empire.

[12] A. Leo Oppenheim (tr.) ANET[3], 315.

[13] Elias Bickerman (Studies in Jewish and Christian History, Vol 1 [AGJU 9; Leiden: E. J. Brill, 1976] 72-108) understands the text of Hebrew Ezra 1:2-4 as a herald's pronouncement of the edict, while the Aramaic text of 6:2-5 is the actual legal document.

III. Religious Involvement Under Cambyses

The Udjahoresne Inscription

As Cyrus, conqueror of Babylon, took an especially active role in the religion of that people, so his son Cambyses, conqueror of Egypt, was active in the religious life of the Egyptians. We have a record of this involvement in the form of inscriptions upon the statue of Udjahoresne, an intriguing figure who seems to have been for Egypt what Ezra was for Judah: a legal/religious authority, acting under Persian auspices.[14] In the inscriptions, Udjahoresne is called "the chief physician,"[15] probably owing to his high position, not only in the temple of Neith, but in the House of Life, an institution dedicated to medicine and the healing arts as well as to religious ritual.[16] However, he had also served as the commander of the Egyptian fleet before his defection to the Persians under Cambyses.[17] It was Udjahoresne who composed the titulary of Cambyses in Egypt: Mesutire, meaning Son of Re, the sun god.[18] Under this name, Cambyses ruled as king of Upper and Lower Egypt. In return, the Persian monarch gave Udjahoresne the authority to expel the "foreigners" from the temple of Neith, even to destroy their houses and property, and to restore the temple to its former glory:

> . . . his majesty commanded to cleanse the temple of Neith and to return all
> its personnel to it, (22) the --- and the hour-priests of the temple. His majesty
> commanded to give divine offerings to Neith-the-Great, the mother of god,
> and to the great gods of Sais, as it had been before. His majesty commanded
> [to perform] all their festivals and all their processions, as had been done
> before.[19]

---

[14] Joseph Blenkinsopp ("The Mission of Udjahoresnet and Those of Ezra and Nehemiah," *JBL* 106 [1987] 417) also observes a formal parallel with Nehemiah, suggesting in particular that Neh 13 "was modeled on the Egyptian autobiographical votive inscription."

[15] Miriam Lichtheim, *Ancient Egyptian Literature*, Vol. 3: *The Late Period* (Berkeley: University of California, 1980) 39.

[16] Ibid., 36.

[17] Ibid 37.

[18] Ibid., 38. The name is translated on 40.

[19] Ibid., 38.

In accord with Udjahoresne's instructions, Cambyses fulfilled his duties in the successions of the temple's royal patrons:

> His majesty did every beneficence in the temple of Neith. He established the presentation of libations to the Lord of Eternity in the temple of Neith, as every king had done before.[20]

The Elephantine Papyri

Cambyses's involvement with religion in Egypt extended not only to Egyptians. The papyri that survive from the Hebrew community at Elephantine record that, though Cambyses destroyed other temples in Egypt, he let their temple to Yahu stand.[21] This intriguing reference demonstrates that Persian support of the religions of subject peoples cannot be ascribed to sheer religious tolerance. Cambyses, it is clear, did not support all Egyptian cults; indeed, some he restricted or overthrew.[22]   Further, this reference suggests that Persian involvement was in fact selective and deliberate. Of all the cults of Egypt, Cambyses chose to support the temple of Neith (with its attendant rites) and the temple of Yahu. Significantly, in each case,

---

[20] Ibid., 39.

[21] AP 30

[22] Mary Boyce ("Persian Religion in the Achemenid age," in CHJ 1 [1984] 288) argues that the archaeological evidence does not support the claim that Cambyses destroyed temples in Egypt. She attributes this rumour to Darius, whom she considers a usurper, and claims that it was picked up and passed on as truth by the Greeks. However, the citation in the Elephantine papyri can scarcely be said to derive from Greek influence. Moreover, the Behistun inscription of Darius expresses no ill will toward Cambyses, but only toward Gaumata, who claimed to be Cambyses's brother and seized the throne upon his death (Franz Heinrich Weissbach, Die Keilinschriften der Achämeniden [VAB 3; Leipzig: J. C. Hinrichs, 1911] 17). Perhaps, as J. Maxwell Miller and John Hayes have proposed (A History of Ancient Israel and Judah. [Philadelphia: Westminster, 1986] 450) Cambyses did not literally destroy other temples, but merely curtailed their power and influence. Support for this argument comes from one of the texts of the Demotic Chronicle, cited by de Vaux (Bible, 73), which records a decree of Cambyses restricting full revenue to only three unspecified temples in Egypt, and either discontinuing altogether or reducing the allocations to the other shrines. De Vaux, who views the destruction or rejection of temples by Cambyses as the result of a fit of pique prompted by military reverses in Africa, writes (Bible, 74): "One is tempted to date it to the beginning of Cambyses' stay in Egypt, but it then becomes difficult to reconcile this order with the formal evidence of Uzahor about the temple of Sais." However, if, as we have suggested, this order is but a reflection of selectivity in Cambyses' support of the cults of Egypt, rather than a punitive measure, there is no conflict: Udjahoresne (Uzahor) and his party in the temple at Sais would be among the favored ones.

the cultus represented a community loyal to Persia. Both Udjahoresne and, apparently, the mercenaries at Elephantine had demonstrated their loyalty by defecting from the Egyptian army to the Persian cause.

Cambyses was not alone in this selective support and rejection of local cults. Herodotus records that Darius I destroyed the temple at Didyma in Asia Minor.[23]   Similarly, when Babylon revolted, Xerxes destroyed the city, demolishing the great temple at Esagila and destroying the Marduk image, central to the annual rites that had been re-established by Cyrus himself.[24] Herodotus also records that, though Xerxes looted and set fire to the temple and citadel of Athens following his conquest of that great city, he then permitted the Athenian exiles in his train to go up and sacrifice on the mountain.[25] We are justified, then, in considering the practice of selective intervention in religious affairs to be standard Persian policy.

The Biblical Witness

Cambyses's selective intervention in the religious affairs of Egypt recalls the situation portrayed in Ezra 4:1-3.   Here, the returnees under Zerubbabel the governor and Joshua the high priest reject the overtures of those in the land, where an ongoing cultus is in place, to assist in the building of the temple.   The response of these Persian-sponsored returnees could, with a change of deities, just as easily be the word of Udjahoresne to the "foreigners" in the temple of Neith and the House of Life: "You have nothing to do with us, to build a house for our God.   For we alone will build for YHWH God of Israel, just as King Cyrus, king of Persia, commanded us" (Ezra 4:3).

The conflict brought about in the land by the rebuilding of the Temple and re-installation of the Zadokite clergy is also evident in the Temple texts of Trito-Isaiah and Malachi on the one hand, and the prophecies of Haggai/ Zechariah and the anti-Levite polemic of Ezekiel

---

23 Herodotus 6.20.

24 Herodotus 1.183.

25 Herodotus 8.51-56.

44:1-14, on the other.[26] While Isaiah 56:3-8 imagines a day when
בן הנכר ("the foreigner") and the eunuch may serve in the Temple, in
the Law of the Temple the service of the בני נכר is a great evil (Ezek
44:7), for which the Levites are deprived of the title כהן, and the בני
נכר are unconditionally barred from the restored cult (44:9).[27] In
Israel as in Egypt, it seems, Persian selectivity led to conflict.

IV. Religious Involvement Under Darius I

The Monumental Inscriptions

With the death of Cambyses in Syria, the empire was thrown into
turmoil. Darius, spear-bearer of Cambyses and a member of the royal
house in his own right, finally brought peace by seizing the throne
himself and systematically quashing rebellion after rebellion until his
leadership and might were known and respected. Whether Darius was
legitimate claimant or usurper, there is little doubt that he became,
after Cyrus, the greatest of Persia's kings.[28] Moreover, thanks to his
monumental inscriptions, we know more of Darius than of any other
Achaemenid, and particularly, more of his religious faith.

In Darius's royal inscriptions, only one deity is ever mentioned
by name.[29] Regularly, these inscriptions begin: "A great god (is)
Ahuramazda, who created this earth, who created yonder heaven, who
created man."[30] Darius understood himself as having been chosen for
kingship, appointed to that lofty task by Ahuramazda.[31] Further, as

---

[26] Cf. Paul Hanson, *Dawn of Apocalyptic* (Philadelphia: Fortress, 1975).

[27] Observed by Fishbane, *Biblical Interpretation*, 138.

[28] Indeed, Richard N. Frye (*The Heritage of Persia* [New York: The New American
Library, 1963], 110) claims "that the unity of the Achaemenid empire is the work of
Darius rather than Cyrus."

[29] Boyce, "Religion," 290.

[30] Weissbach, *Keilinschriften*, 85, 87, 99, 101, 103.

[31] As in this text, translated by Roland Kent ("The Recently Published Old
Persian Inscriptions," *JAOS* 51 [1931] 199):
    A great god is Ahuramazda, who created this earth,
    who created yonder firmament, who created man,
    who created welfare for man, who
    made Darius king, one king of many.

king, he believed that his actions, his building projects, his
promulgation of law, were all precisely ordered by the great god:

> To Ahuramazda
> thus the wish was: in the whole earth
> he chose me as the man for himself, made me king
> in the whole earth. I worshipped Ahuramazda,
> Ahuramazda bore me aid; what was commanded to me
> to do, that by my hand was successfully completed,
>   beautiful;
> what was done by me, all that by the will of Ahuramazda
>   I did.[32]

Similarly,

> I am Darius, great king, king of kings, king of this great earth, son of
> Hystapes, the Achaemenian. Says Darius the king: What I did on this earth, I
> did not otherwise (=precisely) as Ahuramazda commanded me. Because
> Ahuramazda commanded me and was a friend to me, what I did, all that by
> the grace of Ahuramazda, whoso shall see that (which was) done by me, to
> him let me seem on the whole earth exalted. May Ahuramazda protect me
> and my country.[33]

The language of choosing here is strongly reminiscent both of the
Cyrus Cylinder, where the god who chooses Cyrus from all the earth is
said to be Marduk, and Ezra 1:2, where it is YHWH who has appointed
(פקד) the Persian monarch to build His temple. Note also the epithet
"who created yonder heaven/firmament," which seems very close
indeed to the epithet of YHWH used throughout the Hebrew biblical
texts of this period and especially in the Aramaic documents of Ezra,
"God of the heavens." Before we can consider what these striking
parallels might mean, however, we need to know more concerning the
identity of Ahuramazda.

From the inscriptions, particularly those of Darius, it is clear
that Ahuramazda is a creator deity: heaven, earth, human being and the
horse are mentioned consistently as his special creations. Ahuramazda
is also a royal figure. His word is law, even for the king--indeed,
especially for the king, whose task is the promulgation of the law and
the maintenance of the divine order established by Ahuramazda. In
Darius's "Restoration of Order" inscription, we read:

---

[32] Roland Kent, "The Record of Darius's Palace at Susa," *JAOS* 53 (1933) 7.

[33] Roland Kent, "Recently Published Inscriptions," 214.

Says Darius the king: Much evil that had been done, that I made (into) good. Provinces, seething, which smote one another, I made that they not smite; (that) these, as they were previously, so they should be, as many as were provinces.

Says Darius the king: that I did by the will of Ahuramazda, that one man the other not smite; I in his place each one put; the law (*datam*) which was mine, of that they had respect; so that the strong the weak neither smite nor harm.[34]

Such a portrayal of the right society was common in ancient Mesopotamia.[35] The chief good in such a system is order, represented and maintained by priest and king, grounded permanently in a theology of creation as the defeat of chaos.[36] Such is portrayed classically in Marduk's victory over the chaos dragon Tiamat, in Baal's defeat of Prince Sea-Judge River, and in YHWH's primordial triumph over the sea as portrayed in texts such as Psalm 29. That same motif is expressed in Genesis 1 without the overtly mythical element of primordial conquest.[37] Something markedly similar, it seems, is expressed here of Ahuramazda. As creator of the world the great god is also the patron of kings: the one, indeed, who gives kingship as a gift to his select one. Both as creator and as kingmaker, Ahuramazda establishes order in the cosmos. Hence, for the Persians the word of the king was law, expressing the divine order established by Ahuramazda.

---

[34] Roland Kent, "More Old Persian Inscriptions," *JAOS* 54 (1934) 44.

[35] Cf. for example the prologue to Hammurabi's "Code" (Theophile J. Meek [tr.] *ANET*³, 164-65). Jonathan Z. Smith (*Map Is Not Territory: Studies in the History of Religions*, [SJLA 23; Leiden: E. J. Brill, 1978] xii) refers to this as "a locative view of the world as elaborated by an imperial figure.".

[36] J. Smith, *Map* , 132-33. Also, Thorkild Jacobsen, *The Treasures of Darkness: A History of Mesopotamian Religion* (New Haven: Yale University, 1976) 191.

[37] Other striking examples of this creation theology are found in Deutero-Isaiah, especially 40:12-17; 43:15; 44:24-27; 45:11-13. Morton Smith ("II Isaiah and the Persians," *JAOS* 83 [1963] 418-420) observes a close parallel between these texts and Yasna 44 of Zoroaster's Gathas. He is rightly cautious about these parallels, though he strongly suggests that Hebrew creation theology is due to Persian influence. I would prefer to say that, here as elsewhere, the prevailing religious tendency in the Near East during the Persian period (that is, the movement toward a monotheism, or at least a henotheism, based upon a royal creator figure associated with the heavens) can be seen in both Israelite and Persian texts.

The Demotic Chronicle

This passion for order is clearly expressed in the so-called Demotic Chronicle. In the reign of Darius I, according to the Chronicle, an assembly of secular and religious leaders was called in Egypt. The purpose of that gathering, as related by the Chronicle, is most interesting:

> As for Darius, it heeded him . . . the land (of Egypt) in its entirety because of the excellence of his character. He issued a decree concerning Egypt to his satrap in (his) third regnal year, as follows: "Let be brought unto me the learned men ...from among the (military) officers, the priests, (and) the scribes of Egypt so that, being assembled together, they may in concert write the law of Egypt which had been (observed) formerly through the forty-fourth regnal year of Pharaoh Amasis, (that is) the fifth pharaonic law, (concerning) the temples (and) the people.[38]

At least in Egypt, then, Darius intervened in the religious and secular establishment, to bring order to both politics and ritual. Doubtless it was in conjunction with this ordering of religious life in Egypt that Udjahoresne was sent back to Egypt, to reform practices in the House of Life.[39]

The Udjahoresne Inscription

A large part of the Udjahoresne inscription is concerned with his commission from Darius "to restore the establishment of the House of Life ___ after it had decayed."[40] The repeated expression, "as had been done before," already evidenced in the portions of the inscription pertaining to the reign of Cambyses, seems to imply that a lapse in the strict observance of the ritual at the temple of Neith had also taken place--or, in any case, that in the eyes of Udjahoresne and his party

---

[38] Wilhelm Spiegelberg, *Die sogenannte demotische Chronik des Pap. 215 der Bibliotheque Nationale zu Paris, nebst den auf der Ruckseite des Papyrus stehenden Texten* (Demotische Studien 7; Leipzig, 1914) 30-31. Translated here from the Demotic text by S. Dean McBride, Jr.

[39] Blenkinsopp ("Mission," 409) observes that since the Udjahoresne inscription mentions Darius's visit of state to Elam, but does not record his visit to Egypt in the fourth year of his reign, it must be dated shortly before 518, which puts his arrival in Susa to reform the Houses of Life at about the time of the Demotic Chronicle, and makes a connection between the two likely.

[40] Lichtheim, *Literature*, 39.

the cult had become corrupted. We learn from another statue inscription, that of Peftuaneith, that a previous reform of the House of Life had taken place under Amasis, last independent Pharaoh before Cambyses's defeat of Egypt under Psammetichus III:

> I renewed the House of Life after its ruin,
> I established the sustenance of Osiris,
> I put all its procedures in order.
> I built the god's boat of pine wood,
> Having found (it) made of acacia wood.[41]

It would appear that Udjahoresne belonged to a group that was disenfranchised by the reforms of Peftuaneith, and was returned to power and prominence by Persian might. Again, we see the Persians involving themselves in the religious life of a conquered people, to the extent of displacing an existing cultus and instating leaders of their own choosing.

Udjahoresne was provided with resources as well as with authority. His inscription reads:

> His majesty had commanded to give them every good thing, in order that they might carry out all their crafts. I supplied them with everything useful to them, with all their equipment that was on record, as they had been before."[42]

Cambyses's practice of state support for selected cults in Egypt appears to have been continued, and even extended, by Darius.

The Biblical Witness

In light of Darius's monumental inscriptions, coupled with the Demotic Chronicle and the Udjahoresne inscription, the full significance of Darius's religious interventions as portrayed in the Hebrew Scriptures can be seen. We have already observed that two edicts of Cyrus are preserved in the book of Ezra. The occasion of the second citation is a search of the archives ordered by Darius at the request of the governors of Abar-Nahara. The governors have asked for a ruling on the attempts of Judah's elders to build the Temple (5:6-17). When

---

[41] Ibid., 35.

[42] Ibid., 40.

Cyrus' old edict is found, Darius issues a proclamation of his own (6:6-12) which makes the state's support for the Jerusalem cult all the more explicit. First, he directs that the building costs of the Temple be paid from the royal treasury: in particular, from the tribute of the province (v 8). Then, Darius further stipulates that whatever might be required for the Temple service is to be provided daily by the province, that sacrifices might be offered לחיי מלכא ובנוהי ("for the life of the king and his sons," vv 9-10).

This action, we now can see, is not at all unusual or extreme. Given the close relationship between the law of the king and the will of Ahuramazda, the intensive search for a purported edict of Cyrus is exactly what we would expect. Nor is the extent of Persian involvement in the Jerusalem cultus remarkable, in light of what we have learned from the Udhahoresne inscription and the Demotic Chronicle of Darius's religious involvements in Egypt. Indeed, the mention in the Udjahoresne inscription of all equipment "on record" being returned by Darius to the cult personnel of the House of Life recalls Cyrus's return of the sacred Temple vessels stolen by Nebuchadnezzar to Sheshbazzar, leader of the returnees from exile (Ezr 1:7-8). Darius, it seems, did as Cyrus had done.

The parallels of the means by which selected temple establishments were supported in Darius's time with the means by which the Jerusalem Temple is supported in Ezekiel 40--48 are striking. In the Law of the Temple, the expenses of the sacrificial cultus are defrayed by the government, from the considerable estates of the נשיא and from the taxes (תרומה) collected from the province (45:13-17). Further Ezekiel 43:12 is an intriguing literary parallel to the Demotic Chronicle. While the Chronicle records Darius's demand for the "law (concerning) the temples" in Egypt, 43:12 (the superscription to the juridical corpus which follows) declares "This is the law of the Temple." This parallel tightens our fix on the redactor of Ezekiel 40--48, and suggests why Ezekiel's original vision was reworked in this fashion. תורת הבית is the effective title of the reworked Temple vision. The text functions, in essence, as the answer to Darius' command for the Judeans: this, indeed, is the law of *our* Temple, in Jerusalem.

Even if such an order as described in the Demotic Chronicle was not given directly to the Judean priestly establishment, Persian concern for an official codification of Egyptian temple laws may have galvanized the YHWHistic priestly communities, both in Babylon and in Palestine, to formulate their own authoritative canons. In Jerusalem, the fruit of this labor was the Law of the Temple incorporated in Ezekiel's vision report; in Babylon, the process of compilation resulted in the Mosaic תורה, our Pentateuch.[43]

When one considers the commissioning of Udjahoresne by Darius, and the reordering of Egyptian religious institutions described in the Demotic Chronicle, the commission of Ezra under Artaxerxes comes immediately to mind. Here, too, a religious official, empowered by Persia but with roots among the native populace, is sent to order the religious life of a people. Here, too, a law is involved, assembled by the priests and scribes. Here, too, we find the Persians footing the bill for the temple cult. In his letter sent by Ezra, Artaxerxes I directed that the treasurers of the province were to provide whatever the law required for the Temple (7:21-23, although in frugal fashion he did set some limits upon this generosity!). Moreover, Artaxerxes declared the Temple personnel exempt from taxation (7:24). In this, he followed the example of his grandfather Darius, who apparently had also granted tax exemptions to clergy. We know, at any rate, from a Greek inscription that such an exemption was given to the φυτουργους ἱερους Απολλονοσ ("gardeners of the temples of Apollo," apparently

43 Blenkinsopp ("Mission," 414) has also proposed a link between the codification of the legal material in the Pentateuch and the Demotic Chronicle. Intriguingly, Eric Meyers ("The Persian Period and the Judean Restoration: From Zerubbabel to Nehemiah," in Patrick Miller, Paul Hanson and S. Dean McBride, Jr. [eds.] *Ancient Israelite Religion* [Philadelphia: Fortress, 1987] 513) suggests that "Persian encouragement to codify laws in the provinces could well have been the impetus to combine Zechariah 1-8 with Haggai into a single composite piece that was probably intended for presentation at the rededication ceremony of the Second Temple." This may be, though the material in Haggai and Zechariah scarcely fills the bill as a "law of the Temple." In any case, Blenkinsopp and Meyers agree that the Demotic Chronicle could well have brought about the assembly, editing and systematization of traditions in Israel.

officials in the cult of Apollo) at Magnesia, and that the Persian satrap Gadatai was taken to task for not providing it.[44]

All available evidence reveals the reliability of the biblical picture of Darius's involvement in the cult at Jerusalem. What is more, evidence from before and after Darius reveals that the policy of intentional, selective intervention into the religious institutions of subject peoples was not unique to Darius, but was rather standard Persian practice.

V. PERSIAN RELIGION: AN EXCURSUS

The God Ahuramazda and Zoroastrianism

The motivations for selective Persian intervention into local temple establishments would doubtless be clearer if we could formulate a comparative picture of the religion of the Achaemenids. Unfortunately, not a great deal is, or can be, known. The names "Assara Mazash" are said to be found on a god list from the time of the Assyrian Assurbanipal, but that evidence is sometimes questioned.[45] It *is* certain that the name Ahuramazda is found in the Gathas, religious poems attributed to Zarathustra in the ancient Zoroastrian text, the Avesta. However, to connect this divine appellation to that mysterious prophetic figure is but to attach a riddle to an enigma.

Dates claimed for Zarathustra range from the sixth century to midway into the second millenia BCE.[46] Moreover, considerable doubt remains as to how quickly the prophet's message became normative for Persian religion, and how soon the organized, formal religion of

---

[44] The complete text of the inscription can be found in Eduard Meyer, *Die Entstehung des Judenthums* (Halle: Max Niemeyer, 1896) 19-20. Meyer observes that while the inscription itself dates from no earlier than Roman times, perhaps the reign of Tiberius, the privileges it describes, and the historical grounds given for them, are doubtless authentic.

[45] Frye, *Heritage*, 119.

[46] The late date is held by later Zoroastrian tradition, which places the prophet 258 years before Alexander, and is accepted at face value by Olmstead (*History*, 102-3), who also identifies Zarathustra's royal patron with Vishtaspa, father of Darius. Frye (*Heritage*, 50-51) prefers to speak less precisely, saying only that the prophet should be dated before the rise of the Achaemenids. Boyce, however ("Religion," 280), on the basis of the archaic language of the Gathas, places the prophet "between 1500 and 1300 BCE, when his people would still have been pastoral nomads on the South Russian steppes."

Zoroastrianism developed out of those teachings. While Boyce ascribes a full-blown Zoroastrianism to the entire Achaemenid period,[47] Olmstead proposes a pure religion of the prophet, gradually polluted by primitive ritual elements.[48] Frye is skeptical that much at all can be known about the religion of the early Achaemenids. He proposes a complex picture of rival cults and teachings, those of Zarathustra's followers among them, which by the Sasanian period had gradually mingled into something that can be called Zoroastrianism.[49] Of these three views, Olmstead's seems the least probable. If the first stage in the development of Zoroastrianism was the "pure" religion of the prophet, how can we explain the acceptance of such elements as the use of *haoma*, an intoxicating beverage absolutely forbidden by the prophet? It is far simpler to posit a polytheistic, highly ritualized faith to which the ethical, henotheistic teachings of Zarathustra became in time attached.

Boyce claims archaeological support for her views, consisting most notably of the following artifacts: the fragments of two fire-holders from the ruins of Cyrus's capital at Pasargadae; the depiction of fire altars in the funerary carvings of Darius; two stone plinths on a plain at Pasargadae, which Boyce takes to be markers of an outdoor sanctuary such as is used in Zoroastrian worship; the tomb of Cyrus, which she claims is built so that the impurity from the body cannot contaminate any of the elements; and an ossuary from the time of Artaxerxes II, providing evidence for the Zoroastrian practice of the exposure of the dead.[50]

This evidence, however, is certainly open to other interpretations. Boyce herself grants that the veneration of the hearth-fire was a common Indo-European custom,[51] so that the presence of fire altars need not imply a full-blown Zoroastrianism. The tomb of Cyrus and

---

[47] Boyce, "Religion," 280-81.

[48] Olmstead, *History*, 105-6.

[49] Frye, *Heritage*, 142-44.

[50] Boyce, "Religion," 285-86; 302.

[51] Ibid., 285-86.

the ossuary of Artaxerxes II, far from indicating a Zoroastrian presence, witness to a variety of and a development in Persian burial customs. In any case, exposure of the dead was practiced by Magians and Bactrians as well,[52] and does not by itself evidence Zoroastrian beliefs. Finally, as Boyce admits, no evidence supports her suggestion that the plinths at Pasargadae mark a Zoroastrian worship site.[53]

Textual evidence cited by Boyce throughout her article is likewise unconvincing. Evidence for various practices of various origins that became part of Zoroastrian religion is not evidence for a full-blown Zoroastrianism; the part does not, logically, imply the whole. Moreover, her radical pre-dating of Zarathustra's career raises unanswerable questions. In particular, one wonders why, if Zarathustra had taught on the Russian steppes around 1500 BCE, no mention of him, or of Ahuramazda, is found in the Vedic literature of the Aryans in India. The position of Frye, then, seems most tenable-- which, unfortunately, leaves us with no solid base for understanding Persian religion in the early Achaemenid period but the inscriptions themselves.

Iconographical Evidence

At this point the iconography of the Persians becomes highly significant. At Behistun, a carving above the inscription shows Darius receiving the homage of vassal kings. He is facing an elaborate winged disk, his right hand outstretched in supplication toward it. The symbol, also found at the royal palace in Persepolis,[54] seems to be related to the Egyptian *aton*, the solar disk. Boyce relates that this symbol is found also above the door of Darius's tomb, with the king portrayed again in an attitude of reverence, his right hand outstretched. She finds here a reflection of Zoroastrian practice, which enjoins that prayer be said facing sun, moon, or fire.[55] Frye,

---

52 Frye, *Heritage*, 146.

53 Ibid., 286.

54 Frye, *Heritage*, figs. 30 and 67.

55 Boyce, "Religion," 290.

however, rightly identifies this symbol as the iconographic representation of Ahuramazda.[56]

As ruler of the sky, as the young and vigorous principle which abolished chaos and established order, Ahuramazda was the sun. It is certainly intriguing, then, that Cambyses's titulary meant "son of Re," the sun god. Recall, too, that the one Greek cult we know with a certainty to have been supported by Darius was the cult of Apollo. Solar imagery may also have been a part of the cult of YHWH from early days.[57] The Temple, after all, was given an eastern orientation, facing the rising sun. Royal seals and scarabs from the reign of Hezekiah that incorporate solar motifs have been found, raising the possibility that YHWH, as king, may have been associated with the sun.[58] We also have the intriguing mention of the horses and chariots of the sun, removed from the Temple precincts in Josiah's reform (2 Kings 23:11). In later antiquity, the identification of YHWH with the sun is

---

[56] Frye, *Heritage*, figs. 30 and 67.

[57] Mark S. Smith ("The Near Eastern Background of Solar Language for Yahweh," *JBL* 109 [1990] 30-33) argues that Psalm 84 in particular, joined with the common idea of "seeing" God or God's glory and the use of the expression זרח ("rise") for YHWH's appearing, indicates that solar language for YHWH has a long history in the Jerusalem Temple. Despite the later polemical references to such language and imagery in 2 Kings 23:11, Ezekiel 8:16, and Job 31:26-28, Smith believes that the practices described in these texts are part of "a form of solarized Yahwism" (Smith, "Solar," 29).

[58] Three types of seal impressions have been identified: the four-winged scarab (usually regarded as the earliest royal seal), the two-winged scarab, and the winged sun disk. A. D. Tushingham ("A Royal Israelite Seal (?) and the Royal Jar Handle Stamps," *BASOR* 200 [1970] 71-78 and 201 [1971] 23-35) associates the four-winged scarab with Hezekiah, and the two-winged with Josiah. H. Darrell Lance ("The Royal Stamps and the Kingdom of Josiah," *HTR* 64 [1971] 315-332) concurs, countering the suggestion of Aharoni that all the למלך stamps be assigned to the reign of Hezekiah. More recently, Nadar Na'aman ("Hezekiah's Fortified Cities and the LMLK Stamp," *BASOR* 261 [1986] 5-24) has observed that the distribution of the למלך seal impressions corresponds to the plan of the 15 fortified cities described in 2 Chron 11:5-10. Although these fortifications are attributed to Rehoboam by the Chronicler, all are within Judean territory; indeed, Na'aman observes (5) that the cities are "strategically located to protect the kingdom of Judah from an attack on its western front." Hence they must rather belong to a Judean monarch, specifically to Hezekiah or Josiah. Since the pattern of fortification, and of occupation, does not fit the situation of Josiah's wars, Na'aman attributes the city list to the time of Hezekiah's defense against Assyrian invasion in 701 BCE, and suggests that the למלך stamps are Hezekiah's royal seal. Mark Smith ("Solar," 34-38) suggests connections with royal language linking the king with the sun god throughout the Near East, especially in the Late Bronze Age; on the basis of Ugaritic texts and the Amarna letters, he suggests New Kingdom Egypt as the ultimate source of this ideology.

far more marked. At Beth Alpha, Naaran (Ain Duk), and Hamat
Tiberius, synagogues have been found with circular floor mosaics
depicting the zodiac. These zodiacal mosaics all have at their center a
representation of Zeus Helios driving the solar chariot; association
with YHWH seems at least implicit.[59]   These striking parallels
become all the more significant when viewed in the general context of
popular religion and divine titles in the Near East after the fifth
century.

The God of Heaven

Ahuramazda fits an ancient Near Eastern type: the creator/ruler
deity, identified or associated with the sun and the sky. As has already
been noted, the title used of YHWH in the Persian period documents
of the Bible, and especially in the Aramaic portions of Ezra, is "God of
heaven." The use of this title was at one time thought almost certain

---

[59] Erwin R. Goodenough, *Jewish Symbols in the Greco-Roman Period*
(Bollingen Series 13; Princeton: Princeton University, 1953-68), describes the mosaics
from Beth Alpha (vol. 1: *The Archaeological Evidence from Palestine*, 248; vol. 3:
Illustrations for Volumes 1 and 2, fig. 640), Naaran (1:255; 3: fig. 644) and Hamath
Tiberius (vol. 12: *Summary and Conclusions*, 45). He also describes portions of mosaics
at Yafa (1:217) and Isfiya (1:258; 3: fig. 658), where enough remains to suggest that the
same circular zodiac, centering on Helios, was a part of these synagogues as well.
Finally, Goodenough observes that "the zodiac seems the basis for one of the paintings
in the Dura synagogue, where Moses takes the place of Helios." (12:152) This motif, so
characteristic of Palestinian synagogues after the third century in particular, could not
have been mere ornamentation. Goodenough observes that it was just at this time that
astral and solar symbolism was coming into its own in nearly all Greco-Roman
religious traditions (12:45); hence the symbol was still vital as a religious symbol, and
could no more have been divorced from its symbolic import than such potent symbols
of our day as the swastika, which could never be used as mere "decoration!" (12:72)
Goodenough proposes, rather (vol. 8: *Pagan Symbols in Judaism*, 177), that the symbol
has been appropriated for its symbolic import, "that these astronomical symbols, and
Helios himself, meant something in the Judaism of these Jews, something which could
be as central in their thinking as the zodiac panels are physically central in their
floors." As we have proposed above, Goodenough (8:215) sees a link to the notion of
YHWH as royal sky deity: "The zodiac in the synagogues with Helios in the center,
accordingly, seems to me to proclaim that the God worshipped in the synagogue was the
God who had made the stars, and revealed himself through them in cosmic law and
order and right, but who was himself the Charioteer guiding the universe in all its order
and law." Lee Levine (*Ancient Synagogues Revealed* [Detroit: Wayne State University,
1982] 9) suggests another possibility. The *Sefer Harazim* ("Book of Secrets"), a magical
text composed in the Byzantine period by a Palestinian Jew, lists the angels an adept
may petition for specific requests; chief among these was Helios, from whom one could
"learn the secrets of the universe." However, it seems doubtful that such prominent
display would have been given in the synagogues to an angelic figure, however exalted.
Cf. also the discussion of the synagogues at Hammath-Tiberius (by M. Dothan, 63-69)
and Dura-Europas (by L. I. Levine, 172-177) in Levine, *Ancient Synagogues*.

evidence that the documents were either inauthentic, or at best drafted by Jews and merely signed by the Persian monarch. However, the presence of the title at Elephantine has cast new light on its significance.[60]   Apparently, "God of heaven" was a genuine Persian means of addressing the God of the Jews in both Judah and Egypt, with intriguing connections to the standard epithets of Ahuramazda. The authenticity of the Cyrus Cylinder has been doubted for reasons similar to those given for the rejection of the Persian edicts in Ezra. Boyce flatly states, "the words of this declaration were clearly composed by Babylonian priests."[61]   However, the close parallels in language among the Cylinder, the accounts in Ezra, and the Darius inscriptions make it highly unlikely that any but Persian hands are behind the Cylinder.

The title "God of heaven" must also be seen in parallel with the title *Baal Shamin*, "Lord of Heaven." This divine name occurs in the Semitic inscriptions of Phoenicia, Syria and Palmyra throughout this period, in reference to a supreme divine being.[62]   Javier Teixidor observes that from the fourth century onward these inscriptions no longer make reference to any council of the gods, but at most to the angels of the high god. Teixidor discerns here a trend toward monotheism, specifically toward monotheism of the royal type, with a supreme god associated with the heavens worshipped in virtual

---

[60] *AP* 27, 30, 31, 32, 38, 40.

[61] Boyce, "Religion," 287. This point could also be made on the basis of the often-observed similarity in language between the Cyrus Cylinder and Deutero-Isaiah, generally attributed to a common Babylonian court style (M. Smith, "II Isaiah," 415). Morton Smith, however, who going still further posits a direct literary dependence between the two texts ("II Isaiah," 416-17), suggests that behind both the Cyrus Cylinder and the Cyrus texts of Isaiah 40--48 is a common document: a work of political propoganda, circulated by Persian agents in Babylon before that kingdom's fall to Cyrus (418). In any case, it is clear that we need attribute the Cylinder to none other than Persian hands.

[62] The evidence is presented in Javier Teixidor, *The Pagan God: Popular Religion in the Greco-Roman Near East* (Princeton: Princeton University, 1977). Although much of his evidence comes from late antiquity (particularly that of the Bel cult at Palmyra, from 32 CE and later), he does establish a much earlier basis for the spread of the cult of Bel/Baal Shamin through the Near East. In any case, it is certain that the inscriptions, rising out of popular religious sentiment, do not owe themselves to religious innovation, but to the tradition of generations.

independence of the other, minor deities who may also have been recognized.[63]

If Teixidor's analysis of the inscriptional evidence is correct, our thesis gains considerable force. A virtual monotheism--centered on a sky god of the Marduk-Baal-Zeus Helios type--does seem to have emerged in the Persian period. Doubtless, this tendency toward monotheism was supported by the Persians. Indeed, the close parallels among the language used of Marduk on the Cyrus Cylinder, the language used of YHWH in Ezra and the language used of Ahuramazda in the inscriptions of Darius point toward the close association of these three deities, each of whom was, in fact, a type of "God of Heaven." For Cyrus, perhaps Marduk and YHWH, as royal creator deities, were equated with Ahuramazda. The pattern holds, too, with respect to the Egyptian parallels. The House of Life, as we have seen, was identified with the god Osiris, associated with the Pharaoh, and with the sun.[64] The Persian patronage of the temple of the mother goddess Neith seems at first contrary to this principle. However, as Neith was the mother of the son-god Re,[65] it seems quite natural that she might become syncretistically associated with the sky god Ahuramazda. Moreover, the particular act of Cambyses with regard to that temple, in which he was said to do "as every king had done before," was the re-establishment "of libations to the Lord of Eternity," that is, Osiris.[66] In these cases as well, then, it does not strain credibility to see a possible identification of the deities involved with Ahuramazda. The Persians, in their support of these particular cults, may have been acting not only from motives of political expediency, but from genuine piety.

---

[63] Teixidor, Pagan God, 13-17.

[64] The process by which Osiris, originally a chthonic deity, became identified with solar imagery is described by James Henry Breasted, Development of Religion and Thought in Ancient Egypt (New York: Harper, 1959) 142-164.

[65] At any rate, she was celebrated as such at Sais (Lichtheim, Literature, 38). Cf. also W. Helck and E. Otto, Kleines Wörterbuch der Aegyptologie (Wiesbaden: Otto Harrassowitz, 1956), 242-43; and Siegfried Morenz, Egyptian Religion (tr. Ann E. Keep; Ithaca: Cornell University, 1973) 266 and 269.

[66] Lichtheim, Literature, 39.

Support for this hypothesis comes from the reign of Xerxes, son of Darius. The Daiva Inscription of Xerxes, found at Persepolis, gives fascinating insight into Persian religious attitudes. This intriguing statement follows an account of Xerxes's conquests:

> And among these countries was (a place) where previously Daivas were worshipped. Then by the will of Ahuramazda I destroyed that Daiva-sanctuary, and I made proclamation, "Daivas shall not be worshipped!" Where previously Daivas were worshipped, there I worshipped Ahuramazda with due order and rites.[67]

Both Boyce and Frye agree in understanding this to be a statement, not about the religious practices of non-Aryan subject peoples, but about Aryan practice.[68] The Avestan *daeva* refers to the old gods, dark beings whose worship Zarathustra had condemned.[69] Xerxes showed no tolerance at all for *daiva*-worship. As seen above, the touchstone for Persian religious tolerance seems to be conformity to the image of Ahuramazda. Worship of gods perceived as rivals to Ahuramazda could not be permitted, even if practiced by native Aryans. On the other hand, alien cults, if their gods reflected his characteristics, could be actively supported.

VI. The Significance Of Persian Religious Involvement

The means by which the Persians supported the Jerusalem Temple establishment are typical of Persian action when that government supported a cult. They ordered the rebuilding of the Temple, provided funds and materials for rebuilding and maintaining the restored sanctuary, and arranged for the return and installation of a formerly disenfranchised priesthood. But the Persians clearly did not support every cult. By supporting and re-establishing formerly disenfranchised priesthoods, the Persians also rejected the established cult leadership in each area: thus, the Marduk priests in Babylon supplanted priests of the moon god loyal to Nabonidus; the

---

[67] Boyce, "Religion," 293. A different translation is given by Oppenheim (*ANET*[3], 317); curiously, he renders the Old Persian *daiva* as "Evil Gods."

[68] Boyce, "Religion," 294 and Frye, *Heritage*, 144.

[69] Boyce, "Religion," 294.

Udjahoresne party replaced the members of Peftuaneith's reform movement in the House of Life, with their ties to the old royal house in Egypt; and the exiled Zadokite priests from Babylon were imposed upon the people of the land in Judah. Thus, Persian involvement in the Jerusalem Temple establishment cannot be attributed to general religious tolerance.

The Persian involvement in the religion of Judah is neither anomalous nor accidental. When Cyrus sent the captives home with their religious relics and a charge to rebuild their Temple, he set in motion a pattern that his successors would follow. So Darius provided funding for the Temple's actual construction and maintenance, and (at any rate implicitly) gave the impetus for the codification of Temple law. Artaxerxes, by sending Ezra, was likewise acting in keeping with the established practices of the empire. Judah fits the pattern of Persian involvement quite nicely. The Persians installed the exiled Zadokites in the rebuilt temple in Jerusalem, as they had installed the Marduk priests in Babylon and the Udjahoresne party in Egypt, doubtless certain that by returning these disen-franchised elements to prestige and power, their loyalty to Persia would be assured. As Darius, seeking to maintain a stability in the empire that mirrored the divine order established by Ahuramazda, sought from the priests of Egypt an ancient and authoritative law by which the people would live and the temples be ordered, so the Zadokite clergy of the restored Jerusalem cultus set about the codification of their own תורת הבית. As Darius had sent Udjahoresne, so Artaxerxes sent Ezra, law in hand, to his unruly folk in Judah. Yet the Persian choice of this cult to support, in this place, cannot finally be attributed merely to a desire to keep the peace. In the God YHWH, alone without peers, divine warrior against chaos, serene and supreme creator and preserver of all, the Persians thought they recognized Ahuramazda, "who created the earth, who created yonder heaven."

Chapter Four

THE ROLE OF THE נשיא IN
THE LAW OF THE TEMPLE

The bulk of the legislation promulgated in Ezekiel 40--48 is concerned with the proper conduct of the sacrificial cult in the Temple; all else is related to this central organizing principle. Hence, the proper priesthood, essential for the conduct of right worship, is set forth. Even the scheme for land division, as will be seen, functions more as a religious doctrine than as a proposal for land reform. But while the program set forth in the Temple Vision focuses on cultic matters, it nonetheless presupposes, and indeed alludes to, a particular political context. A political leader, the נשיא, figures prominently, and although his role is sketched with primary reference to religious rather than secular affairs, clear intimations of the power wielded by this office are found throughout the text.

In the Law of the Temple, the נשיא is, in brief, the chief patron of the liturgy, responsible for supplying the materials required for the sacrificial cultus. Though evidently a figure of great wealth and influence, the נשיא is given little else to do in these texts, at least explicitly. The very title נשיא seems a curious choice: if the office has political significance, why is it not designated by the term מלך ("king"), or even פחה ("governor")? A consideration of the usage of נשיא throughout the Hebrew Bible may help us understand the use of this title, in this context.

I. The נשיא Outside Of Ezekiel

Most occurrences of the term נשיא are in Priestly material, particularly in the book of Numbers (fifty-six occurrences). Here, נשיא is the technical term for the leader of a clan.[1] The נשיאים are

---

[1] Cf. E. A. Speiser, "Background and Function of the Biblical נשיא" *CBQ* 25 (1963) 111-17, for a discussion of the usage and etymology of this term, particularly as

mentioned alongside Moses (Ex 16:22), Moses and Aaron (Num 1:44;
4:34, 46), Moses and Eleazar (Num 27:2; 31:13; 32:2), Joshua and
Eleazar (Jos 17:4), and Phineas and Eleazar (Jos 22:14, 30), always as
authorities in subordination to a greater authority. In Numbers 17,
though each נשיא lays a rod before the Divine Presence in the tent,
only the rod of Aaron miraculously blossoms; sacerdotal privilege is not
to be given to the clan chiefs, but rather is reserved for Aaron and his
house alone.

The נשיאים are most often cited in groups, as if lacking
independent authority (the sons of Ishmael [Gen 17:20; 25:16], the
נשיאים of Midian [Jos 13:21], or Abraham as one among, even if
highest of, the נשיאים recognized by the Hittites [Gen 23:6]). Even
when given independent reference and status, they seem minor rulers
(Hamor in Gen 34:2).[2] It is quite interesting that in the one instance
(apart from Ezekiel) that a king of Israel is called a נשיא (Solomon in
1 Kgs 11:34), the point of the text is the limitation of kingly authority.
Solomon is denied the right to have a son succeed him as king over
the united northern and southern kingdoms; rather than king of all
Israel, he has become solely the נשיא of the tribe of Judah. Most
intriguing for us is the use of נשיא in Ezra 1:8 to refer to Sheshbazzar,
the leader of the returning exiles, and manifestly a person under
Persian authority.[3] In the Hebrew Scriptures at large, then, the נשיא
is possessed of authority over the clan or tribe, yet is also under the
sacerdotal authority of the priest, and the political authority of the
leader (where such exists) of all Israel. The title נשיא is thus plainly

---

contrasted with מלך. Speiser describes נשיא as a passive participial form of the verb
נשא, functioning as a *nomina professionis* ("Background," 114): hence, the נשיא is
one elevated, or elected, from among the people.

[2] The legislation of Ex 22:27 does not contradict this understanding of the
נשיא, since, as Speiser ("Background," 115) notes, the legislation refers not to a king
per se, but rather to the elected head of "a combination or confederation of tribes." Such
a figure would still have been subject to the people who had elected him, and,
particularly, to the will of YHWH regarding his election--expressed, of course, by the
priests.

[3] Gese (116, n. 9) proposes that this is a mistake, deriving from the misidentifi-
cation of Sheshbazzar with Zerubbabel. This is, however, mere speculation: there is no
textual or exegetical warrant for denying the title נשיא to Sheshbazzar.

distinguished from the title מלך, since the latter may refer to the sole ruling figure.

II. The נשיא In Ezekiel 1--39

When we turn to Ezekiel, however, the situation becomes far more complex. After Numbers, the term נשיא appears more often in Ezekiel (thirty-three occurrences, sixteen in 40--48) than anywhere else in the Hebrew Scriptures. Of these, only three (bracketing out for the moment 40--48) fit the pattern identified elsewhere: the נשיאים of Kedar in 27:21, the מלכים ונשיאים of Edom in 32:29, and the נשיאי הארץ allied with the mythic enemy Gog in 39:18. Twice, the expression is used uncharacteristically of the leaders of mighty foreign powers, elsewhere designated מלכים: the kings of Tyre (26:16) and Egypt (30:13). Zimmerli has proposed that 26:16 refers not to the rulers of Tyre, but to the subject princes of coastal regions, and that 30:13 should read in the plural, referring to court officials rather than the Pharaoh, which resolves these two uncharacteristic references.[4] More difficult is the designation of the mythic enemy Gog as נשיא ראש (38:2-3; 39:1). In this instance, Zimmerli suggests that "already in his title Gog is introduced not as the ruler of a great united empire, but as the leader of a number of national groups."[5]

נשיא as the Title of Israel's Monarch

Most numerous, and most puzzling, are the many attributions of the title נשיא to the king of Israel (12:10, 12; 19:1; 21:17, 30; 22:6; 34:24; 37:25). Ezekiel uses the term מלך only twice to designate Israel's monarch: 7:27 and 17:12.[6] In each instance, מלך is used in a more technical sense, as a title contrasted with other titles: the

---

[4] Zimmerli, 2:30 and 2:125, respectively.

[5] Ibid. 2:305.

[6] The use of מלך in the superscription (1:2) belongs to the redactor, not the prophet. מלך in 37:22 and 24, even if authentic (as Cooke [402] and May [271] affirm; denied by Eichrodt, 511-12; Zimmerli, 2:271-72; Wevers, 196; and Hals, 273-74), designates the future Davidic messiah, not the past or present kings of Israel's history. As has been shown, in 43:8-9 the term belongs to the redaction of the Temple Vision, and does not reflect Ezekiel's particular concerns.

נְשִׂיאִם (here probably "clan elders" or "court officials") in 7:27, and שָׂרִים ("princes") in 17:12. Clearly, in these contexts, the use of נָשִׂיא would be confusing or impossible. Wherever he has a choice, then, Ezekiel calls the kings of Israel נְשִׂיאִים. Zimmerli and Speiser both suggest that this use of נָשִׂיא reflects a deliberate archaizing, a return to the leadership patterns of pre-monarchic Israel.[7] This seems most likely, particularly since it explains the most curious transformation of the title נָשִׂיא in Ezekiel's work: the use of נָשִׂיא as a messianic title.

נָשִׂיא as a Messianic Title

In 34:24 and 37:25, as part of a promise of return to the land, the assurance is given that David (called עַבְדִּי, "my servant") will be נָשִׂיא. Clearly these two texts are a crux; little wonder then that they have been used by many recent commentators as the key for the understanding of the נָשִׂיא in the whole of Ezekiel, and particularly in the Temple Vision.[8]

May considers both texts, as well as the references to the נָשִׂיא in 40--48, to be the work of Ezekiel's redactor: in his view, the future Davidid of these texts and the נָשִׂיא of the Temple Vision are the same figure.[9] While Zimmerli considers 34:24 an authentic saying of Ezekiel, he, too, stresses that, in the later redaction of Ezekiel, נָשִׂיא has become a title of messianic expectation, finding its fulfillment in 40--48.[10] However, for Zimmerli the נָשִׂיא as messiah is something of an afterthought, included only because he must be: the prophet "cannot see the consummation of Israel's salvation without a divine affirmation of the royal house of David."[11] This scion of David is

---

[7] Zimmerli, 2:218 and 2:277-78; Speiser, "Background," 111.

[8] E.g., May, 53; Zimmerli, 2:278-79; Levenson, Program, 87, 94.

[9] May, 53.

[10] Zimmerli, 2:278.

[11] Ibid. 2:278-79.

explicitly a servant figure, on the fringes of what for Ezekiel is the real center of future expectation: the restored sanctuary.[12]

For Jon Levenson, the interpretive crux is the analogy drawn in 17:22-24: "YHWH is to the messiah as Nebuchadnezzar is to Zedekiah."[13] As Zedekiah is king only by the sufferance of his suzerain, so, in Ezekiel's vision of Israel's future, the messiah will reign only insofar as his rule remains subject to the stated will of YHWH. Therefore no administrative structures are provided in the Temple Vision: "In a theocracy, one need devote no attention to the mechanics of government."[14] Nonetheless, Levenson insists that the position of the נשיא in the Temple Vision is one of great honor, involving special Temple privileges as well as the designation of the נשיא as patron of the liturgy.[15]

Hals, too, finds in the נשיא of the Temple Vision the Davidid of Ezekiel 34:24 and 37:25.[16] However, in his assessment, no positive reconstruction of a role envisioned for this figure is possible:

> To put it crassly, the prince's value is solely to be one unlike the past kings (see 43:7-9), one whose cultic role is modest, whose property rights are so modest as to be minimal (see 45:7-8a and 48:21-22), and whose further role in connection with property is presented in a totally negative way.[17]

The נשיא, as replacement for the king, is meant only to undo the past damage of kings such as Manasseh. He represents, perhaps, a return to the pristine days of the tribal confederacy, when there were no kings in the land.[18]

---

[12] Ibid. 2:279.

[13] Levenson, *Program*, 80.

[14] Ibid. 113.

[15] Ibid.

[16] Hals, 252, 274, and 288. Note, however, Hals's observation (288) that "the prince's Davidic role referred to in 34:23f. and 37:24 is left unmentioned throughout chs. 40--48.

[17] Ibid. 288.

[18] Ibid.

Whatever claim Ezekiel wanted to make concerning messianic expectation by designating the future Davidid as נשיא (and here, the proposal of Zimmerli does in fact make good sense), the נשיא of the Law of the Temple is another figure altogether. For all Levenson's ingenuity and Hals's pessimism, the text itself presents the נשיא, not as a theological or political abstraction, but as an actual historical figure. True, the use of this title by Ezekiel's redactors has definitely been affected by the prophet's use of it the body of his book; the נשיא of the Law of the Temple may well have been a "messianic" figure, if that term is used in its narrowest sense, to apply to a descendant of the royal house of David. However, he belongs most immediately to historical and political reality, rather than eschatological hope or proto-apocalyptic fancy.

III. The נשיא In Ezekiel 40--48

His Role in the Cult

In the Law of the Temple, the נשיא plays an important role in Temple liturgy. We first encounter the נשיא in an insert into the original theophany, at 44:3. Although YHWH had commanded that the outer eastern gate by which the Glory had entered be forever closed, the redactors hasten to observe an exception: though he may not actually use the gate, the נשיא may sit in it and eat the sacred meal before YHWH. This privilege is accorded to the נשיא alone: no one else may approach the entryway of the divine Presence. In the major section on entrances and exits in 46:1-15, it is observed that the נשיא is to stand at the doorpost of the eastern gate of the inner court every sabbath and new moon, and whenever else he offers the שלמים נדבה נדבה עולה או ("voluntary burnt offering or peace offering," v 12), at which times this gate is to be opened. While the sacrificial cult of the Temple is carried out within the inner court on high holy days, it is the נשיא alone, standing before the people as they throng in the outer court, who watches the priests come and go. The gates of the complex thus become the setting of a liturgical drama, in which the נשיא plays a cardinal role as both the provider of the sacrifice and the sole witness of the sacrificial act. This is in keeping with the other cultic responsibility given to the נשיא in 46:1-15: the leading of the sacral procession into the Temple courts on high holy days (46:10). Clearly, in these texts the נשיא plays an important cultic function.

What is more, these texts strongly suggest that practice here described was actually performed. Why would a redactor of the text, in mere fancy, qualify the express prohibition of YHWH in 44:2? What unreal circumstance, whether envisioned as social reform or apocalyptic reality, could justify this? Only a *real* practice, either too deeply entrenched in the traditions of the people to excise or supported by individuals too powerful to oppose, could prompt the sort of backpeddling evidenced in 44:3. That the latter situation is the case here is indicated by the repeated descriptions of the נשיא's wealth.

The נשיא as Temple Patron

As befits the role of patron of the liturgy, the נשיא is a figure of significant wealth. Twice (in 45:7-8 and 48:21-22) the estates of this figure are described: the inheritance given the נשיא alone is comparable to the inheritance given elsewhere to an entire tribe. Out of this great wealth, the Temple Vision states, the נשיא is to provide for the maintenance of the cult. This is for the priestly redactors the primary function of the נשיא. The cultic calendar in 45:18-25 states that the prince is to provide the bull for the sin offering at passover (45:22); in 46:4-8 the regular offerings for the sabbath and the new moon are recorded as provided by the נשיא. Indeed, it is made clear in 45:16-17 that the נשיא is to provide for *all* the offerings, on sabbaths and new moons as well as on high holy days, out of his own holdings and out of the תרומה ("contribution") of the people. Hence, the נשיא apparently has the authority to levy taxes. From the viewpoint of the priestly legislators and redactors who have designed these laws, the purpose of this contribution is the support of the sacrificial cultus. Therefore, they give to it the designation תרומה: a sacral offering rather than a secular tax. All the same, the תרומה is collected by a secular authority, which sounds more like a tax than a voluntary gift. We have, then, a portrayal of a state-supported cult: a state church, if you will.

In this regard, the נשיא of the Temple Vision is portrayed in continuity with the נשיא in the bulk of scripture. A prominent task of the נשיאים in the priestly material of the Pentateuch is the provision for the cultus. In Exodus 35:27, it is the נשיאים (apparently people of greater than average affluence) who are to provide the precious stones for the ephod and the priestly breastplate, as well as spice, anointing oil, and incense for tabernacle service. Similarly, Numbers 7 offers a detailed account of the offerings the נשיאים brought לחנכת המזבח ("for the consecration of the altar," v 11). However, of particular interest for us is the specifically cultic task entrusted to Sheshbazzar, leader of the returnees from exile following Cyrus' edict and called הנשיא ליהודה ("the chief/prince of Judah") by the Persians: the return of the sacred vessels of the Temple stolen by Nebuchadnezzar (Ez 1:7-8). As we have already seen, this role of the state in the religious affairs of Judah continued under Persian auspices.

The Prophetic Critique of the נשיא

Further evidence for the historicity of the נשיא in the Temple Vision is the criticism levelled at this figure in these chapters. At three points in the Temple Vision, the נשיאים are subjected to prophetic critique: 45:8; 45:9; and 46:18. In the first and last cases, the critique is connected with the description of the prince's estate: the נשיא is to be content with the generous inheritance he is given, and not seek to extend his lands at the expense of the inheritance of his people. Moreover, 46:16-18 limits the capacity of the נשיא to diminish his own inheritance by insuring that gifts of land given to individuals outside the princely family revert to the estate of the נשיא at the jubilee. Apparently, the legislators thought that keeping the נשיא wealthy was one way to guard against official greed and graft.

The second critique, in 45:9, introduces the second major task ascribed to the נשיא: the proper maintenance of true weights and measures. Verses 10-12 read naturally as the extension of v 9. The נשיא shall not oppress the people or evict them (in continuity with the first prophetic critique, relating to the land); rather he shall execute משפט וצדקה ("justice and right practices"): especially, by ensuring a just system of measurement. This is no niggling demand.

Just weights and measures are repeatedly urged in the Hebrew Bible, and the usage of false weights called an abomination, abhorred by God.[19]   Moreover, in the ancient Near East the maintenance of standard weights and measures is typically related to royal responsibility.   Thus, in the prologue to the ancient Sumerian law-code of Ur-Nammu, we read that among his other mighty accomplishments, Ur-Nammu "fashioned the bronze *silâ*-measure, he standardized the one mina weight, (and) standardized the stone-weight of a shekel of silver *in relation to* one mina."[20]   That the נשיא should be taken to task on this issue, then, serves once more to emphasize the political significance of this office.

These texts read very much like actual critiques of actual rulers, engaged in questionable economic practices.[21]   To argue, as Levenson has done, that they are mere empty formalities seems forced and awkward.[22]   Read as they stand, these texts seem to suppose an actual figure, called נשיא, standing both in cooperation and in tension with the priestly establishment.   The priests depend upon the נשיא for the

---

[19] Lev 19:35-36; Deut 25:13-16; Prov 11:1; Amos 8:5, Mic 6:10-11.

[20] J. J. Finkelstein (tr.), *ANET*[3], 523-24.

[21] So also Gese, 116: *"Andersiets zeigt die spätere Einschränkung der nasi-Gewalt, wie wir sie in den Stücken 45, 8b- 9; 46, 16-18 vor uns haben, dass wir es bei dem nasi wahrscheinlich mit einer historischen Figur zu tun haben"* ("On the other hand, the later restriction of the power of the נשיא, as we have before us in 45:8b-9 and 46:16-18, shows that in the case of the נשיא, there is a possibility that we have to do with a historical figure").

[22] Levenson (*Program*, 113-14) views this prophetic critique either as directed against the נשיאים of old "as if they were still a reality" (*Program*, 114), comparing this text to the critique of the רעים in chapter 34, or as an advance corrective and limitation on the power of the future נשיא. Neither is particularly convincing. In the first place, it is not clear that Ezek 34 must be dated after the fall of Jerusalem, in which case the critique leveled here against the shepherds of Israel could well be seen as a realistic prophetic complaint against the abuses of the Jerusalem hierarchy in those last bitter days. Further, even if a dating after the fall is granted, the intent and structure of this text is markedly different from the critiques of the נשיא in the Temple Vision. There, specific abuses are targeted, apparently with the aim of seeking their correction. In Ezek 34, however, the express point of the scathing criticisms leveled at the רעים of Israel is made clear in v 11: "For thus says YHWH: I, yes, I myself will search for the sheep and seek them out." YHWH, the true shepherd, will care for Israel, as all its false shepherds had failed to do. As for Levenson's second possibility, the simple reading of the texts shows no awareness that the critique is not real. Only if one assumes at the outset the unreality of the text can this conclusion be reached.

maintenance of the liturgy: he provides, from the taxation of the province and from his own estate, the materials necessary for the sacrificial cultus to continue; moreover, he guarantees the proper weights and measures, hence ensuring that the proper sacrifices are offered. Yet, the priests are not afraid to call the נשיא to accounts, and fulfill their teaching function by insisting upon his ethical behavior.

IV. The System Of Weights And Measures

The system of weights and measures set forth in 45:10-12 as the prince's special responsibility offers its own argument for a specific historical setting of the Temple Vision. In 45:12b, M reads עשרים שקלים חמשה ועשרים שקלים עשרה וחמשה שקל המנה יהיה לכם (literally, "twenty shekels, twenty-five shekels, fifteen shekels shall be your mina": or, a sum of sixty shekels). Many commentators and translators have altered the text in light of G, which reads οἱ πεντε σικλοι πεντε, και οἱ δεκα σικλοι δεκα, και πεντηκοντα σικλοι ἡ μνα εσται ὑμιν ("five shekels [shall be] five, and ten shekels [shall be] ten, and your mina shall be fifty shekels"), on the grounds that the text of M is circumlocutious and confused.[23] However, Ezekiel's style, and the style of his school, is customarily rather turgid. Moreover, the reading found in M is suggestive of the system of weights and measures set forth in the Elephantine papyri. On the basis of AP 15, which deals with the bride price in this Egyptian Jewish colony, Cowley has arrived at the following table of weights:

> 1 karash=10 shekels
> 1 shekel=4 quarters
> 1 quarter=10 hallurin[24]

According to a Babylonian cuneiform inscription on a trilingual weight in the British Museum, two karša was the equivalent of one-third of a

---

[23] E.g., Cooke, 498-99; Wevers, 225; Eichrodt, 567; Zimmerli, 2:474; Hals, 324. This approach is also advocated by the editors of the BHS and has been followed by the translators of the RSV and, to a degree, the NEB.

[24] AP, xxxi.

mina, which, again, gives sixty shekels to the mina.[25] This sexagesimal system was of Babylonian origin, and apparently very ancient.[26] It was not, however, used prior to the exile in either Israel or Egypt, where a decimal system (in Israel, fifty shekels to the mina) instead obtained.

It is, of course, possible that Ezekiel himself or his disciples could have used the Babylonian system in a work composed in exile. However, that they would have done so is highly unlikely: why, if the text is indeed a plan for reconstruction after the exile, or even more if it is seen as a portrayal of life in the messianic age, should the system of weights used by the Babylonian oppressors be made the standard? If, on the other hand, the text is read realistically, as detailing an actual system put into practice in an actual cultus, it is more likely that the imposed, non-Israelite system of the dominant power would be used--particularly if, as was the case in Restoration Judah, that dominant power was footing the bill.

Unfortunately, most of the Persian-period weights that have been found in Palestine are anepigraphic; we lack, therefore, concrete evidence as to what system of weights and measures they are meant to employ.[27] However, as Ephraim Stern has observed, "It is very likely that the system of weights employed by the Persian government in

---

[25] Weissbach, 105.

[26] Jacob Lauterbach ("Weights and Measures," in *The Jewish Encyclopedia*, Isidore Singer, ed.; Vol. 12 [New York: Funk and Wagnalls, 1916] 484) notes concerning an Egyptian inscription of Karnak, listing the tribute exacted from Syrian vassals: "Although the sums are given according to Egyptian weight, the odd numbers clearly indicate that the figures were computed originally by some other system, which can easily be shown to have been Babylonian."

[27] Ephraim Stern, *Material Culture of the Land of the Bible in the Persian Period 538-332 B.C.* (Warminster, England: Aris and Phillips, 1982) 216-217. The two exceptions are not especially helpful. A set of weights from a workshop at Ashkelon contains four dice-shaped weights inscribed with numbers, but their meaning is unknown. A rectangular weight of smooth limestone found by Meshorer at Tell el-Shukaf is inscribed פים in standard Persian-period Aramaic script. Stern (*Material*, 217) notes, however, that at 112 grams this weight is many times larger than the pre-exilic פים (around 7.8 grams). He proposes that it may therefore be part of a local system, used alongside the official Persian for local transactions. Similarly, in Egypt, weights according to "the stones of the king" (*AP* 5, 1.7) and "the stones of Ptah" (*AP* 11, 1,2) seem to have been used alongside the Persian standard. It would make sense, however, that the state-supported Temple cult would need to keep accounts by the officially sanctioned Persian system.

this period was uniform throughout the Persian realm, including Palestine."[28] Certainly, the fact that the system used in *AP* 15 (dated by Cowley to about 441 BCE, in the reign of Artaxerxes)[29] is Babylonian rather than Egyptian suggests that, at least in this southwestern province of the Persian Empire, the Babylonian sexagesimal system was the standard weight, replacing the indigenous decimal system.[30] Herodotus records that Darius standardized the systems of weights with regard to the sending of tribute, specifying that those paying in silver were to do so by the Babylonian talent; for this reason, Herodotus records, Darius was called καπηλος ("shopkeeper," "tradesman," or perhaps even "huckster").[31] The businesslike concern of Darius for standard weights and measures is further indicated by the discovery of engraved weights at Persepolis. The weight cited above, and a weight of green diorite, labelled in Persian as 120 karša, in Babylonian as 20 minae, both are inscribed with the imprimatur of Darius: "I am Darius, the great king, son of Hystapes, the Achaemenid."[32] As the karša was ten shekels, both weights, approved

---

[28] Stern, *Material*, 215. F. M. Cross ("Samaria Papyrus 1: An Aramaic Slave Conveyance of 335 BCE Found in the Wâdī ed-Dâliyeh," *EI* 18 [1985] 7-17) observes that the slave conveyances which make up the bulk of the Samaria Papyri presuppose a 50-shekel mina. SP 1, line 3 gives the price paid for Yehohanan the slave as 35 shekels, while line 10 stipulates that the penalty for violation of contract will be 7 minas. Since the standard penalty (following Neo-Assyrian convention) appears to be ten times the selling price, this yields 350 shekels to 7 minas, or 50 shekels to the mina. Note, however, that these are private transactions, not the business of state. Such local systems, as observed above, also prevailed in Egypt and, apparently, in Judah; the presence of a Persian standard, based on the Babylonian talent and used for state business, is not ruled out by this evidence.

[29] *AP*, 44.

[30] The decimal system did, eventually, win out, becoming the standard throughout Asia Minor (Lauterbach, "Weights," 484).

[31] Herodotus 3.89. The translation "shopkeeper" for καπηλος is from David Grene, *Herodotus: The History* (Chicago: University of Chicago, 1987) 252. "Tradesman" is used by Aubrey de Selincourt, *Herodotus* (Middlesex, England: Penguin, 1954) 243. The rendering "huckster" is from A. D. Godley, *Herodotus* (LCL; Cambridge: Harvard University, 1921), 2:117.

[32] Erich H. Schmidt, *The Treasury of Persepolis and other Discoveries in the Homeland of the Achaemenians* (OIC 21; Chicago: University of Chicago, 1939) 62. This latter weight's inscription reads a bit more fully, "I (am) Darius, the great king, the king of kings, the king of the lands, the king of this earth, the son of Hystapes, an Achaemenid."

by Darius, assume a system of 60 shekels to the mina. That this same system is suggested in the Temple Vision makes a strong case for dating this document as well, in its final form, to the reign of Darius in the Persian period. In such a setting, the obligations of the נשיא as secular leader would certainly entail enforcing the great king's standards.

V. The נשיא As Governor Of A Persian Province

If "נשיא" does indeed represent an actual office in Persian-period Yehud, what might that office have been? The only "secular" powers attributed to this figure in the Law of the Temple are taxation and the maintenance of just weights and measures, and even these are given direct sacral links. The נשיא is described repeatedly as a figure of great wealth, not always administered justly--yet even this wealth, from the perspective of the priestly redactors, is for the sake of the Temple, as the נשיא is its patron and benefactor. The primary task of the נשיא in these chapters, indeed we may go so far as to say the real function of the role in the Law of the Temple, is the provision for the sacrificial cult.

This, however, is only what we would expect to find in a text like the Law of the Temple. The political exigencies of the state are relevant to our redactors only to the extent that they impact upon the Temple and its liturgy. The fact that they do not tell us more of the practical, political tasks of the נשיא does not mean, therefore, that the office was devoid of such tasks. Indeed, if we attempt to read this material realistically, to discern the political, historical reality behind the liturgical concerns of the text, we are led to a real political office: namely, the governor of Persian-period Yehud.

Hölscher identified the נשיא as "the highest secular personage in Judah" in the post-exilic period.[33] In support of this analysis, he cited not only the application of this title to Sheshbazzar, but also the designation of Ostanes, brother of the high priest, as נשיא in the

---

[33] Hölscher, 211: "*die oberste weltliche Persönlichkeit in Juda*."

Elephantine papyri.[34]   Messel, going further, identifies the נשיא with the פחה, observing that both titles are applied to Sheshbazzar in Ezra (נשיא in 1:8; פחה in 5:14).   He suggests that the latter title was the *Amtsbezeichung* ("official designation" for the office), while the former was an *Ehrentitel* ("title of honor").[35]

Gese disputes this proposal, on the grounds that the program laid out in Ezekiel 40--48 is an internal, Judean affair while the governorship was a foreign, Persian institution.   Indeed, he rejects the whole notion that these chapters form a *Verfassungsentwurf* ("draft constitution") on these very grounds: the structure of the state in the post-exilic period was established by foreign, rather than domestic, authority.[36]   Gese is, of course, correct.   However, the fact that both political and religious institutions of the post-exilic period were installed by Persian authority does not damage but supports our analysis of the text. If these texts do reflect Persian intervention, then they must be from the Persian period, and are to be read as realistic depictions of the society of that time, rather than as exilic projections. Moreover, we know from the Demotic Chronicle that Darius, at any rate, did not attempt to quash the independent legal and religious traditions of the provinces, but rather supported them.   The attempt of the Zadokite priests to come to terms with their heritage in the setting of Persian domination need not be any less "Judean" for reflecting that setting.

We have already seen in Sheshbazzar the use of the title נשיא for a Persian governor.   Moreover, we know that Sheshbazzar, as leader of the first returnees to the land following the edict of Cyrus, was given a cultic charge: the return of the sacred Temple vessels to Jerusalem. Finally, we know that state support of the cult was Persian policy. These parallels strongly suggest that the נשיא of the Law of the Temple was the Judean governor, under Persian hegemony.

---

[34] Hölscher, 211-12; the reference is to *AP* 30.

[35] Cited by Gese, 116.

[36] Gese, 117.

This interpretation fully accounts for what is said about the נשיא in the Temple Vision. The duties of the provincial government with regard to the funding of the Temple cult have already been stated; such coincide nicely with the expectations placed upon the נשיא. The wealth of the Persian governors of Yehud, and their practice of taxation, are negatively described in Nehemiah 5:14-19. Nehemiah makes a point of refusing to expand his lands or tax the people for his own profit, practices followed, he writes, by previous governors--and, intriguingly, practices specifically addressed in the prophetic critiques of the נשיא in the Law of the Temple. Even the system of weights and measures described in the Temple Vision is highly suggestive of the system we know to have been in use in the Persian period. All of this supports the proposal that נשיא is a title of the Persian-period governor of Judah.

VI. The Title "נשיא" And The Title "פחה"

There is, however, no extra-biblical citation of the title נשיא for Judean governors in the Persian period, and no biblical citation after Sheshbazzar. The usual title given such officials was "governor" (פחוא, פחת, פחה).[37] In a Lihyanite inscription found at the el-Ula oasis (identified with ancient Dedan) one Abd is designated as the *p ḥt* ("governor") of Dedan.[38] Sheshbazzar (Ezra 5:14), Zerubbabel (Haggai 1:1, 14) and Nehemiah are all identified as "governor" (פחת in Haggai, פחה elsewhere). Nahman Avigad notes the occurrence of פחוא on jar-handles, seals and bullae from the Persian period, and on this basis

---

[37] Thierry Petit ("L'évolution sémantique des termes hébreux et araméens *pḥh* et *sgn* et accadiens *pāḥatu* et *šaknu*," *JBL* 107 (1988) 53-67, 56-57) observes that, in the Persian period, "*Il appert que* pehâ *a le sens précis de "gouverneur" d'un certain territoire, d'un district*" ("It appears that פחה had the precise sense of 'governor' of a certain territory or district"). It was distinct from "satrap" in that, while the satrap governed very large territories, the פחה could have responsibility over a smaller district, such as Yehud. Petit notes that Tattenai, the official over all of Abar-Nahara, was also given the designation פחה, but proposes that this is a special case, prompted by the joint governance of Babylon and Abar-Nahara; the title satrap was here reserved for the official over the combined territories.

[38] W. F. Albright ,"Dedan," in *Geschichte und Altes Testament* (BHT 16; Tübingen: J. C. B. Mohr [Paul Siebeck], 1953) 4.

fills in the gap between Zerubbabel and Nehemiah with Elnathan, Yeho'ezer and Ahzai, all "governors" (פחוא) of Yehud.[39] The Elephantine papyri identify Bagohi as פחת of the province in about 408 BCE;[40] and on the basis of the Yehud coins, we know that Yeheziqiyah became governor (פחה) after him.[41] Similarly, in Samaria, we know from the seal-impression of Sanballat on a bulla found in Wâdî ed-Dâliyeh that the title of the Sanballatids was "governor" (פחת).[42] Nowhere does the title נשיא appear.

This may have been due to the ferment that took place throughout the Persian empire, and especially in Judah, early in Darius's reign. As Darius attempted to make his throne secure in the face of Egyptian and Babylonian revolts, and old structures seemed on the verge of collapse, the time was ripe for messianic speculation. Haggai and Zechariah exalted Zerubbabel as messiah designate (Haggai 2:20-23; Zech 4). Similarly, the first edition of the Chronicler's history preserves a wisdom tale inviting comparison of Zerubbabel to Solomon, and indeed attributing the return from Exile and the rebuilding of the Temple to him (1 Esdras 3:1--5:6).[43] Yet, in the final form of that history, Zerubbabel is all but invisible. Perhaps in the interim some action was taken by the Persian government--it is certainly not to be expected that the Persians would ignore the use of language with imperial overtones, however quixotic. Zerubbabel may have been forcibly removed by the Persians, or he may merely have

---

[39] Nahman Avigad, *Bullae and Seals from a Post-Exilic Judean Archive* (tr. R. Grafman, *Qedem* 4 (Jerusalem: Ahva Co-op., 1976) 37.

[40] *AP* 30 and 32.

[41] Cf. especially John Wilson Betlyon, "The Provincial Government of Persian Period Judea and the Yehud Coins," *JBL* 4 (1986) 634, 638, 642.

[42] Frank M. Cross, "Papyri of the Fourth Century B. C. from Daliyeh," in *New Directions in Biblical Archaeology*, David N. Freedman and J. C. Greenfield, eds. (Garden City: Doubleday, 1969) 41-62; figs. 34-35.

[43] On the basis of evidence from Qumran, Frank Cross ("A Reconstruction of the Judean Restoration," *Int* 29 [1975] 191; 195-97) has proposed that the *Vorlage* of 1 Esdras 1:1--5:65, plus 1 Chron 10--2 Chron 34, made up the first edition of the Chronicler's history.

been warned, in no uncertain terms, to watch himself. In either case, Zerubbabel failed to live up to expectations, and was forgotten.

Careful as our redactors seem to have been to avoid the implication of dynastic or imperial aspirations (hence, the prohibition of memorial stelae for royals in 43:7b-9), the נשיאים themselves seem not to have been so careful. The practice which is twice the target of prophetic denunciation in the Law of the Temple, namely the giving of land to individuals outside the family of the נשיא, is strongly reminiscent of the old covenant of grant described by Weinfeld: in brief, it is a kingly act![44] The cult privileges accorded the נשיא sound more appropriate to royalty than to a mere government official, as do the tracts of land apportioned to this figure. Then, there are those references in Ezekiel 34:24 and 37:25, with which the redactors of the Temple Vision were of course familiar. They were certainly not blind to the exalted connotations, however muted, that the use of נשיא would have in the context of Ezekiel's prophecy. However, both Sheshbazzar and Zerubbabel were descendants of David, inheritors of kingly dignity and worthy of the respect due that ancient line. In the tension between respect for the Davidic dynasty and care not to offend their Persian overlords, the title נשיא doubtless seemed the best compromise: a title descriptive of the cultic task of the נשיא which for the priestly establishment was of paramount concern, and reminiscent of Israel's ancient and honorable past, yet lacking dynastic or imperial overtones.

So far as can be determined, no Davidid served as governor of Yehud after Zerubbabel, although Elnathan was connected with the Davidic lineage through his wife.[45] Perhaps, after the messianic hysteria connected to Zerubbabel, and in light of the kingly prerogatives being claimed by the נשיאים, the Persians thought it best

---

[44] Moshe Weinfeld, "The Covenant of Grant in the Old Testament and in the Ancient Near East," *JAOS* 90 (1970) 184-203.

[45] Based on a seal described by Avigad (*Bullae*, 11-13), inscribed לשלמית אמת אלנתן פ(ח)...: "Belonging to Shelomith maidservant of Elnathan (the governor)." Avigad concludes only that the Shelomith of the seal must be a functionary of the government of Elnathan. Meyers ("The Persian Period," 509-510) notes that Shelomith appears in 1 Chron 3:19 as daughter of Zerubbabel, and suggests that she may have been married to Elnathan--a possibility not ruled out by Avigad.

to alter their policy of using persons of the royal line as governors. The title נשיא would then have fallen into gradual disuse, replaced even within Judean circles by the purely secular title "governor." This would strengthen the case for setting the Temple Vision in the reign of Darius, following Zerubbabel's governorship.

Chapter Five

PRIESTHOOD AND CULT IN THE LAW OF THE TEMPLE

I. Priests And Levites In Ezekiel 40--48

In the strongest possible terms, the Law of the Temple restricts altar service to the Zadokites, the old Jerusalemite priestly house. To a degree, this restriction is but the continuation of the two-stage division of the clergy described in 40:44-46, where it is explicitly stated that the altar clergy are "the Zadokites, those from among the Levites who draw near to YHWH to serve him" (40:46). However, in the judgement oracle of 44:1-14 this distinction between Zadokite and ordinary Levite is honed to razor sharpness. Here, because they had permitted the participation of the בני נכר ("strangers, aliens") in the sacrificial cult and participated themselves in idolatrous worship, the Levites are denied the right of priestly access to YHWH. Rather, they are made Temple servitors, given in particular the tasks of guarding the Temple gates and killing the sacrifices (vv 11, 14). In the following verses, the Zadokites are singled out as הכהנים הלויים ("the Levitical priests"), and given exclusive rights to the sacrificial worship of YHWH. It is they alone who may draw near (קרב) to the divine Presence; they alone who may offer YHWH the fat and the blood, serving the Deity at table.

This exclusive right of the Zadokite clan to altar service has already been prefigured by our redactor in the expansion to the Temple description at 42:13-14 (which makes no mention of or provision for the Temple clergy, but speaks only of the priests who may draw near [קרב] to YHWH), and in the altar dedication at 43:19 (which directs that the sacrifice to consecrate the altar be performed by הכהנים הלויים אשר הם מזרע צדוק הקרבים אלי ["the Levitical priests of Zadok's lineage, who may draw near to me"]). Zadokite preeminence is assumed in the description of the Temple kitchens

122   The Law of the Temple

(46:19-24), which distinguishes between הכהנים ("the priests," v 20) and משרת הבית ("those who serve in the Temple," or "Temple servants," v 24). Finally, in the land division text, the land given the priests is distinguished from the land given the Levites, a distinction clarified in 48:11 by a recollection of the judgement oracle at 44:1-14: לכהנים המקדש מבני צדוק אשר שמרו משמרתי אשר לא תעו בתעות בני ישראל כאשר תעו הלויים ("The sacred preserve shall be for the priests, the Zadokites who kept my charge and did not go astray like the Levites, when the people of Israel did"). Note that, in all of these citations and unlike 40:44-46, the title כהן is reserved exclusively for the Zadokites, and denied the Levites. Note also, however, that the Zadokites are themselves designated הכהנים הלויים ("the Levitical priests") in 43:19 and 44:15. Hence, while only Zadokites are priests, the Zadokite priesthood is nonetheless understood to be of Levitical descent.

The Responsibilities of the Zadokite Altar Clergy

As the duties of the ordinary Levite are spelled out in 44:11 and 14, so the duties and privileges of the Zadokite are given explicit statement in 44:15-31. The priest's primary responsibility, of course, is the sacrificial cult (vv 15-16). In the keeping of that sacred charge, the priest is to wear linen vestments, and to change his clothing before going out of the inner court, so as to avoid the communication of dangerous holiness (vv 17-19). This stipulation has also been prefigured in 42:13-14, which describes the chambers where the priest is to change his vestments. The concern for sancta contagion here expressed is also behind the provision for special kitchens in the inner court, where the priests can prepare the sacred meal (46:19-20); the sacred meal is to be consumed in the chambers also used for the vesting of the clergy (42:13-14).

The priest's special status as the one given access to the divine Presence is the factor behind most of the legislation affecting him. He is distinctive in appearance, even without his vestments, as his hair is specially trimmed (v 20). His conduct, too, is distinctive. When serving in the inner court, he abstains from wine (v 21). He may marry only a virgin of unquestioned bloodline or the widow of a priest (v 22). He is obligated to remain ritually pure: hence, he cannot come into contact with the dead, unless the deceased is a member of his immediate family (vv 25-27), and must avoid carrion (v 31). The privilege of access to the divine Presence carries with it the responsibility of stringent observance of the boundaries between sacred and common, clean and unclean.

Growing out of his cultic responsibilities, the priest has a vital obligation to teach (vv 23-24). He must not only himself know and observe the distinctions among sacred, common, clean and unclean, but must teach the people to observe them as well. So also, it is the priest's task to teach the people their place in the regular liturgical cycle of feasts and sabbaths. The priest's teaching role is backed by judicial authority: in lawsuits, it is the priests who are to serve as judges (v 24). Perhaps to guarantee the priest's objectivity and independence, and certainly in continuity with ancient tradition (Numbers 18:20-32; Deuteronomy 18:1; Joshua 13:14), the priest is given no inheritance in the land (vv 28-30). He is to live on the portion of the sacrifices allotted him, especially on the gifts of first fruits. The provision of a place for the priests in the sacred preserve (45:3-4; 48:10) does not alter this, as this land is not the property of the priests, but a trust held for all priests and for the sanctuary which is at its center. The livelihood of the priest is inextricably linked to the wellbeing of the Temple.[1]

This description of the priesthood is, on most points, in continuity with what is said of the priesthood elsewhere in biblical tradition. However, there are also points of strong discontinuity--in particular, regarding the restriction of priestly vocation to the Zadokites. A summary of Temple priesthood as portrayed elsewhere will bring out these similarities and differences, and enable us to come

---

[1] The amount of detail here makes it difficult to understand Hals's assertion that the Zadokite priesthood is entirely a negative construct, meant only to undo past Levitical abuses (288); that "the presumed inner priestly polemic in this section does not reflect some historically reconstructible development within the exilic and postexilic priesthood, but rather a grandiose, eschatological affirmation of heightened holiness" (320). If this was indeed the case, why would the text present so much positive information about the duties and livelihood of the Zadokite priests?

to some conclusions concerning the relationship between the Law of the Temple and other biblical legislation relating to the priesthood.

II. The Levitical Priesthood In Deuteronomy And The Deuteronomistic History

In Deuteronomy, the priests are generally called הכהנים הלויים: the *Levitical* priests (e.g., 17:9, 18; 18:1; 24:8). This identification is doubly appropriate, for in D's legislation not only are all priests Levites but it also appears that all Levites are, at least potentially, priests. Deuteronomy 18:1 identifies הכהנים הלויים with כל שבט לוי : "the entire tribe of Levi." No mention is made of any restriction on this priestly service owing to blood line: that is, unlike the Law of the Temple, D does not restrict priestly service to any one Levitical family. Instead, the one restriction placed upon a Levite's service as a priest has to do with his location: only in the Jerusalem Temple can the Levite offer sacrifices.[2]

D restricts sacrifice to המקום אשר יבחר יהוה אלהיכם ("the place which YHWH your God will choose"): that is, the place where YHWH establishes (שכן) his Name (e.g., Deut 12:5, 11; 14:23; 16:2, 6,

---

[2] G. Ernest Wright ("The Levites in Deuteronomy," *VT* 4 [1954] 325-30) argued that here and elsewhere, Deuteronomy rather*distinguishes* between "the Levites," referring to "clergy who are scattered throughout the country... people without property and dependent upon the liberality of the landowners" and "the priests the Levites," referring to altar clergy at the central sanctuary ("Levites," 328). He concluded, therefore, that the difference on this point between D and P has been greatly exaggerated, as both maintain a distinction between Levites generally and altar priests in particular ("Levites," 330). In his response to Wright, John Emerton ("Priests and Levites in Deuteronomy," *VT* 12 [1962] 129-138) rejected this thesis on two primary grounds. First, on grammatical grounds, Emerton demonstrated that the expression לכהנים הלויים כל שבט לוי in Dt 18:1 must be read by placing the two terms in simple apposition; to see the first term as a smaller entity within the latter, as Wright did, would be to accept a reading "without parallel in Deuteronomy" ("Priests," 134). Second, Emerton observed that one may accept a distinction in Deuteronomy between Levites generally and altar priests specifically and still be left with a most significant question: "does Deuteronomy recognize an impassible and hereditary distinction between altar-priests and ordinary Levites?" ("Priests," 131). To Wright's argument that the word "Levite" standing alone refers to landless clergy living in the land, whose primary function was to teach, Emerton poses a similar question: granting that priesthood entails more than altar service, can it be shown that those Levites who taught did so "without having any connexion with a sanctuary and without the right to act as altar priests" ("Priests," 132)? To each question, it seems, the answer must be "no." Emerton concludes that "Deuteronomy confers the priestly office on the whole tribe of Levi" ("Priests", 138).

11).[3] This restriction is rendered all the more forceful by the command that all outlying altars and cult sites be utterly destroyed (Deut 12:1-3), so that the very possibility of cultic service outside of the Jerusalem Temple is eliminated. Thus, only Levites present in the Jerusalem Temple may offer sacrifice, for only there may sacrificial service be conducted.

D does not make permanent the distinction between Jerusalem clergy and the Levites in the outlying provinces. Deuteronomy 18:6-8 stipulates that any Levite may make his way to Jerusalem, and serve as a priest equal in status with the other priests there. However, this practice is not encouraged. The Levite is only admitted when comes בכל אות נפשו ("with all the desire of his soul"). This expression is used in 1 Samuel 23:20 to describe Saul's desire for David's life, and in Jeremiah 2:24 for the unrestrainable passion of the wild ass. It suggests driving passion, uncontrollable need. Therefore, the provincial Levite is accepted at the Temple when he *must* come, "when he is driven by dire necessity and has no alternative but to

---

[3] The M of Deut 12:5 has the unique noun form לְשִׁכְנוֹ: ("to his dwelling?"). However, in light of the form characteristic of D, and reflected by the G of this text (ἐπικληθηναι), it is better to read the Piᶜel infinitive with ל prefix and third masculine singular suffix: לְשַׁכְּנוֹ. Adam Welch (*The Code of Deuteronomy: A New Theory of Its Origin* [London: James Clarke, 1924] 30) proposed that המקום be read distributively ("every place"), so that D "does not, any more than the Book of the Covenant, demand a solitary place of sacrifice... Yahweh has located his name in certain places, and these are reserved for his worship." G. Ernest Wright (*IB*, vol. 2 [1953] 324), while rejecting this distributive reading, nonetheless held that the formula calls only for a central shrine, not for one exclusive shrine. More recently, Gottfried Seitz (*Redaktionsgeschichtliche Studien zum Deuteronomium* [Stuttgart: W. Kohlhammer, 1971] 212) has proposed that the unspecific early rendering of this formula (מקום with the article, בחר in the imperfect, and the divine Name) has been rendered specific and exclusive by the addition of the phrase לשכן שמו שם: a curious argument, since even if his developmental scheme is granted, it is difficult to see how even in its early form the formula could be read as any less exclusive. The simplest reading of the text can lead to but one conclusion: D demands that sacrificial worship be conducted only at the place chosen by YHWH and sealed by the establishment of the divine Name, a demand that calls not merely for centrality, but exclusivity. With R. E. Clements (*God's Chosen People: A Theological Interpretation of the Book of Deuteronomy* [London: SCM, 1968] 78) and S. Dean McBride, Jr. ("Polity," 240), we must conclude that the only referrent for such a call is the Jerusalem Temple erected by Solomon. In his unpublished dissertation, McBride observes ancient Near Eastern parallels for the establishment of the Name, particularly in the practice of erecting stelae over conquered territories in the king's name. A virtual presence of the king is thereby asserted: to this point, the stele proclaims, the royal person and authority extend.

come."[4] Priesthood, while the right of every Levite, is to be exercised only by the few who cannot stay away from the Temple.

Offices and Orders Within the Levitical Priesthood

Levitical priests in the land.   There are some indications, however, that the Levite could exercise some priestly functions without becoming a Temple priest in Jerusalem.   Deuteronomy 21:5 gives to Levitical priests the responsibility of assisting in the ceremony of atonement for a city when a corpse is found in an open field.   The responsibilities of these Levites are clearly stated: they minister (שרת) to YHWH, pronounce the blessing, and act as the final judicial authority in lawsuits and assault cases.   Sacrifice is not involved.[5] Similarly, Deuteronomy 24:8 gives the responsibility for diagnosing and treating leprosy to Levitical priests, though surely it is not expected that the Jerusalem clergy are to handle this mammoth task all by themselves. We may find here a reflection of non-sacrificial priestly service: a suggestion, that is, of a differentiation within the Levitical priesthood.[6]

The chief priest.   Another significant indication of distinctions within the priesthood in the legislation of Deuteronomy is the mention

---

[4] Menachem Haran,*Temples and Temple-Service in Ancient Israel: An Inquiry Into Biblical Cult Phenomena and the Historical Setting of the Priestly School* (Oxford: Clarendon, 1978; reprint Winona Lake: Eisenbrauns, 1985) 62.

[5] Note that the neck of the heifer used in the atonement ritual is broken by the city elders, not by the Levites. As David P. Wright ("Deuteronomy 21:1-9 as a Rite of Elimination," *CBQ* 49 [1987] 391) observes, not only is the slaughter of the heifer not called a sacrifice, it is performed by a free-flowing wadi, not at an altar or sanctuary, and the priests enter only after the slaughter is accomplished. Wright terms this an elimination rite, that is "a reenactment of the homicide in order to eliminate bloodguilt from the community" ("Rite," 389). He finds numerous parallels between the rite described in Dt 21:1-9 and the elimination rites of the Hittites and Mesopotamians, which are also connected with bodies of water thought to bear away impurity ("Rite," 401-3).

[6] Aelred Cody (*A History of Old Testament Priesthood* [AnBib 35; Rome: Pontifical Biblical Institute, 1969] 130) observes that this conclusion is not precluded by Deuteronomy; however, he is skeptical that such was actually the case. Wolf Baudissen ("Priests and Levites," in *A Dictionary of the Bible, Dealing with its Language, Literature and Contents Including the Biblical Theology*, James Hastings, ed.,Vol 4: *Pleroma-Zuzim* [New York: Charles Scribner's Sons, 1902] 75) has proposed that these texts are drawn from older legislation, presupposing a priesthood scattered throughout the land, and have not been brought into conformity with the stipulations limiting priestly service to the Levites of Jerusalem.

of הכהן ("the priest") in Deut 17:12 and 26:3. These passages seem to concern a priestly figure of special dignity, analogous to the high priest of P. In the prologue to the Deuteronomic Code, such a figure is assumed, for when Aaron died, we are told, ויכהן אלעזר בנו תחתו ("his son Eleazar became priest after him;" Deut 10:6). Since Eleazar was already a priest, this must mean that he became *the* priest, the high priest.[7] The Levitical priesthood of D is, then, not quite the undifferentiated monolith it at first appears.

When we turn to the Deuteronomistic History, we again find evidence of a chief priest. The most usual expression for this figure, as in D, is simply הכהן ("the priest"), a title attributed to Jehoiada (e.g., 2 Kings 11:9-10, 15), Uriah (2 Kings 16:10-11, 15; also Isa 8:2), and Hilkiah (2 Kings 22:10, 12, 14).[8] The expression כהן הראש ("chief" or "head priest") is also used in 2 Kings 25:18, of Seraiah. To consider these references exilic or post-exilic insertions, influenced by P's high priest, would be strange indeed, as P's title is הכהן הגדול ("high priest"): if these are indeed insertions, why do they not use the later title?[9] Also intriguing in this light is 2 Kings 19:2, which speaks of זקני הכהנים: "the elders of the priests." As Baudissen has observed, these "can be nothing else than the chiefs of groups."[10] The presence of such intermediate authorities supports the existence of an ultimate authority, or chief priest. We find here further evidence that in the First Temple, perhaps already by the time of Hezekiah, the priesthood was divided into subgroups.

The Levites as bearers of the Ark. On three occasions in DtrH הלויים appear as the bearers of the Ark: 1 Samuel 6:15,[11] 2 Samuel

---

[7] As Baudissen ("Priests," 75) has observed.

[8] So H. J. Katzenstein, "Some Remarks on the Lists of the Chief Priests of the Temple of Solomon," *JBL* 81 (1962) 377-384.

[9] So Baudissen, "Priests," 73. The later title is, in fact, used of Jehoiada (2 Kings 12:11) and Hilkiah (2 Kings 22:4, 8; 23:4), in what are, evidently, priestly expansions to the text (so Cody, *Priesthood*, 103).

[10] Baudissen, "Priests," 74.

[11] Because of the abruptness with which the Levites appear in this text, most commentators consider their mention a later insertion: e.g., Baudissen, "Priests," 74;

15:20, and 1 Kings 8:4. This is in keeping with Deuteronomy 10:8, which assigns to the Levites responsibility for bearing of the Ark, as well as service (שרת) to YHWH and the giving of the blessing. Deuteronomy 31:25 ascribes the task of bearing the Ark to "the Levites," while 31:9 speaks of the Ark as carried by הכהנים בני לוי ("the priests, the sons of Levi"). Carrying the Ark is understood, then, as a form of priestly service.[12]

In 2 Samuel 15:24, the Levites appear in the company of Zadok the priest. This text is doubly significant. On the one hand, it suggests a subtle distinction between Zadok, cited by name, and the Levites who bear the Ark. The distinction is not between priest and Levite, since for D and DtrH the bearing of the Ark is a priestly service. It is rather a distinction of dignity, Zadok (together with Abiathar) having been placed over the service of the Jerusalem shrine by David. On the other hand, 2 Samuel 15:24 suggests an identity between Zadok and the Levites in whose company he is found,[13] which

---

George B. Caird (IB, vol. 2 [1953]) 910; P. Kyle McCarter (I Samuel [AB 8; Garden City: Doubleday, 1980]) 136. McCarter further observes that Josephus apparently did not know of the mention of the Levites at this point (Antiquities 6.15), since he suggests that the men of Beth-shemesh were stricken by YHWH because they had offered sacrifices, but were not priests. On this basis, and on the basis of G, McCarter (I Samuel , 131) rejects the M of v 19a, and reconstructs the text to read "But the sons of the priests did not join in the celebration with the men on Beth-shemesh..." McCarter's reconstruction may well be correct. However, it is clear from the text that the men of Beth-shemesh were punished, not because there were no priests among them, but because they looked into the Ark. The mention of Levites in Beth-shemesh is certainly not strange, as Beth-shemesh was one of the Levitical cities (Josh 21:16); nor is it strange that the sacrifice described is performed by the men of Beth-shemesh, and not by the Levites: after all, for the Deuteronomistic editor of our text, the Levites could perform sacrifices legitimately only in the Jerusalem Temple--not yet built at the time this text is set.

[12] In contrast to P, where the bearing of the Ark is a task given to Levites as a group subservient to priests (Num 3:31; 4:4-20).

[13] So Haran, Temples, 78. The genealogies in 1 Chronicles 5:30-34; 6:35-38; 24:3, which trace Zadok's line to Eleazar, are usually rejected by scholars as without historical foundation (so Cody, Priesthood, 89); it must indeed be conceded that they are late, and due to the frequent repetition of names in priestly lineages, corrupted by haplography and dittography (so Frank M. Cross, "The Priestly Houses of Early Israel," in Canaanite Myth and Hebrew Epic: Essays in the History of the Religion of Israel [Cambridge: Harvard University, 1973] 212). Similarly, the Zadokite genealogy in 2 Sam 8:17 is generally regarded as confused: the order Zadok-Ahitub-Ahimelek-Abiathar contradicts 1 Sam 22:9, 20, which present Abiathar as the son of Ahimelek the son of Ahitub. Most follow Wellhausen's proposal (described by Cody, Priesthood, 89) that the original order was Abiathar-Ahimelek-Ahitub, and Zadok; a Zadokite partisan has reversed the order, to give preeminence to Zadok and to provide him with a genealogy. The conclusion, that Zadok had no priestly lineage in Israel, is given

reinforces the identification of the Zadokites as Levitical priests in the Law of the Temple.

The third mention of "the Levites" in DtrH is in 1 Kings 8:4. Here, unlike the earlier two references, a distinction is made between priests and Levites. As the context is the transport of the Tent of Meeting, the Ark, and the holy vessels into the Temple, the explicit mention of the Levites is in line with P, which consistently gives to the Levites the physical work of transporting the Tent and its contents. In contrast, we are told in v 3 and again in v 6 that the priests are the bearers of the Ark: again, in keeping with D's understanding of priestly service. This mention, then, is most likely a later priestly insertion. However, we still find in the first two instances mention of Levites engaged in the bearing of the Ark: a service that, while accorded priestly dignity by D, is not connected with the sacrificial cult.

The guards of the threshold and כהני המשנה. Another distinction among priestly offices in DtrH is introduced in 2 Kings 12:10. Here we find הכהנים שמרי הסף: "the priests who guard the threshold." These figures appear again in 2 Kings 22:4, 23:4 and 25:18, without the designation הכהנים. Two tasks are explicitly given

---

classical expression by Wellhausen (*Prolegomena* , 139): "The B'ne Zadok of Jerusalem as contrasted with the B'ne Eli whom they superseded were originally illegitimate (if one may venture to apply a conception which at that time was quite unknown), and did not inherit their right from the fathers, but had it from David and Solomon." Of particular influence has been the proposal of H. H. Rowley ("Zadok and Nehushtan," *JBL* 58 [1939] 113-41) that Zadok was the priest of the Jebusite Jerusalem, and was retained as priest by David following his conquest of that city. Cross has effectively rebutted Rowley's arguments. The comparison of the name Zadok with Melchizedek, priest of Salem, he shows to be without warrant, names with the element צדק being "extremely common in Amorite, Ugaritic, Canaanite, and Hebrew" ("Priestly Houses," 209). Nor need one postulate a Jebusite priest to account for Canaanite influences on Israel's cult: after all, YHWHism had sprung from roots in the cults of 'El and Baᶜl ("Priestly Houses," 211). Cross wonders ("Priestly Houses," 210) at the appointment of a Jebusite priest "by David, a primitive Yahwist of well-documented piety. Why would David who obviously attempted to draw all the old League traditions to his new religious establishment, turn and invite a pagan priest as one of the high priests of the national cultus?" It is this question that must, finally, put to rest all speculation about an extra-Israelite origin for Zadok. Moreover, Cross suggests that we do have, in the corrupted text of 2 Sam 8:17, a legitimate patronymic for Zadok. He proposes that, on ordinary text-critical principles, we can reconstruct an original text identifying "Zadok son of Ahitub and Abiathar son of Abimelek" ("Priestly Houses," 213-14). The Ahitub identified as Zadok's father would not, of course, be the Ahitub who was Abiathar's grandfather; rather, we find here yet another instance of the tendency in priestly circles to use and reuse the same stock of names ("Priestly Houses," 214).

them in the texts: they are to guard the doorway into the inner court, where the altar is, and they are to collect the contributions of the people for the upkeep of the Temple. As Baudissen has observed, the guardians of the threshold are to be distinguished from the post-exilic doorkeepers.[14]   According to Ezra 2:42, 139 doorkeepers returned from exile. Yet, 2 Kings 25:18 speaks of only three guardians. The most striking difference between the two offices, however, is the designation of the guardians as priests.

The assignment of guard duty before the threshold to a priest is very interesting, as this task is given to the Levite in P (Num 3:14-39; 8:25-6) and the Law of the Temple (Ezek 44:11, 14). This martial aspect of the Levitical priesthood is not out of line with D, either. After all, as the prologue to the Deuteronomic Code reveals, D was familiar with the tradition that associated the Levitical priesthood with that clan's slaughter of the idolaters who worshipped the golden calf (Deut 10:8). Moreover, D gives to the Levitical priesthood the task of addressing the troops before they go into battle (Deut 20:2). In the guardians of the threshold, then, we find yet another office within the priesthood, not associated specifically with the performance of sacrifice.

Our final indication of distinctions within the Levitical priesthood comes in 2 Kings 23:4, which, together with Hilkiah and the guardians of the threshold, mentions כהני המשנה ("priests of the second order").[15] This expression also appears in 25:18, where we are told that Seraiah the chief priest and the three guardians of the threshold were taken captive together with Zephaniah, a כהן משנה.[16]

---

[14] Baudissen, "Priests," 74.

[15] Baudissen ("Priests," 74) proposes that the singular should be read here, with the Targum and in keeping with 2 Kings 25:18, which mentions only one כהן משנה. He understands this figure as a representative of the chief priest. However, the plural is supported by G; one may just as easily conclude that the figure in 25:18 is one representative of the class described in 23:4.

[16] Variously rendered "the second priest" (RSV) or "the deputy priest" (JPS); however, in light of 2 Kgs 23:4, this phrase should be read as "a priest of the second order" (cf. n. 15, above).

Already in the First Temple period, evidence of a very complex
subsystem within the one category "Levitical priest" can be found. At
the head of the priestly class is הכהן, *the* priest. Other subgroupings
are headed by the elders of the priests. Then, there are the guardians
of the threshold, and the second order of the priests: groups twice
mentioned together, and in company with the chief priest. Finally,
there are "the Levites," bearing the Ark in procession in Jerusalem,
and "the Levitical priests" outside of the city, serving a vital function in
the land: arbitrating disputes, pronouncing blessings, taking part in
occasional rituals, and diagnosing leprosy.

D/DtrH and the Law of the Temple.

This analysis of the priesthood in D and DtrH provides a
tremendous boost to our understanding of the Temple Vision. The
dramatic contrast between Ezekiel 40:45-46, which divides the כהנים
into Temple clergy and altar clergy, and 44:1-31, which rejects the
Levite and reserves the title כהן exclusively for the Zadokite altar
clergy, has already been observed. Now, the proposal that 40:45-46 is
part of Ezekiel's original vision, and reflects the state of the
priesthood at the close of the First Temple period, can be expanded.[17]

Since Wellhausen, the assertion that the division between priest
and Levite began with the Second Temple and is first reflected in P
has become nearly an article of faith. However, as Baudissen early
argued and the evidence reveals, orders of the priesthood were
already in existence in First Temple times. Particularly interesting is
the identification, in 2 Kings 23:4, of a second order of priests. These
are closely associated with the guardians of the threshold, whose
duties were keeping guard over the inner court, thereby preserving its
sanctity, and collecting the money for Temple repairs and upkeep.
The duties of the second order are nowhere stated so explicitly. The
context of 23:4, however, is suggestive. Hilkiah, the second order,
and the guardians have been summoned by Josiah to cleanse the
Temple: to remove from it all the cult images and appurtenances given
to the worship of Ba^cl, Asherah, and the host of heaven. This suggests

---

[17] See above, chapter 2, pp. 31-33.

that the duties of the second order were related to the maintenance of the Temple itself--as does the association of this group with the guardians, who were responsible for collecting funds for Temple maintenance. As priests, they would of course have been distinct from the Temple menials: the Gibeonites (Josh 9:23), the Nethinim (Ezra 2:43; 8:20), and the servants of Solomon (Ezra 2:55). Indeed, the role of the כהני המשנה may at least in part have involved the supervision of these Temple servants. Perhaps, either alone or in company with the other Levitical priests whose tasks did not involve performance of sacrifice, these are the כהנים שמרי משמרת הבית of Ezekiel 40:45.[18]

It is intriguing to note the continuities between the priesthood in the Law of the Temple and that depicted in D and DtrH. Many priestly duties are held in common: notably, sacrificial service and the responsibility to teach תורה and preside over courts of law. Also, the association of Zadok with the Levites lends support to the identification of the Zadokites as Levitical priests in 43:19 and 44:15. Other duties considered priestly tasks in D are, however, removed explicitly from such consideration in the Law of the Temple; in particular, keeping guard over the threshold.[19] The Ark being lost forever, the Law of the Temple makes no mention of its portage. However, שרת, the term used explicitly of the service of Levitical priests, and in the context of the Ark, is made in the Law of the Temple a non-priestly task, its object being no longer YHWH, but the people (Ezek 44:11). Note that guarding the threshold and service (שרת) are still Levitical tasks, performed by Levites; they have, however, been deprived of their priestly distinction. Between 40:45-46 and 44:1-14, something happened. However, before whatever has effected this change can be determined, the structure of the priesthood in P must be considered.

---

[18] Baudissen ("Priests," 78) early proposed "that the distinction of כהנים of two grades was familiar to Ezekiel from already existing relations."

[19] Doubtless it is also significant that the Law of the Temple knows nothing of a chief priest; the significance of this omission is discussed below, p. 153.

III. Priests And Levites In The Priestly Work

For the Priestly writers, the priesthood is the exclusive province of Aaron and his descendants. As for D the terms "priest" and "Levite" are virtually interchangeable, so for P the expression בני אהרן ("sons of Aaron") is synonymous with "priest" (e.g., Exod 28:40-41; 29:44; 40:12-15). The priestly dignity of the Aaronids is traced back to the revelation at Sinai, which for P is the revelation of a cult. In the midst of the detailed description of the Ark, the tabernacle and all the sacred vessels and implements (Exod 25:1-27:19; 30:1-37), the sacred vestments to be made for Aaron and his sons are also described, and a ritual is established for the priests's ordination (28:1-29:46).[20] The Ark, the Tent and the sacred vessels are all consecrated to YHWH by anointing with oil (30:26- 29); Aaron and his sons, too, are anointed, for the same reason (29:27; 30:30). For P, Aaron and his sons were priests at the beginning, joined inextricably to the sanctuary and its cult, and the sons of Aaron would continue as priests forever.

Ithamar and Eleazar

This guarantee of eternal priesthood, given without distinction to Aaron and his sons in Exodus 29:9, is in Numbers 25:13 extended in particular to Phineas, the son of Eleazar, in reward for his zeal for YHWH at Baal-peor. Indeed, from the Eleazarite line within the Aaronid family comes הכהן הגדול ("the high priest"): Aaron is succeeded by his eldest surviving son Eleazar, who in turn is

---

[20] The expression for the ordination offering is מלאים ("fill-offering"; Exod 29:22). The term derives from the expression "fill the hand," used everywhere for the installation of priests (e.g., the narrative concerning Micah's Levite in Judges 17, and Exod 28:41, from P). The origin of the expression is much debated. However, Wellhausen's assertion that "filling the hand" referred to payment, and his conclusion from this that anyone at all could be chosen by a patron and paid to perform as a priest (*Prolegomena*, 129-30) does not fit the evidence. Baudissen's proposal, that the expression refers to the priest's right to take up the sacrificial portions ("Priests," 71), seems more likely, and is starkly appropriate to the setting in Exod 32. Cody (*Priesthood*, 153) notes the relationship of this expression to the Akkadian *mullû qâta*, "meaning to entrust someone with something abstract," and also to the use of the expression "fill the hand" at Mari for spoils of war, and particularly for the slain. These parallels would seem to support the interpretation of Baudissen, that to "fill the hand" of the priest meant to entrust the priest with the sacral responsibility of sacrifice. Intriguingly, this same expression is used of the altar in the altar consecration ritual of the Law of the Temple (Ezek 43:26).

134 The Law of the Temple

succeeded by his first-born Phineas. The descendants of Ithamar are nowhere denied the right of priesthood, which belongs always to the entire house of Aaron. Still, an evident distinction is made between the priestly lines of Eleazar and Ithamar, reminiscent of the twofold clergy described in Ezekiel 40:44-46.

The closer we examine the evidence, the stronger this impression grows. As the youngest son of Aaron, Ithamar is consistently mentioned last in the lists of Aaron's sons (Exod 6:23; 28:1; Num 3:2, 4; 26:60; 1 Chron 5:29; 24:1, 2). When the two lines of Aaronid priestly descent are mentioned, Eleazar comes first, Ithamar second (Lev 10:6, 12, 16; 1 Chron 24:3, 4, 6; Ezra 8:2). This suggests a lower ranking, reminiscent of כהני המשנה, for the Ithamarite priesthood. Particularly intriguing are the tasks assigned to Eleazar and Ithamar in P. Eleazar is responsible for supervision of the Kohathite Levitical clan, which carries the most holy objects and accoutrements from within the Tabernacle (including the golden altar and the Ark) when the tribes are on the move (Num 4:2-16; 7:9); he is personally held responsible for the oil, the incense, and the regular meal offering. Ithamar, on the other hand, is given responsibility for the Gershonites and the Merarites, who do the heavy work of hauling the tent, its frame, and other bulky (and less sacred) items (Exod 38:21; Num 4:28, 33; 7:6-8). In brief, Eleazar is associated with the most sacred cult vessels, particularly those pertaining to sacrificial service; Ithamar is associated with non-sacrificial items. From this, McBride concludes that Ithamar is a construct, his name perhaps derived from that of Merari, representing Levitical priestly claims recognized by the Aaronids.[21] The Ithamarites of P, like the כהני המשנה of DtrH and the Temple clergy of Ezekiel, may represent a class of priests involved in non-sacrificial service, distinct from the more narrowly-defined altar clergy.

If this is so, then the attachment of the house of Eli to Ithamar's line in 1 Chronicles 24:3 is highly significant. Judges 18:30-31

---

[21] S. Dean McBride, Jr., "Jeremiah and the 'Men of ᶜAnatot,'" a paper presented to the Colloquium for Old Testament Research at the Colgate-Rochester Divinity School, 23 August 1973.

identifies Jonathan, cult founder at Dan, as the grandson of Moses. We
are further informed that his descendants continued as priests for the
Danites until the Assyrian exile, serving at the Dan temple until its
destruction. This strongly suggests that the Elide line, which served
at Shiloh, traced its lineage to Moses, not Aaron--which would, of
course, still make it a Levitical priesthood. This proposal, first made
by Wellhausen and Baudissen, has been considerably elaborated by
Frank Moore Cross.[22] Cross reconstructs a long-standing, often bitter
rivalry between two priestly houses. One, tracing its descent from
Moses and preserving old Midianite traditions, held sway at Shiloh and
Dan, as well as in local shrines in ᶜArad and Kadesh. The other held
Aaron to be its founder, and was in power at Bethel and Hebron.
David's selection of Zadok and Abiathar as priests at the central
Jerusalem shrine was a diplomatic attempt to mediate between these
two great priestly houses: the Mushite priesthood at Shiloh
represented by Abiathar, and the Aaronid priesthood at Hebron,
represented by Zadok. The establishment by Jeroboam I of two
national shrines (at Dan and Bethel) with two priesthoods can be seen
as yet another instance of this same tactic. It is possible, therefore,
that the Ithamarites in the Aaronid lineage of P are in fact
representative of the old Mushite line of Eli and Abiathar, baptized
into Aaronid ancestry by the priestly redactors.

The Restrictions, Duties, and Obligations of the Priesthood in P

In P's scheme, all priests are Aaronids. This does not mean,
however, that any Aaronid can serve as priest. Just as sacrificial
animals presented to YHWH are to be without defect (e.g., Lev 22:17-
25), so, too, the priests must be free from any physical deformity (Lev
21:17-21).[23] Further, even a qualified Aaronid loses his right to act as
priest if he incurs ritual defilement, and cannot serve as priest again
until cleansed. If, while ritually unclean, he eats the sacred portion,

---

[22] Cf. Wellhausen (*Prolegomena* , 142) and Baudissen ("Priests," 71) with Cross,
"Priestly Houses," esp. 195-215.

[23] Intriguingly, even the deformed Aaronid is still possessed of a degree of
holiness, for while barred from service as a priest, he may still eat the sacrificial
portion to which the priests are entitled (Lev 21:22).

he is outcast (Lev 22:1-7). Little wonder, then, that so much attention is paid, particularly in the Holiness Code, to the careful distinctions among the sacred, common, clean and unclean: indeed, as in the Law of the Temple, it is the priest's responsibility to teach the people to observe these distinctions (Lev 10:10-11).

As in the Law of the Temple, the priests are also to avoid defiling contact with the dead, save for their immediate family (Lev 21:1-4); indeed, it is in this context that P prohibits the priest from shaving his head, cutting his sidelocks, or committing some more severe self-mutilation in his grief (Lev 10:6; 21:5). The priests are forbidden to marry divorced women or harlots, again, because such contact would bring defilement (21:7-8), and are directed to avoid wine when serving in the sanctuary (Lev 10:8-10). Special obligations are laid upon the high priest, who cannot defile himself even to grieve for his father or mother, and is forbidden to marry any woman who is not a virgin (21:10-15). All of this, save the special provision for the high priest, is very reminiscent of the provisions in the Law of the Temple.

As we would expect, the duties of the priest are spelled out in much greater detail in P than in D. Foremost among these, of course, is the conduct of the massively complex sacrificial cult. Only the priests may offer any sacrifices at all (e.g., Lev 1:7-9, 11-13, 17; 2:2, 9, 16), though the preparation of the sacrifice, including the killing and dismembering of the animal in the case of blood sacrifices, is left to the person bringing the offering. Only the priests may enter the sanctuary (Exod 30:20), or indeed even approach the altar (Num 18:7); anyone else attempting this is killed. Yet, the priests have duties outside the sanctuary as well. As in D, the priests pronounce the blessing of YHWH (Num 6:22-27), diagnose and treat leprosy (Lev 13:1-14:57), and teach. The high priest is given the special obligation of entering the most holy place once a year, on the Day of Atonement, to sprinkle the כפרת with blood and so atone for the priests and the congregation (Lev 16). He is also entrusted with the sacred lot, so that in P only the high priest may perform the oracular function given elsewhere to all priests (Exod 28:30; Lev 8:8; Num 27:26).

The Levites

Characteristic of P is the special status of the Levites, who occupy an intermediate position between the laity and the priesthood. The Levites have a certain sanctity, since they alone are able to handle the sacred cult appurtenances when the tabernacle is disassembled for transport (Num 1:51; 18:4, 22). However, they do not officiate in the sacrificial rites. Therefore, P knows of no ordination for the Levites; the expression "fill the hand" is not used of them. Instead, they are themselves regarded as an offering to YHWH, taking the place of the first-born of Israel (since, in P's sacrificial system, the firstborn belong to YHWH; so Num 3:11-12, 40-51). In a special ritual of purification, they are consecrated to YHWH's use, and are presented to YHWH as a תנופה ("wave offering" or "elevated offering," usually performed to consecrate the priestly portion of the sacrifice to YHWH for the priest's use; e.g., Exod 29:22- 28; Lev 7:29-36).

In P's system, the Levites perform two functions. The first is keeping guard (שמרי משמרת, always used in P in the sense of keeping watch).[24] The Levites camp all around the Tabernacle, to prevent unauthorized access (Num 1:50-53), and beyond this, specific Levitical clans are given responsibility for guarding specific cult objects when the tribes are on the move and the disassembled Tent is in transit (Num 3-4).

The second function of the Levites, according to the Priestly work, is the עבדה ("work"). In P, this term never loses its sense of physical labor.[25] It is used consistently, not for cultic service, but for the work of disassembling, transporting, and reassembling the Tabernacle and its contents (see especially the many uses of עבדה in Num 4). Milgrom argues for the essential historicity of the עבדה:

---

[24] Haran, *Temples*, 60, 181-182; and Jacob Milgrom, *Studies in Levitical Terminology, I: The Encroacher and the Levite; The Term 'Aboda* [UCPNES 14; Berkeley: University of California, 1970) 8-9. Both Haran (*Temples*, 60) and Milgrom (*Studies* , 14) give the expression שמרי משמרת this meaning in Ezek 40:45-46 as well. However, while Haran understands those who keep guard over the בית (i.e., the entire Temple complex) to be Levites, Milgrom urges that. since both have chambers in the inner court, both must be priests.

[25] As Milgrom (*Studies* , 61-76) has demonstrated; see especially the summary statement on 65, and the composite of all texts relating to the Levitic עבדה, 72-76.

138 The Law of the Temple

until the building of the permanent Temple in Jerusalem, the portage of Tent and Ark continued to be the Levites's task.[26] In the texts of the Second Temple, עבדה has shifted in meaning, being used for the Temple cult in general, and for religious service rather than physical labor. "These facts," Milgrom urges,"lead to but one conclusion: the עבדה passages in P are old, pre-exilic materials which were allowed to experience reinterpretation but no inner editorial change."[27]

D/DtrH and P Compared

This conclusion of Milgrom's ought not be too surprising. Setting aside for a moment the characteristic vocabularies of the D and P traditions, and taking into consideration each source's peculiar concerns, it becomes clear that the priesthood in P and the priesthood in D are strikingly similar. Both traditions know only of Levitical priesthood. Both restrict sacrifice to the priest, and give to the priest the responsibility to teach and to participate in certain atoning rituals, as well as responsibility for the diagnosis and treatment of leprosy. Already in D, we have found evidences of P's הכהן הגדול, although the restriction of the sacred lot to this figure, and the institution of the Day of Atonement which in P is this figure's greatest responsibility, are not prepared for in D. Further, evidence exists in D and DtrH of distinctions within the priesthood, and in particular, for priestly offices not involving sacrifice. The duties given the Levite in P, שמרי משמרת and the עבדה, are also Levitical tasks in D.[28] Indeed, while in P the Levites at large no longer may become priests, the inclusion of the Ithamarites in the Aaronid lineage

---

[26] Milgrom, *Studies*, 68-72; he notes especially 2 Sam 7:6 (YHWH going about among the people in a tent) and two texts from the Chronicler, 1 Chron 23:25-26 and 2 Chron 35:3, which speak of the Levites's work coming to an end with the Temple's construction.

[27] Milgrom, *Studies*, 87.

[28] The institution of the Tabernacle is P's unique concern; D does not speak of the Levitical responsibilities relating to its disassembly, transport,and reassembly. This is as we would expect. Save for the institution of the cult by Moses, D has no interest in the history of the cult before the settlement, or indeed before the permanent establishment of the Jerusalem Temple. However, as we have seen, it is the responsibility of the Levites to carry the Ark in D.

suggests that P as well recognized the existence of clergy whose duties did not involve sacrifice.

The Comparison of P and the Law of the Temple

The parallels between the priesthood in P and in the Law of the Temple are legion, ranging from a general philosophical compatibility and similarity of themes to very particular, nearly word-for-word correspondences. Both restrict priesthood to a single Levitical clan. Neither considers the other Levites priests. But of particular note are the point by point similarities between the instructions to the priests in Ezekiel 44:15-31 and the instructions to the priests in the Holiness Code (especially Lev 21:1-22:9), which make it clear at least that a common tradition underlies these two texts, and raise the possibility of literary dependence, one way or the other. The conclusions one draws from these similarities will have a decisive effect on the date and setting ascribed to P and to the Law of the Temple, and indeed upon the way that the entire history and development of the priesthood is perceived.

In his classic reconstruction of the history of Israel's priesthood, Wellhausen considered Ezekiel 40--48 the major turning point between pre-exilic priesthood, shared by all Levites, and post-exilic priesthood, limited to the family of Zadok.[29] This distinction, though taken for granted in the Priestly Code, had, according to Wellhausen, never been made before Ezekiel: hence the heat of the prophet's rhetoric in 44:1-14. It was Ezekiel's concern to provide a moral argument for the shift in fortunes which had made the Jerusalem Temple the exclusive shrine of YHWHism, and its priestly family the exclusive priesthood. However, according to Wellhausen, the polemic of 44:1-14 "does not explain the fact, but is merely a periphrastic statement of it."[30] The Levites's only crime is that they are not Zadokites.

---

[29] Wellhausen, *Prolegomena*, 124. For a concise summary of the debate regarding the history of the priesthood, cf. Julia M. O'Brien, *Priest and Levite in Malachi* (SBLDS 121; Atlanta: Scholars, 1990), 1-23.

[30] Ibid.

The three stage history of the priesthood as reconstructed by Wellhausen (first no priests, then Levitical priests, then Aaronid priests) continues to exert considerable influence, as do the assumptions therefore made about the anti-Levitical stance of the Temple Vision. However, it is by no means clear that Wellhausen's reconstruction is correct. There is no reason to doubt the great antiquity of priestly service in Israel. Further, we have seen ample evidence of offices and distinctions in the priesthood in the pre-exilic period, both in D/DtrH and in the doubtless pre-exilic institution of the Levitical עבדה in P. The division of the priesthood into temple clergy and altar clergy described in Ezekiel 40:44-47 is presented without polemic or valuation of ministries: both temple clergy and Zadokite altar clergy are called כהנים ("priests"). This positive valuation of Levitical priesthood from Ezekiel, a Jerusalemite priest, supports the notion that some form of twofold priesthood must have existed already, in relative amity, in pre-exilic times.[31]

This brings us to the final plank of Wellhausen's three-part plan: the proposal that P is dependent on Ezekiel 40--48. The assumption back of this theory, of course, is that P is a late document, reflecting a setting after the exile. Difficulties with this assumption have already emerged in Milgrom's convincing argument that the Levitical עבדה was an actual, pre-exilic institution. Indeed, after comparing the linguistic elements of both P and Ezekiel with unquestioned examples of early and late biblical Hebrew, Avi Hurvitz concludes that P is the earlier text: "Apparently it was from the P document as we now have it, that Ezekiel drew--directly--the material included in both of these compositions."[32]

This conclusion, which turns Wellhausen's theory on its head, has much to recommend it. It is indeed difficult to see how one can

---

[31] So also Baudissen, "Priests," 78. Note, though, that Baudissen assumes a commonality of authorship for Ezek 40--48.

[32] Avi Hurvitz, *A Linguistic Study of the Relationship between the Priestly Source and the Book of Ezekiel: A New Approach to and Old Problem* [CRB 20; Paris: J. Gabalda, 1982) 150. Hurvitz does grant, however (*Relationship*, 151), the possibility that each draws independently from "additional common sources," to which P is more faithful.

derive the priesthood and cult as portrayed in P from the Law of the
Temple. The absence of the high priesthood from these texts, taken
by Wellhausen and others to indicate that this institution did not
emerge until after the exile, cannot in fact be so understood, since
evidence for a chief priest in pre-exilic times can be found in D and
DtrH. In this respect, then, P is closer to D than to the Law of the
Temple. Nor could the laws in Leviticus 21:1--22:9 have been derived
from Ezekiel 44:15-31. The text from the Holiness Code lacks any
mention of the requirements that the priests teach תורה, abstain from
wine (both of these provisions are in Lev 10:9-11), or serve as judges
(apparently, this provision is not even found in P, but is found in D
[e.g., Deut 21:1-5] and E [Exod 21:6; 22:7-8]). In the Leviticus text,
vestments are mentioned in connection with the high priest, who
does not appear at all in the Law of the Temple; and the law relating to
cutting the hair comes in the context of regulations restricting
mourning practices--not, as in the Law of the Temple, as an injunction
to good grooming. Finally, Ezekiel 44 bears no hint of the lengthy list
of disfigurements that can bar a priest from service, an important
aspect of the Leviticus 21 text. Despite the many similarities to be
found here, the differences rule out any dependence of this text on
the Law of the Temple.

Zadokite and Aaronid Priesthood. The most important reason
for denying the dependence of P's priesthood upon the portrayal in
the Law of the Temple, however, is P's identification of the priestly
line with Aaron. No facile identification of the Aaronids with the
Zadokites is possible. First, it is clear that the Zadokite line is a
singular entity. However, the Aaronid line is bifurcated, Aaron being
succeeded by his two sons Eleazar and Ithamar. Why would P, if it is
indeed dependent upon the Law of the Temple, introduce a second
son, since Zadok obviously can be the descendant of only one of
these?[33] It does not do, as proposed by Cooke and Eichrodt,[34] to
suggest an expansion of the priesthood after Ezekiel: in light of the

---

[33] An argument advanced by Haran, *Temples*, 75.

[34] Cooke, 482-3; Eichrodt, 566.

142   The Law of the Temple

radical exclusivity evident in both the Law of the Temple and in P, how could such an expansion have taken place?

Second, it is evident that the Zadokite priesthood is limited in geographic range: always and everywhere, the house of Zadok is the priestly house of Jerusalem. Not so the Aaronid line, which in Joshua 21:9-19 is associated with the villages and pasturage of greater Judah. Haran suggests that, while the upheavals and cultic abuses during the reign of Manasseh and following the death of Josiah could well explain the narrowing of the priesthood to the Jerusalemite clergy alone, "neither Ezekiel's ideology nor historical circumstance could offer any justification for expanding the priestly right to include people from the provinces."[35] Once again, the provisions of P cannot be derived from the Law of the Temple.

Neither, however, is it possible to derive the Law of the Temple from P. The reasons given above for denying the dependence of the priestly legislation in the Holiness Code upon the Law of the Temple also work the other way round: if the Law of the Temple is dependent, why does it not mention the disqualifying disfigurements of Leviticus 21? The difficulty with attempting to argue for the dependence of the Law of the Temple on P can be seen most clearly in the laws relating to the cult.

The Cult. It is not difficult to find discrepancies between the Law of the Temple and cultic legislation articulated in the P strata of the Pentateuch. Variations between the laws in the Temple Vision and those in Mosaic תורה prompted the rabbis to hold our text somewhat in question. For example, b. Menaḥot 45a notes a conflict between Ezekiel 46:6-7 and Numbers 28:11 with regard to the proper offering for the new moon. The Law of the Temple requires a young bull, six lambs, a ram, together with a grain offering of one ephah for the bull, another for the ram, and "as much as he is able" (RSV) with the lambs; each ephah of grain is to be mingled with a hin of oil. On the other hand, the P text calls for two bulls, a ram, and seven lambs, with a grain offering of three-tenths of an ephah for the bull, two-tenths for

---

[35] Haran, "Law-code," 65.

each ram, and a tenth for each lamb. The amount of oil to be mixed with the flour is unspecified, but the text additionally stipulates libations of one half of a hin of fine wine for the bull, a third for the ram, and a quarter for each lamb, plus a goat as sin offering.

More major differences are also evident, particularly in the cultic calendar (Ezek 45:21-25). The Law of the Temple knows only three major annual observances, in addition to the daily offerings, sabbaths and new moons. The first, set on the first day of the first month, is evidently Yom Kippur.[36] It is explicitly designated as a time to atone for the Temple, and for the inadvertent sin of the people. This atonement is made by sacrificing a bull on the first and seventh days of the month, and placing its blood on the sanctuary doorposts, the four corners of the altar, and the doorposts of the gate (assumedly the eastern gate) of the inner court. The Day of Atonement in P, however, takes place on the tenth day of the month. The ritual in P is far more complex, involving the goat for Azazel as well as other sacrifices. The major differences, however, are the absence of the Ark with its כפרת and the absence of the high priest.[37] The second annual observance, and the only one named, is פסח, which does fall where it is supposed to according to P, though the offerings differ (cf. Num 28:16-25). The third observance, called simply החג ("the feast"), is from its date evidently the old autumn festival, or booths. This festival was already known in 1 Kings 8:2 and 12:32 simply as *the* feast. However, the building of the booths that in P represents the most characteristic feature of this feast is nowhere mentioned in the Law of the Temple (Lev 23:33-36). Note finally that the festival of weeks is altogether absent. Thus, while formally similar to P's cult, the cult

---

[36] With Zimmerli, 2:482; *contra* Haran, "Law-code," 68-69, who states that the Day of Atonement was long lost and unknown by Ezekiel's time.

[37] The involvement of a high priestly figure, at least in the source from which this law was derived, is suggested by the use of the second singular תקח ("you will take") in 45:18, and הכהן (which, it has been shown, can refer to the chief priest in D and DtrH) in v 19. However, in our present text, no high priest is anywhere in view, and the literary referrent for the singular verbs, as in the altar consecration text, has become the visionary.

portrayed in the Law of the Temple is on fine points entirely different.[38]

As these striking divergences reveal, literary dependency alone cannot explain the relationship between the Law of the Temple and P. Levenson has attempted to find in these texts a deliberate reformation of P. Observing that Ezekiel 40--42 "finds its only close biblical parallel in Moses' vision of the tabernacle,"[39] Levenson suggests that the "very high mountain" of 40:2 is typologically not only Zion, but Sinai as well.[40] Ezekiel is thus a new Moses, spelling out a new תורה for a new Israel in a new age.[41] This new תורה is necessary, because the first תורה was fundamentally, and deliberately flawed. Levenson cites Ezekiel 20:25-26:

> I gave them statutes that were not good, and ordinances by which they could not have life; and I defiled them through their very gifts in making them offer by fire all their first-born, that I might horrify them; I did it that they might know that I am the LORD" (RSV).

In Ezekiel's view, "God deliberately imposed upon them a sinful liturgy."[42] The law in the Temple Vision comes as a new תורה, by which the people may find life.

Against Levenson's ingenious proposal, it must be observed that the Law of the Temple nowhere presents itself as a corrective or reform. Only in 44:1-14 and related texts do we find a polemic here-- and it is directed at cult functionaries, not at cult practices. Further, even if one accepts Levenson's exegesis of 20:25-26, the specific agent of defilement in that text (the sacrifice of the firstborn) is nowhere

---

[38] Haran ("Law-code," 62) states, "There is not the slightest resemblance between the two in the actual quantities prescribed for the public daily offerings, for the additional offerings on Sabbaths, New Moon days, and holidays, or for the grain-offerings and the proportions of wheat blended into them."

[39] Levenson, *Program*, 40.

[40] Ibid. 41.

[41] Ibid. 38.

[42] Ibid. 39.

addressed in the Law of the Temple.[43]   Indeed, neither Moses, nor
Mosaic תורה, are anywhere invoked.   Finally, the myriad variations
between the cult as described in P and in the Law of the Temple bear
primarily on minor matters: the numbers of animals offered, or the
quantities of grain or oil.   It is very difficult indeed, then, to think of
the Law of the Temple as a deliberate reformation of P.

What, then, is the relationship between P and the Law of the
Temple?   Such similarities as do obtain, especially when these two are
compared with D, make it clear that there must be some relationship,
though not one of direct dependence.   The most likely conclusion is
that both derive from a common tradition.[44]   Already, in the laws
related to the נשיא, evidence for dating the redaction of the Temple
Vision to the early period of the Restoration has been discerned.   In
that period, too, an excellent motivation can be found for the
collection of the traditions in the Law of the Temple.   The Demotic
Chronicle preserves a summons from Darius I to the Egyptian priests,
to collect the laws of their temples.   Intriguingly, תורת הבית (Ezek
43:12) is the effective title of the law code in Ezekiel 40--48 as well.   I
propose that both the Law of the Temple and the Mosaic תורה were
prepared in response to such a summons.

This proposal has numerous advantages.   It accounts for the
impetus behind the composition of the Pentateuch, and explains how
this multi-faceted document came to be designated as the תורה.   The
authoritative polity of the Restoration would appropriately be called
Law: not in a narrow juridical sense, but in the broad sense of the
establishment of order--as a natural rendering of the Persian concept
of *dat*, so important to Darius in particular.   Even the ancient tradition
that the תורה is to be written only in the square Aramaic script is
perfectly reasonable if the document was compiled and promulgated

---

[43] As the author has argued elsewhere (Steven Tuell, "The Temple Vision of
Ezekiel 40-48: A Program for Restoration?," *PEGLBS* 2 [1982] 97).

[44] So Fohrer-Galling, 155, who suggest that Ezekiel and the redactor of the
Holiness Code had access to the same sources; and Haran, "Law-code," 62-63. Indeed, as
the mention of the priestly role in the law court and the use of the phrase הכהנים
הלויים reveals, our redactor also seems to have had access to Deuteronomic traditions.

146   The Law of the Temple

under the Persians, who used Aramaic as their official administrative language.[45]

Finally, this proposal accounts for the curious anomaly of the legislation in Ezekiel 40--48: the only legislative material in the Hebrew Bible not attributed to Moses. If the Priestly redactors of תורה and the Temple Vision were virtual contemporaries, both the numerous parallels and the puzzling differences between them are readily accounted for. The traditions used by the two would have been very similar, if not identical. However, working in two different locales, under different editorial philosophies, the decisions made as to structure and significance would have understandably differed. Darius had ordered the Egyptian priesthood to write the law of their people and temple as of their last great figure of authority. For the Jerusalem priesthood, this seems to have been Ezekiel, the great prophet-priest of the exile; their תורה was woven into his grand vision of the Temple. The priesthood in exile, however, looked further back: beyond Zedekiah, Jehoiachin, and even David, to Moses. Their law was placed into the context of the old epic of JE, and concluded with Deuteronomy, severed from its place as the prologue to the Deuteronomistic History. In this way, they made sense of their history, made peace with the still-lively Levitical traditions, and addressed the need of their people for a statement of purpose and identity. It would have been this work that Ezra brought with him to Jerusalem. The Law of the Temple in Ezekiel 40--48 was in a sense a Pentateuchal first draft, assembled, as was that great document, by priestly editors from a variety of sources, yet skillfully woven into a unified whole.

IV. Evidence for a Restoration Dating

If the laws relating to the priesthood and cult found in the Law of the Temple were indeed assembled soon after the third year of Darius I, it ought to be possible for us to uncover evidences of that dating. This evidence will not, however, be found in the specific cult

---

[45] m. Megillah 1.8.

ordinances themselves, since most of these were likely (as their similarity to the P legislation reveals) drawn from a pool of old priestly tradition. Our best evidences, then, are to be found in the most distinctive elements of the Law of the Temple, which are most likely original to our redactors and hence reflective of their social and historical setting.

The High Priest

One such element is the absence of a chief priest. Since we know that there was a high priest throughout the Second Temple period, even (as Haggai/Zechariah make very plain) early on, this would seem to argue against the proposed dating. Remember, however, that a long-term establishment is not being proposed here. If the Law of the Temple did serve as an official statement of Judean religious polity, it was superseded by the law brought to the land by Ezra. Further, we must ask when a polity without a high priest could most reasonably have been promulgated. We have observed that Zerubbabel, regarded so highly in Haggai and Zechariah, seems to have become a problem once it became clear that Darius's throne was secure. Perhaps this ill will was also directed at Joshua, the high priest, who is virtually linked with Zerubbabel in Haggai and Zechariah.[46] If so, then the silence of the Law of the Temple concerning the high priest is perfectly reasonable.

Zadokite Exclusivity and the Anti-Levite Polemic

The most characteristic aspect of the priesthood in the Law of the Temple is the absolute restriction of priestly dignity to a single Levitical house: the Zadokite altar clergy. This, as we have seen, is totally anomalous. The norm, for both D and P, is a two-stage priesthood. The First Temple was served, apparently, by two orders of Levitical priests: one performing sacrifices at the altar, the other overseeing the routine concerns of the Temple and its liturgy. It is

---

[46] In every instance but one (Hag 2:20), when Zerubbabel is mentioned in Haggai, so is Joshua (1:1, 12, 14; 2:2, 4). Zechariah has a highly exalted view of Joshua (3:1-10); he and Zerubbabel together are designated בני היצהר (literally, "sons of oil;" 4:14), a title with strong messianic overtones.

this situation that Ezekiel describes in 40:44-46. If P's edition of the
Pentateuch can be taken as the normative statement of the Second
Temple cult, then this same situation seems to obtain in the period
after the coming of Ezra. Note that in the list of returnees under Ezra
in Ezra 8:2 we find descendants of both Eleazar and Ithamar. In
contrast, the list in Ezra 2:36-39 speaks only of the priests of the
house of Joshua, the high priest: Eleazarites, or Zadokites, alone.
Apparently, following their standard policy of selecting a
disenfranchised priestly house and instating it with full financial and
political support, the Persians at first selected only the Jerusalemite
line of Zadok to preside over the Jerusalem Temple cult.   It is in this
light that the judgement oracle against the Levites in Ezekiel 44:1-14
must be viewed.

Attempts to demonstrate that 44:1-14 is not a judgement against
the Levites have been unsuccessful. Milgrom, Duke, and Fishbane have
each proposed that the judgement is in fact directed against the
people of Israel, addressed in v 6.[47]   Because of their idolatries,
supported by the Levites, the people are no longer permitted to kill
their own sacrifices. That task is given to the Levites (v 11), who are
otherwise restored to their historical responsibilities of service and
guard duty: responsibilities they had earlier shirked by the
employment of בני נכר. According to Duke, the statement that the
Levites are to bear their guilt and shame (v. 13) is to be understood in
connection with a common motif in Ezekiel: the shame brought by
God's gracious acts of restoration, which call sharply to mind one's
unworthiness (cf. 16:53-63; 20:39-44; 36:31-32; 39:25-29; 43:10-
11).[48]   Duke denies, therefore, that there is any degradation of the

---

[47] Milgrom, *Studies*, 83-85; Duke, "Punishment," 67-70; Fishbane, *Biblical
Interpretation*, 140. Fishbane, however, holds that this apparent concern is a pretext;
the "primary issue" in this text is "the exclusive elevation of the Zadokites to the
priesthood."

[48] "The gracious restoration of the Levites to their position of cultic
responsibility would remind them of their previous abominations and humble them"
(Duke, "Punishment," 70). For an excellent treatment of this motif, cf. Margaret Odell,
"Be Ashamed When I Forgive You: The Restoration of Honor in Ezekiel," presented to the
SBL Annual Meeting, 1990.

Levites in this text; 40:13-14 merely restates Levitical duties, in
neutral language reminiscent of Numbers 18:3. Note, however, that
while Numbers 18 properly requires the Levites to remain at a
distance from the holy things, it does not forbid the Levites to serve as
priests: that they will not do so is presupposed in the context. This,
by contrast, is precisely what Ezekiel 44:13 *does* stipulate. Former
priestly service by the Levites is presupposed in the accusation (v 7),
which states that בני נכר have been present in the sanctuary
(בהקריבכם את לחמי חלב ודם "when *you* offer my food, the fat and the
blood"). Since this accusation clearly addresses sacrificial personnel,
the claim that the people are judged here rather than the Levites
appears untenable. The people are of course punished as well, by
being denied any role in the sacrifice whatever. But the Levites are
particularly condemned, losing the right to serve as priests.

Exactly what is it that the rejected Levites are said to have done
to merit this punishment? Two specific offenses emerge. The first is
stated in the opening words of the accusation, as the head of the
abominations of Israel: בהביאכם בני נכר ערלי לב וערלי בשר להיות
במקדשי ("You brought aliens, uncircumcised of heart and flesh, to be
in my sanctuary"). The Levites, charged from of old with keeping
guard over the sanctuary, have not been true to that charge. In
addition, the Levites are accused of serving (שרת!) the גלולים:
Ezekiel's term of choice for idols (e.g., 6:3-6; 8:10; 14:3-4). The text
does not tell us when these offenses were committed, but *where* they
were committed is clear enough. The first offense, the involvement of
the בני נכר in cult service, can only be associated with the Temple.
In his vision of abominations (8:10), the prophet saw גלולים set up
and worshipped in the Temple itself, suggesting that the second
offense as well took place there.[49] If the setting is the Temple, then
the issue at stake is priestly authority: who may enter the sanctuary,
and how is the cult to be conducted?

---

[49] Baudissen ("Priests," 78) claims, on the contrary, that "by the non-Zadokite
Levites, Ezekiel means the former priests of the high places," an interpretation also
reached by Cooke (480) and Hals (288; 319). However, Haran (*Temples*, 104-6)
demonstrates that גללים cannot be taken as in any way identical to "high place,"
being everywhere used for idols.

The identity of the בני נכר in 44:7, 9 is unclear. However, since many interpreters agree with Wellhausen that the accusation is but a pretext for the restriction of altar service to the Zadokites, not many genuine attempts to identify this group have been made. Generally, the בני נכר have been assumed to be foreign cult servitors (i.e., the Gibeonites of Josh 9:23, or the Nethinim of 1 Chr 9:2), though there is no evidence of such ever being connected with the sacrificial liturgy.[50]   Julie Galambush proposes that this text refers to Egyptian priests left behind by Psammeticus II, participating in the Jerusalem Temple cult.[51]   However, this would not explain the Levites being considered guilty, and the Zadokites innocent of the offense.

A possible solution is presented by the use of בני נכר in Nehemiah 9:2. When Ezra called the people to the first celebration of the feast of Booths conducted according to his תורה, we are told that ויבדלו זרע ישראל מכל בני נכר ("the descendants of Israel were separated from all בני נכר"). Here, the reference is not to foreigners in a generic sense, but in particular to non-Israelites living in the land. The particular "foreigners" with whom Nehemiah 9:2 is concerned are likely the same people in the land whose offers to help rebuild the Temple are rebuffed in Ezra 4:1-3: persons of mixed heritage, the product of intermarriages among ethnic Israelites and the people resettled in Israel by Esarhaddon. These same persons may be the ones perjoratively labelled בני נכר in Ezekiel 44. Those taking part in the cult in the land prior to and soon after the Zadokites' return were people of mixed blood--foreigners, by the Zadokites' rendering. Worship alone would not have condemned all foreigners (Deuteronomy 23:4-8 stipulates that while Ammonites and Moabites are absolutely denied a place in the congregation, Egyptians and Edomites may be admitted after their families have been among the people Israel for three generations), but more than worship is at stake. Ezekiel 44:7 accuses the Israelites of permitting בני נכר to serve as cult personnel

---

[50] So Cooke, 479; Eichrodt, 564; Wevers, 220; Zimmerli, 2: 453-54; and Hals, 319.

[51] Julie Galambush, "Who Broke Whose Covenant and How in Ezek 44:7," presented to the SBL Annual Meeting, 1990.

involved in the act of sacrifice. It is possible, then, that the בני נכר
were none other than Levites who had not gone off into exile, and
whose families had intermarried with the people in the land. Their
line, the accusation goes, is impure and defiled, mingled with the
blood of foreigners. The character of the invective in this passage is
not unusual. In the Udjahoresne inscription, we read that Cambyses
gave Udjahoresne the authority to expel the "foreigners" from the
temple of Neith in Egypt, even to destroy their houses and property,
and to restore the temple to its former glory.[52]   Similarly, the
accusation levelled against Jeroboam in I Kings 12:31 is that the
priests he installs at Dan and Bethel are not Levites. Rival cult
personnel are, of course, illegitimate. Their bloodlines are impure,
they are not descended from proper priestly families. They are, in a
word, *foreigners*.

With this in mind, it is very interesting that Trito-Isaiah freely
accepts, even delights in, the Temple service of the בן נכר (Isa 56:3,
and esp. 6-8), stating explicitly that he may serve (שרת) YHWH (v 6)
and that his sacrifices upon the altar will be acceptable (v 7).   As
Fishbane has proposed, this suggests a post-exilic debate on the status
of Temple personnel.[53]   Another party to this debate, evidently, is
Malachi, who rejects the unclean priesthood and sacrifices of the
rebuilt Temple as a perversion of YHWH's covenant with *all* the house
of Levi (Mal 2:1-9). The other Levitical houses were doubtless
horrified at the Zadokites' exclusivistic claims. The Zadokites in turn,
emboldened by the support of the Persian colossus, accused their
enemies of idolatry, and even denied their claim to priestly descent.
This Zadokite dominance did not last. With the Mosaic תורה of Ezra,
the old balance was restored. However, for the tumultuous first years
after the return, the תורה of the Temple in Ezekiel 40--48 was
the תורה, the source of stability and meaning in a world of shifting
allegiances and the constant threat of annihilation.[54]

---

[52] Lichtheim, *Literature*, 3:38.

[53] Fishbane, *Biblical Interpretation*, 138.

[54] This position has been succinctly stated by S. Dean McBride, Jr., "Biblical
Literature in Its Historical Context: The Old Testament," in *Harper's Bible*

Commentary, ed. James L. Mays (San Francisco: Harper and Row, 1988) 22-23.
McBride's full thesis regarding the Persian dating of the Law of the Temple and the
parallel, somewhat later edition of Ezra's תורה (our Pentateuch) was presented in two
papers: "The 'Law of the Temple' and the Pentateuchal תורה," presented to the Chicago
Society of Biblical Research, April 1981; and "The Polity of Ezekiel 40-48," an invited
paper presented to the annual meeting of the Society of Biblical Literature, December
1983.

Chapter Six

THE BOUNDARIES AND DIVISION OF THE LAND
IN THE LAW OF THE TEMPLE

The final chapters of the Temple Vision, 47:13--48:35, deal with the boundaries of the land and its division among the twelve tribes. In the laws regarding the נשיא and the cult, reflections of a Restoration setting can be seen, giving them a specificity and realism denied by those who would consider these chapters the ideal program of a future age. Here, however, the idealization seems, at first sight, undeniable. From the "premonarchical" borders to the over-precise division of the land among tribes whose existence was a mere memory, these texts would seem to evade any attempt at a realistic reading. Still, it is possible to detect in the scheme for land division as well evidence for a realistic setting in the Judean Restoration. Here, too, clues are given whereby the life and faith of a people may be recovered.

I. The Borders Of The Land In The Law Of The Temple And In P

The borders laid out in 47:13-20 and 48:1, 28 are generally assumed to represent the same Priestly traditions which underlie Numbers 34:1-12 and Joshua 15:1-4.[1] These boundaries cannot be explicitly identified with the territory occupied or controlled by Israel in any particular era. Even at its height, the Davidic empire apparently did not extend north of Sidon along the Mediterranean coast, nor did it ever control all the coastal cities. On the other hand, Israelite settlements in the Transjordan are as old as Israel, yet neither Numbers 34 nor Ezekiel 47 include territory east of the Jordan. The

---

[1] Albrecht Alt, "Das System der Stammesgrenzen im Büche Josua," *Kleine Schriften zur Geschichte des Volkes Israel*, Vol 1 (München: C. H. Beck, 1953) 196; Martin Noth, "Studien zu den historisches-geographischen Dokumenten des Josuabuches," *ZDPV* 58 (1935) 239-47; cf. also Zimmerli, 2:528; Levenson, 115-16; Eichrodt, 591; Wevers, 230; Gese, 99; May, 329; Magne Sæbø, "Grenzbeschreibung und Landideal im Alten Testament Mit besonderer Berucksichtigung der min-Cad-Formel," *ZDPV* 90 (1974) 35. Cooke (525) holds that the vision of Ezekiel is the original, from which the boundaries in P are derived.

frequent claim that these are but ideal boundaries[2] does not resolve our difficulty, but merely begs the question: why should these boundaries be regarded as ideal?

Aharoni has proposed that these borders derive originally from old Egyptian sources, representing in fact the extent of Egyptian holdings in Syria-Palestine at the time of Israel's settlement in the land. As such, he holds, these boundaries naturally came to represent for Israel the extent of the land the nation rightly should inherit, and so they were remembered.[3]

A major advantage of Aharoni's proposal is its explanatory force: the extended northern border, the elimination of the Transjordan and the use of these curious boundaries in the Law of the Temple as well as by P are all accounted for. However, a comparison of the border stations described in Ezekiel 47:13-20 and those described in Numbers reveals significant differences. Of the nine southern boundary markers in Numbers (the wilderness of Zin, the border of Edom, the Salt Sea, the Ascent of Akrabbim, Kadesh-barnea, Hazar-Addar, Azmon, the Brook of Egypt, and the Mediterranean), the Law of the Temple has only three (the Brook of Egypt, the Mediterranean and Meribath-Kadesh [apparently identical with Kadesh-Barnea, though the difference in nomenclature is certainly significant]), and adds Tamar. The obvious western border, the Great Sea, is found in both texts. In the north, the Numbers text and the Law of the Temple again differ.

---

[2] So John Marsh, "The Book of Numbers," *IB*, Vol 2 (1953) 299, N. H. Snaith, *Leviticus and Numbers* (Greenwood: Attic, 1971) 201.

[3] Yohanan Aharoni (*The Land of the Bible: A Historical Geography* [tr. A. F. Rainey; Philadelphia: Westminster, 1967] 61-70) suggests that an actual ancient document establishing the borders of Canaan, written in Egyptian or Akkadian and preserved perhaps at Shiloh, is behind all three lists. He derives the idea of a written source behind the Num 34 and Jos 15 text from Martin Noth; Noth's view, however, is less elegant. He identifies a single written source, a list of *Grenzfixpunkte*, behind both Jos 15:2-4 and Num 34:3-5 ("*Studien*," 187; reconstruction 191). The southern border description in Ezekiel 47 is, then, an abbreviated version of Num 34 ("*Studien*," 239 n. 2). The northern border description, however, is understood by Noth as deriving from an Assyrian *Vorlage*, namely the system of Assyrian provinces and provincial boundaries ("*Studien*", 241-42; 245). Magne Sæbø suggests that a particular model for the land, that of Greater Canaan, has been given an eschatological application in the Temple Vision ("Grenzbeschreibung," 37). Sæbø also observes that, in the Assyrian provincial system as over against the systen laid out in the Temple Vision, the provice of Subutu/Subat was interposed between the provinces of Damascus and Hamat (33).

Both begin at the Great Sea and move inland, both cite Lebo-Hamath[4] and Zedad, and both wind up at Hazar-enon. However, the Ezekiel text is as fulsome on the northern border as Numbers is on the southern: the list goes on to include Hethlon, Berutha, and Sibraim, with the added note that these lie on the border between Damascus and Hamath. The Numbers passage cites only an unknown Mount Hor[5] and Ziphron. Further differences arise in the east. The Numbers text cites a series of unknown locations: Shepham, Riblah, and Ain. Only when we reach the shore of Yam-Kinneret are we back on familiar ground. The Law of the Temple uses the boundaries of set territories (Hauran, Damascus, and Gilead) to trace the eastern border back to the Jordan. In short, while the territory enclosed by the borders in Ezekiel 47 and those in Numbers 34 is roughly equivalent, the borders are marked off by strikingly different means. Many of the correspondences (the Jordan, the Wadi 'el-ᶜArīš, the Great Sea) are obvious geographical markers. It does not do to say, with Aharoni, that Ezekiel has merely updated the list according to the sites of his own day.[6] If this were the case, one would expect some more explicit associations between the lists, perhaps an identification of the prophet's current sites with the traditional ones. One certainly would not expect the degree of divergence found here. It seems doubtful, then, that the writer of the Ezekiel text was simply following an ancient tradition.

A possible clue to what the writer *was* doing may be found in the most patently obvious difference between the lists of Numbers 34 and Ezekiel 47. The Priestly writer begins in the south, with a clearly marked border, then moves west to the Sea. The northern border is sketchy, as is the eastern border until the Sea of Chinnereth. The redactor of the Law of the Temple begins in the north and describes the northern border in some detail. The description moves to the

---

[4] Reading Ezek 47:15 here with G, assuming a misplacement of חמת following instead of preceding צדדה in M.

[5] Aharoni (*Land*, 67) suggests one of the peaks in the Lebanese range north of Byblos, perhaps Ras Shaqqah.

[6] Ibid. 63.

eastern border, again described with some precision, then follows the Jordan south to the tip of the Salt Sea. From here, the southern border is tenuously drawn west to the Meditteranean Sea. The two accounts are almost direct opposites, beginning at opposite points, moving in opposite directions, each strong where the other is weak and weak where the other is strong. The reason for the southern orientation in the Numbers account is clear: the text purports to describe the land from the perspective of a people who have come from Egypt, to the south. Many of the sites used as border markers would have been familiar ones to any Judean. The Syrian territory to the north and east, however, was never conquered or settled by Israel. How then can we account for the fulsomeness of the Temple Vision at just this point? From what point of view does the northern orientation of the Law of the Temple's boundaries become clear? As Aharoni found in the Numbers list the perspective of the great power to the south, so I propose that we find in the boundaries of Ezekiel 47 the perspective of a great power to the north and east. The point of view in this text is Persian. The borders are those of the Persian satrapy Abar-Nahara.[7]

II. The Origins Of Abar-Nahara

The designation "land beyond the River" for the region of Syria/Palestine goes back to the Assyrian conquest. The Assyrians referred to this region as *ebir nari*, that is, the lands beyond the Euphrates. A prism from the reign of Esarhaddon reads:

> I called up the kings of the country Hatti and (of the region) on the other side of the river (Euphrates) (to wit): Ba'lu, king of Tyre, Manasseh (Me-na-si-i), king of Judah (Ia-u-di), Qaushgabri, king of Edom, Musuri, king of Moab, Sil-Bel, king of Gaza, Metinti, king of Ashkelon, Ikausu, king of Ekron, Milkiashapa, king of Byblos, Matanba'al, king of Arvad, Abiba'al, king of

---

[7] The theory of Noth cited above (p. 157, n. 3), that the writer of Ezekiel 47 was using an Assyrian account of provincial boundaries, is not so far from this conclusion. The Persians seem to have inherited, by and large, the provincial system of the Babylonians, which they in turn had adopted from the Assyrians. I propose, indeed, that the difference between the systems noted by Sæbø ("Grenzbeschreibung," 33) may be accounted for by proposing, either that the old province of Subutu had been absorbed into Damascus or Hamat by Persian times, or that the Persians for some reason decided to abolish it.

Samsimuruna, Puduil, king of Beth-Ammon, Ahimilki, king of Ashdod--12 kings from the seacoast.[8]

The area described as "on the other side of the river" seems to correspond roughly to Syria/Palestine, and not to mean, literally, all the desert, waste, and habitable land between the Euphrates and the sea. This designation apparently survived through the Neo-Babylon era; by the Persian period, Abar-Nahara (the Aramaic equivalent of the Assyrian expression) was the official designation of an administrative division in the Persian empire.

At first, this area was governed together with Babylon by a single satrap.[9] Then, according to Herodotus, the empire was reordered early in the reign of Darius I into twenty satrapies, with Syria/Palestine as the fifth and Babylon/Assyria as the ninth.[10] Oscar Leuze argued persuasively for a Persian rather than a Greek source behind the satrapy list of Herodotus, noting that, as a citizen of Halicarnassus under Persian domination, he would have had ample opportunity to obtain such information first-hand.[11] However, Leuze also states, "We cannot derive from Herodotus the actual date of the establishment of the 20 satrapies, for he himself did not know it, and only set it in the reform of Darius' first year on the basis of his own surmise."[12]

Some evidence suggests that Abar-Nahara was not an independent satrapy in Darius's time. Texts from Babylon in 520 and 519 BCE show that Ushtannu was governor of both Babylon and *ebir nari* at that time.[13] Moreover, the territory lists in Darius's royal

---

[8] *ANET*[3], tr. Oppenheim, 291.

[9] Gobryas administered both Babylon and Abar-Nahara in the reign of Cyrus. Aharoni (*Land*, 357) has proposed that this satrap had responsibility for all the lands of the former Neo-Babylonian kingdom.

[10] Herodotus 3.89-94.

[11] Oscar Leuze, *Die Satrapieeinteilung in Syrien und im Zweistromlände von 520-320* (Halle: Max Niemeyer, 1935) 242 [86].

[12] Ibid. 237 [81]: "*Aus Herodot können wir die wahre Zeit der Einrichtung der 20 Satrapien nicht entnehmen, da er sie selbst nicht kannte und nur auf Grund einer Vermutung die Reform ins erste Jahre des Dareios setzte.*"

[13] A. F. Rainey, "The Satrapy 'Beyond the River'," *AJBA* 1 (1969) 51-78, 53.

inscriptions make no mention of Abar-Nahara.[14]   Many scholars, following Olmstead, have thus suggested that the list of Herodotus reflects the political situation of his own time, and that the establishment of Abar-Nahara as an independent satrapy must be redated to around 482 BCE, following the Babylonian revolt.[15] However, it is worth noting that Olmstead himself cites a cuneiform text from Babylon which refers to one Ta-at-[ta-ni] as *paḥat* (governor) of *ebir nari* in 502 BCE.[16]   Hence, even if only as a sub-province of Babylon, Abar-Nahara had a significant political life and organization in the reign of Darius.   Moreover, in a bilingual building inscription of Darius at Susa, the Old Persian *kara hya Athuriya* ("people of the Assyrians") is rendered in Akkadian as *sabe sa eber nari* ("people of *eber nari*").[17]   On this basis, plus the consistent placing of Athura between Babylon and Egypt in Darius' monumental inscriptions,[18] Rainey concludes that the Persian Athura and the Aramaic Abar-Nahara have the same referent: the land of Syria/Palestine.[19] If this is so, then the arguments against the authenticity of Herodotus's list are considerably weakened, and the historical reliability of the Aramaic portions of Ezra is supported.

III. The Borders Of Abar-Nahara

It is difficult to determine the precise extent of Abar-Nahara. The most detailed account is that of Herodotus:

---

[14] Stressed by Ephraim Stern, "The Persian Empire and the political and social history of Palestine in the Persian period," *CHJ* 1 (1984) 78.

[15] Olmstead, *History*, 291.

[16] A. T. Olmstead, "Tattenai, Governor of 'Across the River,'"*JNES* 3 (1944) 46. Olmstead identifies this figure as the biblical Tattenai of Ezra 5:3, 6; 6:6, 13.

[17] The entire Old Persian text is in Roland G. Kent's *Old Persian* [AOS 33; New Haven: American Oriental Society, 1950) 142-14 (English translation on 143-144). Rainey ("Satrapy," 73-74) credits G. G. Cameron for this observation.

[18] Rainey, "Satrapy," 54; also observed by Stern, "Persian Empire," 78, though he does not draw the conclusions from this placement that Rainey does.

[19] Rainey, "Satrapy," 54.

From the city of Posideium--established by Amphilochus, the son of Amphiaraus, on the border between the Cilicians and Syrians--as far as Egypt (and always omitting the Arabians, who were not subject to tax), there was a tax assessment of 350 talents. In this province was all of Phoenicia, Palestinian Syria, and Cyprus. This was the fifth province.[20]

The Northern Border

The northernmost point of the coast of Abar-Nahara, according to Herodotus, was Posideium on the Cilician border, usually identified as modern Basit.[21]   However, this does not mean that the northern border of Abar-Nahara passed through that city, for, as Rainey observes, Herodotus does not place this city on the border between Phoenicia and Cilicia, but between Syria and Cilicia.[22] This is no mean distinction, for Herodotus states that the regions encompassed by the fifth satrapy were Phoenicia, the island of Cyprus, and Συριη ἡ Παλαιστινη καλεομενη--not, as Aharoni seems to read,[23] Syria and Palestine, but specifically the part of Syria called Palestine, or Palestinian Syria.   This distinction is necessary, as Herodotus elsewhere seems to regard everything along the Mediterranean from Egypt to Asia Minor as Syria.[24]

---

[20] Herodotus 3.91, translated by David Grene (*Herodotus*, 253). This version will be used hereafter for all citations of Herodotus in English.

[21] So Rainey, "Satrapy," 59; and Aharoni, *Land* , 357; Stern ("Empire," 79) proposes also al-Mina at the mouth of the Orontes, about 25 km. north of Basit.

[22] Rainey, "Satrapy," 60.   Rainey, however, does not draw from this the conclusions I have drawn, but places the coastal border of Abar-Nahara just north of Posideium ("Satrapy," 59).

[23] Aharoni, *Land*, 357.

[24] Note especially Herodotus 2.116 ("Syria is the neighboring country to Egypt, and the Phoenicians, to whom Sidon belongs, live in Syria.") and 7.89 ("The Phoenicians lived of old, so they say, about the Red Sea, but they came out of there and settled in that part of Syria that is next to the sea. That piece of Syria, and all as far as Egypt, is called Palestine."). More will be said about this denotation of Palestine shortly; for now, however, it must be noted that while this quoted portion of the text would suggest that Phoenicia was a part of Palestine, Herodotus distinguishes between the two earlier in this very paragraph, as well as in 3.91. Most important for our purposes is the notion that Syria seems here to identify not so much a particular country or people as a large geographical area, in which particular nations (Phoenicia, Palestine) are to be found. Herodotus never identifies his fifth satrapy as Syria; rather (see next footnote) he places the ethnic grouping called Syrians in his third satrapy. This usage is distinct from 3.5, where Συριον is evidently shorthand for Palestinian Syrian. Clearly the range, both geographic and semantic, of the term "Syria" is quite large in Herodotus's writing.

Herodotus lists the ethnic Syrians as part of his third satrapy, together with the Phrygians.[25]   This could suggest that the fourth, or Cilician, satrapy was restricted to a narrow strip of coastline, while the third satrapy curved down and around, encompassing the Syrian desert and bordering on Abar-Nahara along the Mediterranean coast. Posideium would then have been situated in the third satrapy, but at a juncture with Cilicia to the north and Abar-Nahara to the south. A more elegant solution, however, is made possible by Leuze's insight that the border spoken of here is ethnological, not political.[26] Doubtless ethnic Syrians lived within the Cilician satrapy, as they lived in the Phrygian; Herodotus's point would be that Syrians first began to be encountered after Posideium.   The political border between the fourth and fifth satrapies could than have been further south. In any case, as a coastal city of some size, Posideium seems to have been reckoned, together with the rich coastal ports of Phoenicia and old Philistia, as part of Abar-Nahara. The northern border of the province proper, however, would have coincided with the northern border of Phoenicia, which Rainey places at Byblos.[27] This would roughly agree with the northern border of the land according the Ezekiel 47:15-16.

The Southern Border

Herodotus says that, in the south, the fifth satrapy extended to the border of Egypt.   Elsewhere, he describes the Egyptian border thusly:

> The only clear entry pass into Egypt is this: from Phoenicia as far as the boundary of Cadytis is the country of what are called Palestinian Syrians; from Cadytis, a city that in my judgement is not much smaller than Sardis, to the city of Ienysus the seaports are in possession of the Arabians, but from Ienysus as far as the Serbonian marsh, along which the Caspian mountain stretches to the sea, they are again owned by Syrians. Beyond the Serbonian marsh--where, the story goes, Typho was hidden--it is already Egypt.[28]

---

[25] Herodotus 3.90.   Only for the fifth satrapy does Herodotus give geographical borders. For the other nineteen, he instead lists the ethnic groupings administered by each sarapy.

[26] Leuze, Satrapieeinteilung , 257 [101].

[27] Rainey, "Satrapy," 61.

[28] Herodotus 3.5.

We learn two important facts from this description. First, the dividing point between Egypt to the south and Palestinian Syria (hence, Abar-Nahara) to the north was the Serbonian marsh. Second, the coastline from Gaza (Greek Cadytis) to Ienysus was in Arabian hands; this is apparently the territory referred to in 3.91, which was not subject to taxation. Though the tribal identity of these Arabs is not given by Herodotus, the discovery of a silver bowl with an Aramaic inscription at Tell-Maskhûṭa makes the identification probable. The inscription reads זי קינו בר גשם מלך קדר קרב להן עלת ("That which Qainu bar Geshem, king of Qedar, offered to han-ᶜIlat").[29] On the basis of coins from the site, as well as paleography, Rabinowitz dates the inscription to about 400 BCE,[30] which would make the Geshem of the inscription the biblical enemy of Nehemiah, evidently his opponent to the south as Sanballat opposed him to the north and Tobiah to the east (Neh 6:1).[31] Cross suggests that Kedarite influence extended east, west, and south of the Dead Sea, and to the eastern extent of Egypt.[32] Rainey notes the presence of Aegean ointment vessels at Tell el-Khuleifeh (Ezion-Geber). This probably indicates Arabian trade with the West via the ports (particularly Gaza) controlled by the Kedarites, and illustrates that Kedarite influence extended to the tip of the Gulf of Aqaba.[33]

---

[29] Isaac Rabinowitz, "Aramaic Inscriptions of the Fifth Century BCE from a North-Arab Shrine in Egypt," *JNES* 15 (1956) 2.

[30] Rabinowitz, "Inscriptions," 6.

[31] Further, albeit indirect, evidence for this identification comes from an Aramaic inscription at Taymāʾ, published by F. M. Cross ("A New Aramaic Stele from Taymāʾ," *CBQ* 48 [1986] 387-94). The stele was erected by Pṣgw Šahrū, son of the king of Lihyān. Cross proposes that the double name distinguishes this Šahrū from his ancestor, Šahrū the father of Gašmū ("Stele," 390). Dated on paleographical grounds toward the end of the fourth century, this inscription appears to belong to the figure called Šahrū II by Albright ("Stele," 391-92). This additional evidence for the dynasty of Qedar and Lihyān, as Cross observes, "strengthens the case for the equation: biblical Gašmū the Arab = Gašmū son of Šahrū (I) = Gašm the father of Qaynū" ("Stele," 394).

[32] F. M. Cross, "Geshem the Arabian, Enemy of Nehemiah," *BA* 18 (1955): 47.

[33] Rainey, "Satrapy," 61.

The Kedarite Arabs, then, were something of a power in the land, a force in their own right. Leuze, Rainey, and Aharoni seem to assume that the Arab lands were still considered part of Abar-Nahara,[34] but this is not the position of Herodotus. In 3.91 he states emphatically πλην μοιρης της Αραβιον (ταυτα γαρ εν ατελεια): "always omitting the Arabians, who were exempt." In the text we have just considered, a clear distinction is made as to where Arab possessions begin and end, with the note that the interrupted Palestinian possessions resume at this point. Pseudo-Scylax makes a similar distinction. His own estimation of the limits of Συρια και Φοινικη extends from the Thapsakos River in the north to Ashkelon in the south, beyond which is Arabian coastline until Egypt.[35] Rainey has proposed that the Thapsakos is the present day Orontes, which puts Scylax and Herodotus in agreement on the northernmost coastal point belonging to Abar-Nahara.[36] Scylax's southern point is, however, far north of the border given by Herodotus[37] The Arabian holdings south of Ashkelon seem to be outside the satrapal framework. Moreover, the Arabian claims seem to be rather fluid, as considerable Arab aggression and activity on the southern border of this Persian province would lead one to expect. In light of fluctuating Arab claims to the south, it seems reasonable that an arbitrary, somewhat artificial border might be sought for administrative purposes.

---

[34] Leuze, *Satrapieeinteilung* , 259 [103]; Rainey, "Satrapy," 60; Aharoni, *Land*, 358.

[35] Pseudo-Scylax 104, *Geographi Graeci Minores*, Karl Müller, Vol 1 (Paris: Ambrosio Firmin Didot, 1855) 78-79.

[36] Rainey, "Satrapy," 68. Stern ("Empire," 79) identifies Thapsakos with biblical Tiphsah, on the Euphrates (1 Kings 5:4 [Eng. 4:24]). However, as Pseudo-Scylax is a mariner's guide to coastal cities and landmarks, it is difficult to see how an inland site could have been included. Moreover, Scylax states explicitly (Müller, *Geographi*, 79) that the distance from the Thapsakos to Ashkelon is 2700 stadia (about 306 miles). Measured from the mouth of the Orontes, that distance is just about right; Tiphsah, however, is much further away.

[37] Stern ("Empire," 79) remarks, "It is probable that Scylax omits the whole area under Arabian rule."

The Wadi 'el-ᶜAriš, the famed Brook of Egypt, is a natural choice.[38] The Brook of Egypt (*Nahal Muṣur* in Akkadian) appears as a significant landmark in the annals of Sargon II (721-705 BCE) and Esarhaddon (680-669 BCE).[39] Hence, there was also historical warrant for using the Wadi 'el-ᶜAriš as a boundary. Finally, the Wadi is located within the contested strip of desert and coastline, between Gaza and the Serbonian marsh. Again, the borders given in the Law of the Temple make sense in a Persian context.

The Eastern Border

The greatest difficulty arises when we turn to the eastern border, about which neither Herodotus nor Pseudo-Scylax provides information. On analogy with the Assyrian *ebir nari*, we might presume that the Transjordan was included.[40] However, no evidence confirming this has been found. The enemies of Nehemiah are often understood as rivals within the province, but this need not have been the case. Sanballat in Samaria was an internecine rival. However, as has already been shown, the Arab holdings seem to be outside the satrapal framework; Geshem the Arab is not an official within the satrapy. The same may be true of Tobiah the Ammonite.

Two arguments can be raised for placing the eastern border of Abar-Nahara at the Jordan. First is the fact that Herodotus considered Abar-Nahara a coastal, maritime province. That this would be true of Cyprus and Phoenicia is self-evident. However, Herodotus claims the same distinction for what he calls Palestinian Syria. In both 3.5 and 3.91, as we have seen, he describes Palestine as a coastal strip. The argument frequently raised, that Herodotus was merely mapping out the Mediterranean coastline, is true so far as it goes. However,

---

[38] As Aharoni (*Land*, 58) notes, "It is the only geographical obstacle in this area besides the desert itself, and for this reason the Wadi was considered the natural border between Palestine and Egypt.".

[39] *ANET³*, trans. Oppenheim, 286, 290 and note especially 292, where the march from Samaria to the Brook of Egypt is described as a unit, leading up to the desert campaign against Egypt.

[40] So Leuze, *Satrapieeinteilung* , 226 [110], who supposes that the border between Babylon to the east and Abar-Nahara to the west ran through the vast Syro-Arabian Desert

Herodotus claims to have been in the country he calls Palestine;[41] if it had extended inland to any appreciable degree, he would have known this and assumedly made some comment pertaining to the province's inland reaches.   Note further that in 4.39, as part of Herodotus' grand map of the world, he describes Palestinian Syria and Phoenicia as comprising the coast of his "second peninsula" as it passes along the Mediterranean.   In 7.89, Herodotus notes that Phoenicia and Palestine are partners in maritime enterprise, together furnishing 300 triremes for Xerxes's invasion fleet.   Most compelling for our purposes, however, are the following lines:

> The Phoenicians lived of old, so they say, about the Red Sea, but they came out of there and settled in that part of Syria that is next to the sea. That piece of Syria, and all as far as Egypt, is called Palestine.[42]

It is intriguing that here Herodotus seems to use Palestine in a sense inclusive of all the coastland from Egypt north through Phoenicia. Elsewhere, Phoenicia and Palestinian Syria are considered separate provinces.[43]   Particularly to be noted, however, is that the piece of Syria in which the Phoenicians are said to have settled, called here Palestine, is also explicitly said to be παρα θαλασσαν ("next to, alongside of, the sea"). According to Herodotus, the satrapy of Abar-Nahara, which consisted largely of Phoenicia and Palestinian Syria, was a strip of coastland. As we know that the satrapy included Yehud, and hence the central highlands, the mountains are not the eastern border.[44]   The next logical, geographical border is the Jordan--as described in the Temple Vision.

---

[41] Herodotus 2.106.

[42] Herodotus 7.89.

[43] Herodotus 1.105; 2.104; 3.5; 3.91; 4.39.

[44] Aharoni (Land, 364) believes that we can recover from the roster of cities participating in the repair of the walls in Neh 3:1-32 a picture of the administrative division of Yehud. He proposes a division into five districts: Keilah (subdivided into Zanoah and Keilah), Beth-zur (subdivided into Beth-zur and Tekoa), Beth-haccerem, Jerusalem (subdivided into Jerusalem and Gibeon) and Mizpah (subdivided into Mizpah and Jericho).   Michael Avi-Yonah (The Holy Land from the Persian to the Arab Conquest [Grand Rapids: Baker, 1966] 19-23; map 23) prefers a system of six districts, with Jericho serving as the capital of the sixth. In either case Jericho and Senaah in

A second argument for placing the eastern boundary of Abar-Nahara at the Jordan is the apparent strength of the Kedarite Arabs. As Aharoni has observed, "when Transjordan became an unsettled region, a pasturage for desert nomads, then the Jordan Valley and the Dead Sea formed the natural eastern boundary of western Palestine."[45] The reign of Darius was, I suggest, such a time. Evidence of the aggressiveness of the Kedarites on the shifting southern border has already been presented. Herodotus places these Arab lands outside the satrapal framework, noting that the Arabs are not taxed--although he does observe that the Arabians contributed a gift of a thousand talents of frankincense a year.[46] Some have proposed that this so-called gift was in fact but a tax paid in kind rather than in silver.[47] However, Herodotus sharply distinguishes those who paid taxes from those who gave gifts. The latter include the Ethiopians, the people of the Caucasus Mountains, and the Arabians. The first two groups were on the outer fringes of the empire, as Herodotus himself observed. The Arabian tribes, though technically well within Persian borders, dwelled in the waterless, trackless wastes: hence, they too were for all practical purposes a people on the fringe of the empire's authority.

---

the Jordan valley are the easternmost of these cities; none, significantly, are in the Transjordan.

[45] Aharoni, Land, 58.

[46] Herodotus 3.97.

[47] Rainey, "Satrapy," 60; Stern, Material, 252. Israel Eph^{c}al (The Ancient Arabs: Nomads on the Borders of the Fertile Crescent 9th-5th Centuries BC [Jerusalem: Magnes, 1984] 208-210) proposes that the thousand talents (thirty tons!) of frankincense represent the equivalent value of duties collected by the "King of the Arabs" from the spice trade via the southern Palestinian ports. Smuggling being ever a profitable enterprise, Eph^{c}al suggests that oversight of these ports, for reasons "of efficiency and convenience" (Arabs, 210), was given to the Arabs. The δωρα ("gift") he therefore understands to be "a regular tax, though collected differently from the φopos" (the usual term for tax; Arabs, 208). Eph^{c}al goes on, however (Arabs, 208), to state that "those on whom it [the δωρα] was levied were beyond the reach of the Persian administration." This is our point precisely: how would the Persians have gone about collecting such a tax from the desert nomads? Further the amount in itself is surely suspect: as Eph^{c}al observes, this would represent "an extraordinarily onerous levy, as valuable as those extracted from the wealthiest satrapies" (Arabs, 208). Elsewhere (1.183), Herodotus describes a sacrifice of one thousand talents of frankincense burned in a single day on the altar of Bel-Marduk in Babylon; here, as there, the number is doubtless hyperbole.

One might propose, therefore, that the notion of annual "gifts" from these peoples was in fact a face-saving fiction, meant to cover the Persians' failure to exact tribute from them, and passed on uncritically by Herodotus.

The story related by Herodotus concerning Cambyses's invasion of Egypt shows the strength and influence Arabian desert power could bring to bear. The king of Arabia was able to demand, and receive, concessions from the Persian empire in exchange for water and safe passage through the desert.[48] Perhaps among those concessions was considerable independence from Persian authority. Possible evidence for this comes from a Lihyanite inscription found at the el-Ula oasis (identified with ancient Dedan) in which the names Gashmu bin Shahru and Abd, pḥt of Dedan, appear together. W. F. Albright and Rabinowitz both argue that the Gashmu mentioned is the biblical Geshem.[49] Apparently, both Geshem and Abd were persons of sufficient influence that Nuran, the author of the inscription, could use their names to date his writing; significantly, the name of the Persian governor alone did not suffice. Perhaps, in the region of Dedan, both figures needed to be cited, for both wielded power. The situation here proposed, with Arab and Persian claims in the area being held in uneasy tension, would account for this.

Stern cites a number of excavated Persian fort sites in southern Palestine as indicating that "this entire area was under the direct rule of a Persian governor, assisted perhaps by Arab soldiers."[50] But the situation may have been exactly the opposite: a strong Persian presence in the area was necessary to enforce the uneasy peace with the Arabs. The Persians seem to have regarded the Kedarites with something approaching dread. Diodorus notes that in the latter part of the fifth century a fleet of three hundred triremes was sent to Phoenicia, to counter a presumed joint Arab-Egyptian conquest of the

---

[48] Herodotus 3.4-9. For this reason, Herodotus says, the Arabs were called ξεινοι ("friends"); cf. 3.88, 91, 97.

[49] Albright, "Dedan," 4; and Rabinowitz, "Inscriptions," 7.

[50] Stern, "Empire," 81. Cf. also Eph‘al, Arabs, 200.

region.[51]   In short, all available evidence shows that the Arabs of Kedar, the biblical kingdom of Geshem, were an aggressive, potentially hostile force in the region.

Already by the Babylonian period, the Kedarite Arabs had decimated Edom, forcing its people into the Negeb and the highlands of southern Judea.[52] Similarly, Moab had been repeatedly assaulted through the Assyrian and Babylonian periods, and likely was conquered in the Persian period; inscriptional evidence suggests that the conquerors were, again, the Kedarites.[53] It would be strange indeed if, at this point of great strength and influence, they did not annex the grazing lands of Ammon as well. The archaeological evidence supports such an interpretation, as (following a total destruction in the sixth century) the Transjordan seems virtually depopulated.[54] Moreover, excavations at ᶜArâq el-'Amir, identified as the biblical Tyre of the Tobiads, have failed to turn up Persian period remains,[55] which suggests that circumstances in the region were far from stable. As has often been suggested, the title עֶבֶד applied to Tobiah is indicative of an official post, most likely governor under Persian auspices of the

---

[51] Diodorus Siculus 13.46.

[52] Stern, *Material*, 253.

[53] J. T. Milik, "Nouvelles Inscriptions Sémitiques et Grecques du Pays de Moab," *Liber Annus* 9 (1958-1959) 340-341. Although the relevant inscription is in Aramaic, it contains the Arabic *wgr*, "monument," prompting Milik to propose that it was written for an Arab, and in any case establishing an Arab presence in Moab. Ephᶜal (*Arabs*, 200) concludes that "with the collapse in the first third of the sixth century B.C. of the kingdoms of Judah and Transjordan, there was a repetition of what happened in Palestine and its environs after the fall of the kingdoms of Syria and Damascus: waves of nomads penetrated into the settled areas close to the desert borders, this time throughout southern Transjordan and Palestine to the Judean hills."

[54] Stern, *Material*, 252; and also H. L. Ginsberg, "Judah and the Transjordan States from 734 to 582 B.C.E.," *Alexander Marx Jubilee Volume* (New York: The Jewish Theological Seminary of America, 1950) 367-68--both citing the early reconstructions of Nelson Glueck. However, James Sauer, in a recent study ("Transjordan in the Bronze and Iron Ages: A Critique of Glueck's Analysis," *BASOR* 263 (1986) 1-26) challenges this assessment, finding, particularly at Amman, evidence for a flourishing culture in precisely this period. The picture remains ambiguous.

[55] Stern, *Material*, 252.

region of Ammon.[56] The unsettledness of the region suggested by the
archaeological and textual evidence, however, raises the possibility
that Tobiah the "Ammonite slave" may have been under Arab, as well as
Persian, hegemony.   The sort of dual government that prevailed at
Dedan may have also held sway in the Transjordan.

This would explain why in Nehemiah 6:2 it is only Geshem and
Sanballat who approach Nehemiah to discuss a meeting at Ono,
although in 6:1 the autobiographer notes that Sanballat, Geshem, and
Tobiah had received word concerning the completion of Jerusalem's
walls.   Similarly, it is Sanballat and Geshem together who threaten to
expose Nehemiah to the Persians as a rebel (6:5-9).   If Tobiah was
Geshem's vassal, his participation would be assumed.   That Tobiah, and
not Geshem, should be mentioned in connection with the plot to buy a
prophet and thereby coerce Nehemiah into fleeing to the Temple for
sanctuary (6:10-14) is not strange.   After all, Geshem would have had
no influence in the Temple precincts, while the Tobiads had close,
long-standing ties to the Judean upper class (6:17-19) and priestly
establishment (13:4-6).[57]   In any case, the evidence of Arab strength in

---

[56] Albright ("Dedan," 4, n. 5) makes the intriguing proposal that "*Ṭōbīyāh hā-*
ᶜébed hā-ᶜAmmōnī, 'Tobiah, the servant, the Ammonite' ...is a corruption of an
original *Ṭōbīyāhū* (as the name was undoubtedly spelled at that time) *wā-ᶜEbed hā-*
ᶜAmmōnī, 'Tobiah and ᶜAbd, the Ammonite,'" thereby giving the Persian governor an
Ammonite name.   The relationship between Tobiah and this ᶜAbd would then be
parallel to the relationship between Gashmu bin Shahru and the ᶜAbd designated as *pḥt*
of Dedan in the Lihyanite inscription discussed above (see p. 169).   Most, however, have
chosen to let the text stand, and attempt to deduce the meaning of עבד in that context.
C. C. McCown ("The ᶜAraq el-Emir and the Tobiads," *BA* 20 [1957]: 72) observes that
עבד ("slave") is often found on seal inscriptions preceding מלך, suggesting that the
term may apply to a royal official.   Indeed, the Akkadian *arad sharri* and the Old
Persian *badaka* are definitely used in that way: as terms of honor applied to officers of
the king.   Cf. also Benjamin Mazar("The Tobiads," *IEJ* 7 [1957] 137-145; 229-238), and
Avi-yonah (26-27).

[57] Mazar suggests that this family has roots in the region of Gilead going back to
the reign of Tiglath-Pilesar III ("Tobiads," 237).   Apparently, the Tobiad land holdings
continue in an unbroken line down to the Hellenistic Period.   This ancient Jewish
family, involved in power plays at the Temple in the time of Nehemiah, may also have
been involved in the intrigue surrounding the Syro-Ephraimite War (Mazar [Tobiads,"
236] proposes that, before theophoric elements in proper names were changed in the
reform of Josiah, the family name Tobiahu was Tob'el, and suggests an identification
with the Ben-Tab'al of Isa 7:6) and was undoubtedly a leading faction in Temple politics
leading up to the Maccabean revolt (Hyrcanus the Tobiad, a leading supporter of the
Ptolemies, committed suicide when Antiochus IV Epiphanes gained power).   The late

the region lends further weight to the case for placing the effective eastern border of Abar-Nahara at the Jordan.

This impression is reinforced by evidence from the Greek period. Apparently, Alexander and his heirs controlled neither the southern Transjordan nor Northern Arabia, suggesting that at the time of Alexander's conquest the Persians did not control these regions, either. On the basis of city destructions in the region, Eph[c]al dates this loss of Persian control to around 404 BCE, after the death of Darius III.[58] However, Persian control of these Arab lands was likely always tenuous. Eph[c]al reconstructs the region over which the Persians lost control by considering the areas of the Transjordan claimed by the Ptolmies (and hence, by the Egyptians before them). This area, he writes, "can be said generally to have extended north from the Arnon river (Wadi al-Mujib) and to have included a cleruchy (a military colony) in 'the land of Tobiah' to cope with the nomads from the desert":[59] the very region here proposed to have been an Arab stronghold, never effectively held by the Persians.

This is not to suggest that the Persians surrendered all claims in the Transjordan. It is unlikely that they would have abandoned the rich caravan routes through this region, and Tobiah does appear to have been a governor under Persian auspices. However, it seems likely that Arab strength qualified these Persian claims, and that these lands may therefore have been among those outside the satrapal framework.

---

occurrence of the name Hyrcanus (Greek Ὑρκανος) suggests a Persian connection from early on; the name is Persian (*Vurkan*) and, according to Mazar, "characteristic of well-connected families." Another Tobiah, mentioned in the Lachish ostraca, is given the titles "servant" and "arm of the king" (Tobiads," 234), suggesting a royal connection for this family in the waning days of the First Temple; the Aramaic inscription טוביה at [c]Araq el-Emir, dated by Mazar to the beginning of the fifth century (Tobiads," 141-142), further attests the family's long tenure in the land. Little wonder, then, that Mazar, with McCown and Avi-Yonah, proposes that Tobiah was the governor of the Persian province of Ammon. Still, if the reconstruction we have proposed is correct, the power in the Transjordan throughout this period was the Kedarites, not the Persians, and only canny politicians (as, from all evidence, the Tobiads traditionally were) could have survived.

[58] Eph[c]al, *Arabs*, 205.

[59] Ibid, 206.

The Inclusion of Cyprus

The sole remaining incongruity between the borders of the Law of the Temple and the territory of Abar-Nahara is that the latter included the island of Cyprus. As the Assyrian *ebir nari* likely also included Cyprus, this pairing of island with mainland is very old.[60] There is, however, some indication in Herodotus that Cyprus may have been considered practically as separate from Abar-Nahara. In Herodotus's roster of Xerxes's invasion fleet, the ships contributed by Cyprus are listed separately from those contributed by Phoenicia and Palestine.[61] Even if the island was administratively connected to Abar-Nahara, its very isolation must have meant that for practical purposes it was self-governing. Moreover, competing Greek claims to the island doubtless made Cyprus more distant still from the day to day life of the province to which it was nominally attached. Finally, for the purposes of the Law of the Temple, Cyprus would not have been included in any case. Lacking a YHWHist community, it would not have come under the sphere of influence of the Jerusalem Temple and its priests.

IV. The Function Of The Land Divisions

In brief, it is at least possible that the borders given in Ezekiel 47 are the actual borders of the Persian province of Abar-Nahara. This brings us to the scheme for the division of the land within these boundaries among the twelve tribes. Most scholars have seen in this scheme an unrealistic, utopian idea of the land, removed from its realities, grounded in archaic, premonarchic ideals.[62] Clearly, the division portrayed here could not have been carried out. The tribes no longer existed, save as a literary ideal, and the precise, symmetrical

---

[60] *ANET*[3], tr Oppenheim, 291. The ten kings from Cyprus (Iadnana) are counted with the 12 kings of the seacoast (see above, n. 8) as among the kings of *ebir nari* and Hatti. Note, however, that a distiction may be implied among the kings of "Hatti, the seashore and the islands." If so, then this text could demonstrate that Cyprus was indeed distinguished from *ebir nari* by the Assyrians. The intent, however, is unclear.

[61] Herodotus, 7.90. This account is separated from the account of the Phoenician and Palestinian contributions in 7.89 by the description of the Egyptian contingent.

[62] Levenson, *Program*, 115-16; Eichrodt, 591; Wevers, 231; Cooke, 524.

divisions described make no allowance for the assymetry and varying quality of the land itself. But that does not mean that the plan for the division of the land is devoid of realistic content.

A possible entry into this material is gained if the plan is viewed as a religious doctrine, rather than a political proposal. George Lindbeck, under the influence of Geertz's semiotic theory of religion and culture, proposes that religious doctrines function as rules: that is, that they have a primarily regulative, rather than propositional, quality.[63] Doctrines are not so much about facts in the world as about the community which chooses to abide by them. In this sense, as a religious doctrine, the division of the land in 47--48 is quite realistic, and quite serious. For while the division itself could not actually be accomplished, owing to the uneven qualities and asymmetry of the land and the loss of tribal identity, the *intention* to divide the land in these ways was vitally important, reflecting a certain attitude toward God, history and the identity of Israel.

As Levenson has shown, the division of the land is a profoundly theological enterprise.[64] On the one hand, the text connects with the ancient wilderness traditions seen in the battle camp of P (Num 2; 3:21-28). Here as there, the placement of the tribes relative to the sanctuary reflects old conceptions concerning the relative sanctity of the tribes, revealed by the birth-order and mother of each tribe's eponymous ancestor. Hence, in the land allotment, those descended

---

[63] George A. Lindbeck, *The Nature of Doctrine: Religion and Theology in a Postliberal Age* (Philadelphia: Westminster, 1984) 18-19.

[64] Levenson, *Program*, 116-21. Similar arguments, though not so detailed, were advanced by Moshe Greenberg,"Idealism and Practicality in Numbers 35:4-5 and Ezekiel 48," *JAOS* 88 (1968): 59-65. Greenberg argues for the comparative realism of the land division. By arranging seven tribes to the north of Jerusalem, and five to the south, he observes, the true "eccentric position" of the city in the land is allowed for by the composer ("Idealism," 64; an observation made as early as Smend, 392: *"Nur in sofern muss Ez. der Wirklichkeit eine Concession machen, als Jerusalem doch nicht in der Mitte des Landes leigt"* ["Only so far must Ezekiel make a concession to reality, since Jerusalem indeed does not lie in the middle of the land"]). Similarly, Greenberg notes that, as the natural variations of the land fall into longitudinal zones (coastal plain, highlands, valley, desert), only a cross-sectional division such as that described here could hope to result in an equitable division. I hold these texts to represent, not an eschatological hope (Levenson) or future plan (Greenberg), but a present confession about the identity of Israel at a particular point in the people's history. Still, the observations are as applicable to my conclusions as to theirs.

from the hand-maids Bilhah and Zilpah are placed furthest from the Temple, Gad (Zilpah's firstborn) being the southernmost, and Dan (Bilhah's firstborn) being the northernmost, with Asher (Zilpah's second) and Naphtali (Bilhah's second) next in line. Similarly, those placed closest to the Temple are the sons of Jacob by his legitimate wives. The sacred precinct is adjoined to the south by Benjamin, son of the favored wife Rachel, and to the north (!) by Judah: a Leah tribe, and also the tribe of royalty.

On the other hand, the plan for the division of the land also sets out to right old wrongs. Every tribe is given the same inheritance. Regional hostilities are placated by moving the Transjordanian tribes west and Judah north. Thus, all of Israel is placed on an equitable footing under God. Further, if the land claimed was the Persian satrapy of Abar-Nahara, a certain claim about "church-state" relations was being made. The plan for land division in 47--48 is a Judean claim to hegemony over Samaria, albeit that hegemony is religious rather than political. By parcelling out all the lands of Abar-Nahara among the traditional twelve tribes, as Joshua had parcelled out the land in ancient days, the returning Zadokites asserted religious dominance throughout the region.

The Law of the Temple claims for the Jerusalem Temple clergy the same sort of authority granted to Ezra years later: religious authority through the whole of Abar-Nahara. However, this authority is limited, as Ezra's would be. The rights of the other peoples who comprised Abar-Nahara could not be infringed upon. Hence, Ezra's commission was limited לכל ידעי דתי אלהך ("to all who know the laws of your God," Ez 7:25). In the Law of the Temple, an inheritance is granted to הגרים בתוככם ("the alien in your midst," 47:22, 23), an allotment which has the same effect: the authority of the clergy is limited, and the rights and independence of all the people of the land are affirmed.

Although generosity to the גר is a consistent biblical principle, the extent of this provision is unprecedented. Elsewhere, the rights of the alien are guaranteed, but he always remains an alien, in contrast to the native-born, ethnic Israelite. Here, the alien is made co-inheritor of the land with the ethnic Israelite. This provides further support for setting the Law of the Temple in the period of the Restoration. If this text is an exilic proposal for reconstruction, or a vision of the end-time, such generosity is an anomaly. If, on the other hand, this text is a realistic depiction of Restoration society, the land grant to the גר is exactly what one should expect to find. Under Persian rule, respecting the rights of all inhabitants in the land, no other approach would be possible.

Literarily, these concluding chapters of the Law of the Temple return us to the beginning: to the great Temple vision of 40--42. The detailed measurement of the land in 47:13--48:35 not only recalls the measurement of the Temple in 40--42, but reflects the same purpose. The glory and holiness of YHWH are given physical and spacial expression. As in 40--42 the holiness of the Temple is expressed by its marvelous symmetry, so the symmetry of the land's division bears witness to YHWH's ordering, creative presence.   As the sacred precincts were protected by a wall and massive gates, so now that entire complex, indeed Jerusalem itself, is surrounded by a reserve 25000 cubits by 25000 cubits, hedged in by the lands of the priests and the Levites (48:8-22). Most significant, however, is the placement of the Temple at the center of Israel.

Our redactor has appropriately placed this scheme for land division following the vision of the River, which binds Temple to land (47:1-12), thereby affirming theologically the centrality of the Temple in the whole of the land as well as counterbalancing literarily the lengthy measurements and divisions of the opening Temple description. The center of this grand scheme, both literally and figuratively, is the land apportioned for the Temple and its personnel, the city, and the נשיא (48:8-22). Having begun at the northern border and moved south, the author here reaches the center of the land, which contains Jerusalem and the Temple; the description of the southern tribes' apportionments follows. This is a bit off geographically: Jerusalem is not *in* the center of the land. Our writer, however, is no geographer; we are here in the realm, not of real estate, but of religious doctrine.

As Israel is at the center of the earth (Ezek 38:12), so is the Temple at the center of Israel--the center of the center, the core of reality. The Temple as the center of the earth is the meeting place of the divine and the human, the *axis mundi* linking heaven, earth and the underworld, the source of life and fruitfulness.[65]   The message of the great River of Ezekiel's core vision, that life and order and healing come from the Temple, is now communicated in the calm, ordered structuring of the land.   This is the point of the Law of the Temple: that the Temple is the heart of life, the center of the world, the one source of meaning and direction, for it is the place of YHWH's presence.   The Zadokite priest and his patron, the נשׂיא, are by their identification with the Temple identified as well as central figures for the believing community.   The abridgement of this lengthy center section at 45:1-8, placed between the laws regarding priest and נשׂיא, foreshadows this connection from early on.   Nor should the connection surprise us at any rate.   The major concerns of the Law of the Temple throughout are land, priest and נשׂיא; the binding reality behind this triad is, consistently, the Temple.   By means of the restored cult in the restored Temple, celebrated by the right priesthood, maintained by the benevolence and generosity of the נשׂיא, the presence of YHWH once again can be recognized in Israel's midst.   Thus the final words of this section, penned by the old prophet, are an appropriate summation of the legislative masterpiece built upon his vision. To Jerusalem is given a new, sacred name: יהוה שׂמה--"the Lord is there."

---

[65] Mircae Eliade, *The Myth of the Eternal Return, or, Cosmos and History* (tr. Willard Trask; Princeton: Princeton University, 1974) 12-21; and Clifford, *Cosmic Mountain* , 3.

Chapter Seven

CONCLUSIONS AND SUMMARY

The Temple Vision of Ezekiel 40--48 is a complex text, but not an incomprehensible one. Close examination reveals deliberate connections among materials that have often been attributed to separate, isolated layers of redaction. The Temple Vision manifests a definite overall shape, indicating a particular function. Like Deuteronomy and the Book of the Covenant, the Temple Vision is a polity, and functioned as such for a particular society. However, the text cannot easily be explained as the work of the prophet Ezekiel alone, or of any other single author. In particular, the radical contrast between the priesthood as described in the Temple description (40:44-46) and in the Law of the Temple (esp. 44:6-14) can only indicate two separate, and divergent, sources.

The first of these sources is the prophet Ezekiel. Connections between the grand vision of the Temple and the other two visions designated מראות אלהים (Ezekiel's call, and his vision of the destruction of Jerusalem) are readily apparent. In the material assigned to Ezekiel's core vision, there is nothing that does not admit to an early exilic setting, including the bifurcated priesthood of Ezekiel 40:44-46. Comparison with Temple texts from the traditions of Israel and from elsewhere in the ancient Near East demonstrates precedent for the detailed Temple description, the occupation of the Temple by the divine Presence, even for the vision of the river with its abundant fresh waters and paradisial trees.

This core vision is concerned with the problem of the divine Presence, which indeed could be said to be the uniting theme of the entire text of Ezekiel. In the Temple vision, as in the vision of his call, the prophet experiences the full majesty of YHWH's כבוד while in exile, in a foreign land. Though city, king, Temple, and cult be destroyed, this vision is a promise of YHWH's continuing presence--a concrete demonstration of YHWH's promise to be a sanctuary for Judah's exiles (11:16). As the Jerusalem sanctuary had become, for Ezekiel, totally and irredeemably defiled, the perfect archetypal Temple of his vision is a place guarded from defilement, defended by massive fortified gates. Indeed, the gate by which the Divine enters that Temple is sealed for all time. The כבוד will never leave again; the Temple will never again be defiled.

The second source is no less a coherent unit than the first. The entire final form of the Temple Vision demonstrates a grand unity of conception. By careful and artful use of language, the second author of our canonical text has woven legislation into the prophet's vision. The center of the text has been subtly shifted, from the divine promise of presence to the means by which the Presence can be encountered. The closed doors of Ezekiel's vision have been opened. Ancient tradition, current practice, and the author's own insight and innovation have been skillfully combined. A liturgy is set forth, together with a cult calendar and a hierarchy of Temple personnel. The funding of the cult is arranged, and hence its continuance is guaranteed. The land is claimed for YHWH, as Joshua had claimed it.

Within this scheme are evidences of gritty reality. Political problems are revealed in the three prophetic critiques of the leader in the land, the נשיא. Tensions in the Temple leadership are evidenced by the polemic against the Levites, especially in 44:6-14. A new standardized system of measurement is presented. In brief, we have numerous indications that the society depicted in the Temple Vision is no ideal projection, but an actual society, centered on a state-supported Temple in which the secular leadership played an important role. The texts describing the Judean Restoration in Ezra-Nehemiah depict a similar society. When these texts are compared with what can be learned of Persian interventions in the religious institutions of other subject peoples, the veracity of this portrayal is supported.

The identification of the society back of the Temple Vision with Restoration Judea is supported by the evidence. The sixty-shekel mina from the table of weights and measures in 45:10-12 corresponds to the system described in the Elephantine papyri--a system instituted by Darius I, according to Herodotus. The title נשיא, given to the leader of the society portrayed in the Temple Vision, is also given to Sheshbazzar, first governor of the Persian province of Yehud. The restriction of priestly dignity to the family of Zadok is an anomaly: evidently, in both the First and the Second Temple establishments, Temple clergy as well as altar clergy could be designated כהנים. The restriction of priesthood to the Jerusalemite altar clergy can best be explained as a transitional stage between First and Second Temple periods, operative until the time of Ezra's Mosaic תורה. The borders depicted in 47:15-20 roughly coincide to the borders of the Persian province Abar-Nahara, of which Judah was a part. The provision within those borders for land to be given as an inheritance to aliens makes perfect sense in the Persian context, where the Judeans were one people among many in the land, and the power was in the hands of a foreign government.

Particularly suggestive is the Demotic Chronicle, which details the demand of Darius that the Egyptian clergy produce an authoritative code, a law of the temples. As 43:12 explicitly states, in its final form, the Temple Vision is just such a code: it is תורת הבית, the Law of the Temple. I have used this designation particularly for the legislative expansions of our redactor. But in truth, in its final form the entire vision functions as Law of the Temple. The grand vision of the old prophet-priest has become the foundation for an edifice of legislation.

The implications of this proposal are far-reaching. If, as has been suggested, the Law of the Temple is a parallel to the Mosaic תורה, pentateuchal criticism could well make use of this material to understand the development of law and cult in Israel. Histories of the priesthood have long turned to the Law of the Temple as the exception that must prove the rule: any workable reconstruction of the priesthood must be able to account for this aberration. Usually this has been accomplished by some scheme of dependence: either P is derived from Ezekiel (as in Wellhausen's classic structure), or Ezekiel from P (as in the recent work of such distinguished Jewish scholars as Haran, following the magisterial work of Kaufmann). I have proposed, on the contrary, that Ezekiel and P are parallel streams, and their depictions of the priesthood cannot be reduced to literary dependence in either direction. As Wolf Baudissen demonstrated long ago, no viable history of the priesthood can avoid coming to terms with the tremendous complexity of the issue, even in First Temple times.

Seen in its proper historical and literary context, the Temple Vision of Ezekiel 40--48 emerges as neither failed prophecy nor flawed building project; as neither irrelevant appendix to prophecy nor awkward frontispiece to apocalyptic. Rather, it is seen clearly as a courageous confession, in a "day of small things"(Zechariah 4:10) that YHWH is not far off, but near at hand. By placing worship at the heart of life, the Temple Vision lends meaning to the lives of a people lost in the shuffle of world events. From the perspective of our text, the land and people of Judah are not peripheral, but central to YHWH's action, even in a world of great empires. The Temple stands, not only at the heart of Ezekiel's vision, but at the center of the world.

BIBLIOGRAPHY

Aharoni, Yohanan. *The Land of the Bible: A Historical Geography.* Tr. Anson F. Rainey. Philadelphia: Westminster, 1967.

Ahlström, Gösta Werner. "Heaven on Earth--at Hazor and Arad." In Birger A. Pearson, ed., *Religious Syncretism in Antiquity: Essays in Conversation with Geo Widengren,* pp. 67-83. Formative Contemporary Thinkers1. Missoula: Scholars, 1975.

Aistleitner, Joseph. *Die mythologischen und kultischen Texte aus Ras Schamra.* Bibliotheca Orientalis Hungarica 8. Budapest: Akadémiai Kiadó, 1959.

_____. *Wörterbuch der ugaritischen Sprache.* Berlin: Akademie-Verlag, 1963.

Albright, William Foxwell. "The Babylonian Temple-tower and the Altar of Burnt-Offering." *Journal of Biblical Literature* 39 (1920) 137-42.

_____. "Dedan." In Gerhard Ebeling, ed. *Geschichte und Altes Testament: Festschrift fur Albrecht Alt,* pp. 1-12. Beiträge zur historischen Theologie16. Tübingen: J. C. B. Mohr [Paul Siebeck], 1953.

_____. "The High Place in Ancient Palestine." In *Volume du Congrès, Strasborg 1956,* pp. 242-58. Vetus Testamentum Supplement 4. Leiden: E. J. Brill, 1957.

Alt, Albrecht. "Das System der Stammesgrenzen im Büche Josua." In *Kleine Schriften zur Geschichte des Volkes Israel,* Vol. 1, pp. 193-202. München: C. H. Beck, 1953.

Armour, Robert A. *Gods and Myths of Ancient Egypt.* Cairo: The American University in Cairo, 1986.

Avi-Yonah, Michael. *The Holy Land from the Persian to the Arab Conquest.* Grand Rapids, Michigan: Baker Book House, 1966.

Avigad, Nahman. *Bullae and Seals from a Post-Exilic Judean Archive.* Monographs of the Institute of Archaeology, The Hebrew University of Jerusalem, Qedem 4. Tr. R. Grafman. Jerusalem: Ahva Co-op., 1976.

180   The Law of the Temple

Baltzer, Klaus. *The Covenant Formulary: In Old Testament, Jewish, and Early Christian Writings.* Tr. David E. Green. Philadelphia: Fortress, 1971.

Bartlett, John R. "Zadok and His Successors at Jerusalem." *Journal of Theological Studies* 19 (1968) 1-18.

Barton, George A. *The Royal Inscriptions of Sumer and Akkad.* New Haven: Yale University, 1929.

Baudissen, Wolf Wilhelm Grafen. *Die Geschichte des alttestamentlichen Priesterthums untersucht.* Leipzig: S. Hirzel, 1889.

_____. "Priests and Levites." In James Hastings, ed. *A Dictionary of the Bible, Dealing with its Language, Literature and Contents Including the Biblical Theology.* Vol. 4: Pleroma-Zuzim., pp. 67-97. New York: Charles Scribner's Sons, 1902.

Bickerman, Elias. *Studies in Jewish and Christian History.* 3 Vols. Arbeiten zur Geschichte des antiken Judentums und des Urchristentums 9. Leiden: E. J. Brill, 1973-86.

Biran, Avraham, ed. *Temples and High Places in Biblical Times.* Jerusalem: Nelson Glueck School of Biblical Archaeology of Hebrew Union College--Jewish Institute of Religion, 1981.

Bertholet, Alfred. *Das Buch Hesekiel eklärt.* Kurzer Hand-Commentar zum Alten Testament 12. Freiburg: Mohr, 1897.

Betlyon, John Wilson. "The Provincial Government of Persian Period Judea and the Yehud Coins." *Journal of Biblical Literature* 105 (1986) 633-42.

Blenkinsopp, Joseph. *A History of Prophecy in Israel.* Philadelphia: Westminster, 1983.

_____. "The Mission of Udjahoresnet and Those of Ezra and Nehemiah." *Journal of Biblical Literature* 106 (1987) 409-21.

Boyce, Mary. "Persian Religion in the Achemenid age." In *The Cambridge History of Judaism,* Vol 1: *Introduction: The Persian Period,* pp. 279-307. Ed. W. D. Davies and Louis Finkelstein. Cambridge: Cambridge University, 1984.

Breasted, James Henry. *Development of Religion and Thought in Ancient Egypt.* New York: Harpers and Brothers, 1959.

Bright, John. *A History of Israel.* Philadelphia: Westminster, [3]1981.

Caird, George B. "First Samuel." *Interpreter's Bible*, Vol. 2, pp. 855-1,040. Ed. George A. Buttrick. New York/Nashville: Abingdon, 1953.

Caquot, André; Szycner, Maurice; and Herdner, Andrée, eds. *Textes Ougaritiques*, Tome 1, *Mythes et Légendes: Introduction, Traduction, Commentaire*. Paris: Cerf, 1974.

Childs, Brevard. *Introduction to the Old Testament as Scripture*. Philadelphia: Fortress, 1979.

Clements, R. E. *God and Temple*. Oxford: Basil Blackwell, 1965.

_____. *God's Chosen People: A Theological Interpretation of the Book of Deuteronomy*. London: SCM, 1968.

Clifford, Richard J. *The Cosmic Mountain in Canaan and the Old Testament*. Harvard Semitic Monographs 4. Cambridge: Harvard University, 1972.

Cody, Aelred. *A History of Old Testament Priesthood*. Analecta Biblica 35. Rome: Pontifical Biblical Institute, 1969.

Cohen, Martin A. "The Role of the Shilonite Priesthood in the United Monarchy of Israel." *Hebrew Union College Annual* 36 (1965) 59-98.

Cooke, George Albert. *Ezekiel*. International Critical Commentary. Edinburgh: T. and T. Clark, 1936.

Cross, Frank Moore. "Geshem the Arabian, Enemy of Nehemiah." *The Biblical Archaeologist* 18 (1955) 46-7.

_____. "A New Aramaic Stele from Taymā'." *Catholic Biblical Quarterly* 48 (1986) 387-94.

_____. "Papyri of the Fourth Century B. C. from Daliyeh." In David Noel Freedman and J. C. Greenfield, ed., *New Directions in Biblical Archaeology*, pp. 41-62. Garden City: Doubleday, 1969.

_____. "The Priestly Houses of Early Israel." In *Canaanite Myth and Hebrew Epic: Essays in the History of the Religion of Israel*, pp. 195-215. Cambridge: Harvard University, 1973.

_____. "The Priestly Tabernacle." In G. Ernest Wright and David Noel Freedman, eds.,*The Biblical Archaeologist Reader*, Vol. 1, pp. 201-28.   Garden City: Doubleday, 1961.

_____. "A Reconstruction of the Judean Restoration." *Interpretation* 29 (1975) 187-203.

_____. "Samaria Papyrus 1: An Aramaic Slave Conveyance of 335 B.C.E. Found in the Wâdî ed-Dâliyeh." *Eretz-Israel* 18 (1985) 7-17.

Dietrich, Manfried and Loretz, Oswald. "Zur ugaritischen Lexikographie 1." *Bibliotheca Orientalis* 23 (1966) 127-33.

Dietrich, Manfried; Loretz, Oswald; and Sanmartín, J., eds. *Die keilalphabetischen Texte aus Ugarit: Einschliesslich der keilalphabetischen Texte ausserhalb Ugarits,* Vol. 1: *Transkription.* Alter Orient und Altes Testament 24. Neukirchen-Vluyn: Neukirchener, 1976.

Diodorus Siculus, 12 Vols., tr. Charles Henry Oldfather. Loeb Classical Library. Cambridge: Harvard University, 1921.

Driver, Godfrey Rolles. *Canaanite Myths and Legends.* Old Testament Studies 3. Edinburgh: T. and T. Clark, 1956.

Duke, Rodney . "Punishment or Restoration? Another Look at the Levites of Ezekiel 44.6-16," *Journal for the Study of the Old Testament* 40 (1988) 61-81.

Eichrodt, Walther. *Ezekiel.* Tr. Cosslett Quin. The Old Testament Library. Philadelphia: Westminster, 1970.

Emerton, John. "Priests and Levites in Deuteronomy." *Vetus Testamentum* 12 (1962) 129-138.

Eliade, Mircae. *The Myth of the Eternal Return, or, Cosmos and History.* Tr. William Trask. Bollingen Series 46. Princeton: Princeton University, 1974.

Eph^cal, Israel. *The Ancient Arabs: Nomads on the Borders of the Fertile Crescent 9th-5th Centuries B.C.* Jerusalem: Magnes, 1984.

Feigin, Samuel. "The Meaning of Ariel." *Journal of Biblical Literature* 39 (1920) 131-37.

Fishbane, Michael. *Biblical Interpretation in Ancient Israel.* Oxford: Clarendon, 1985.

Fohrer, Georg and Galling, Kurt. *Ezechiel.* Handbuch zum Alten Testament 13. Tübingen: J. C. B. Mohr, 1955.

Frankfort, Henri. *Ancient Egyptian Religion.* New York: Harper and Brothers, 1961.

Frye, Richard N. *The Heritage of Persia.* New York: The New American Library, 1963.

Galambush, Julie. "Who Broke Whose Covenant and How in Ezek 44:7?" Paper presented to the annual meeting of the Society of Biblical Literature, November 1990.

Galling, Kurt. "Erwägungen zum Stelenheiligtum von Hazor." *Zeitschrift des Deutschen Palästina-Vereins* 75 (1959) 1-13.

Geertz, Clifford. *The Interpretation of Cultures.* New York: Basic Books, 1973.

Gese, Hartmut. *Der Verfassungsentwurf des Ezechiel (Kap. 40-48) traditionsgeschichtlich untersucht.* Beiträge zur historischen Theologie 25. Tübingen: J. C. B. Mohr [Paul Siebeck], 1957.

Ginsberg, Harold Louis "Judah and the Transjordan States from 734 to 582 B.C.E." In *Alexander Marx Jubilee Volume,* pp. 347-68. New York: The Jewish Theological Seminary of America, 1950.

Goodenough, Erwin R. *Jewish Symbols in the Greco-Roman Period.* 13 Vols. Bollingen Series 13. Princeton: Princeton University, 1953-68.

Gordon, Cyrus H. *Ugaritic Textbook.* Analecta Orientalia 38. Rome: Pontifical Biblical Institute, 1965.

Goshen-Gottstein, Moshe H. *The Aleppo Codex; Part One: Plates.* Jerusalem: Magnes, 1976.

Greenberg, Moshe. "The Design and Themes of Ezekiel's Program of Restoration." *Interpretation* 38 (1984) 181-208.

_____. *Ezekiel 1-20.* The Anchor Bible 22. Garden City, N.Y.: Doubleday and Co., 1983.

_____. "Idealism and Practicality in Numbers 35:4-5 and Ezekiel 48." *Journal of the American Oriental Society* 88 (1968) 59-65.

Gunneweg, Antonius H. J. *Leviten und Priester.* Göttingen: Vandenhoeck & Ruprecht, 1965.

Hals, Ronald M. *Ezekiel.* The Forms of Old Testament Literature 19. Grand Rapids: William B. Eerdmans, 1989.

Helck, Wolfgang and Erhard, Otto. *Kleines Wörterbuch der Aegyptology.* Wiesbaden: Otto Harrassowitz, 1956.

184   The Law of the Temple

184   The Law of the Temple

Hanson, Paul. *The Dawn of Apocalyptic.* Philadelphia: Fortress,
1975.

_____. "Old Testament Apocalyptic Re-examined." *Interpretation*
25 (1971) 454-79.

Haran, Menahem. "The Law-Code of Ezekiel XL-XLVIII and its Relation
to the Priestly School." *Hebrew Union College Annual* 50 (1979)
45-71.

_____. *Temples and Temple-Service in Ancient Israel: An Inquiry
into Biblical Cult Phenomena and the Historical Setting of the
Priestly School.* Oxford: Clarendon, 1978 [reprint Winona Lake:
Eisenbrauns, 1985].

Hauer, Jr., Christian E. "Who Was Zadok?" *Journal of Biblical
Literature* 82 (1963) 89-94.

Herdner, Andrée, ed. *Corpus des Tablettes en Cunéiformes
Alphabétiques Decouvertes à Ras Shamra-Ugarit de 1929 à 1939.*
2 Vols. Mission de Ras Shamra 10. Paris: Imprimerie Nationale,
1963.

Herntrich, Volkmar. *Ezechielprobleme.* Beihefte zur Zeitschrift für
die alttestamentliche Wissenschaft 61. Giessen: Alfred Töpelmann,
1933.

Herodotus, 4 Vols. Tr. A. D. Godley. Loeb Classical Library.
Cambridge: Harvard University, 1931.

_____. Tr. David Grene. Chicago: University of Chicago, 1987.

_____. Tr. Aubrey de Selincourt. Middlesex, England: Penguin
Books, 1954.

Herrmann, Johannes. *Ezechiel ubersetzt und eklärt,* Kommentar zum
Alten Testament 11. Leipzig: A. Deichert, 1924.

Himmelfarb, Martha. "From Prophecy to Apocalypse: The Book of
the Watchers and Tours of Heaven." In *Jewish Spirituality,* Vol. 1:
From the Bible through the Middle Ages, pp. 145-165, ed. Arthur
Green. World Spirituality: An Encyclopedic History of the Religious
Quest 13. N.Y.: Crossroad, 1986.

Hölscher, Gustav. *Hezekiel: der Dichter und das Buch,* Beihefte zur
Zeitschrift für die alttestamentliche Wissenschaft 39. Giessen:
Alfred Töpelmann, 1924.

Hoonacker, Albin van. "Ezekiel's Priests and Levites." *The Expository Times* 12 (1900-1) 494-98.

_____. "Les Prêtres et les Lévites dans le Livre d'Ezéchiël." *Revue Biblique* 8 (1899) 177-205.

Howie, Carl Gordon. *The Date and Composition of Ezekiel.* Journal of Biblical Literature Monograph Series 4. Philadelphia: Society of Biblical Literature, 1950.

_____. "The East Gate of Ezekiel's Temple Enclosure and the Solomonic Gateway of Megiddo." *Bulletin of the American Schools of Oriental Research* 117 [1950]: 13-19.

_____. "Ezekiel." In *Interpreter's Dictionary of the Bible*, Vol. 2, pp. 203-13. Ed. George A. Buttrick. Nashville: Abingdon, 1962.

Hurvitz, Avi. *A Linguistic Study of the Relationship between the Priestly Source and the Book of Ezekiel: A New Approach to an Old Problem.* Cahiers de la Revue Biblique 20. Paris: J. Gabalda, 1982.

Irwin, William. *The Problem of Ezekiel: An Inductive Study.* Chicago: The University of Chicago, 1943.

Jacobsen, Thorkild. *The Harps That Once... Sumerian Poetry in Translation.* New Haven and London: Yale University, 1987.

_____. *The Treasures of Darkness: A History of Mesopotamian Religion.* New Haven: Yale University, 1976.

St. Jerome. Tr. W. H. Freemantle. A Select Library of Nicene and Post-Nicene Fathers of the Christian Church 2/6. New York: The Christian Literature Company, 1893.

Josephus. 9 Vols. Tr. Henry St. John Thackeray and R. Marcus. Loeb Classical Library. Cambridge: Harvard University, 1926.

Katzenstein, H. Jacob. "Some Remarks on the Lists of the Chief Priests of the Temple of Solomon." *Journal of Biblical Literature* 81 (1962) 377-84.

Kaufman, Stephen A. "Reflections on the Assyrian-Aramaic Bilingual from Tell Fakhariyeh." *Maarav* 3/2 (1982) 137-175.

Kennett, Robert Hatch. "The Origin of the Aaronite Priesthood: A Reply." *The Journal of Theological Studies* 7 (1905-6) 620-24.

Kent, Roland G. *Old Persian.* American Oriental Series 33. New Haven: American Oriental Society, 1950.

186   The Law of the Temple

_____. "The Recently Published Old Persian Inscriptions."
Journal of the American Oriental Society 51 (1931) 189-240.

_____ "The Record of Darius's Palace at Susa." *Journal of the
American Oriental Society* 53 (1933) 1-23.

_____ "More Old Persian Inscriptions." *Journal of the American
Oriental Society* 54 (1934) 34-52.

Klein, Ralph. *Ezekiel: The Prophet and His Message.* Studies on
Personalities of the Old Testament. Columbia: University of South
Carolina, 1988.

König, Eduard. "The Priests and the Levites in Ezekiel xliv. 7-15."
The Expository Times 12 (1900-1901) 300-303.

Kuhrt, Amélie. "The Cyrus Cylinder and Achaemenid Imperial Policy."
Journal for the Study of the Old Testament 25 (1983) 83-87.

Lance, H. Darrell. "The Royal Stamps and the Kingdom of Josiah."
Harvard Theological Review 64 (1971) 315-32.

Lauterbach, Jacob. "Weights and Measures." In *The Jewish
Encyclopedia*, Vol. 12, pp. 483-90. New York: Funk and Wagnalls,
1916.

Lemke, Werner. "Ezekiel." In *Harper's Bible Dictionary*, pp. 293-94.
Ed. Paul J. Achtemeier. San Francisco: Harper and Row, 1985.

Leuze, Oscar. *Die Satrapieeinteilung in Syrien und im Zweistromlände
von 520-320.* Halle: Max Niemeyer, 1935.

Levenson, Jon D. "The Jerusalem Temple in Devotional and Visionary
Experience." In *Jewish Spirituality*, Volume 1: *From the Bible
through the Middle Ages*, pp. 32-61. Ed. Arthur Green.

_____. *Sinai and Zion: An Entry Into the Jewish Bible.* N.Y.:
Winston, 1985.

_____. "The Temple and the World." *The Journal of Religion* 64
(1984) 275-98.

_____. *Theology of the Program of Restoration of Ezekiel 40-48.*
Harvard Semitic Monographs Series 10. Missoula: Scholars, 1976.

Levine, Lee L., ed. *Ancient Synagogues Revealed.* Detroit: Wayne State
University, 1982.

Levy, Jacob. *Chaldäisches Wörterbuch über die Targumim.* Köln: Joseph Melzer, 1952.

Lichtheim, Miriam. *Ancient Egyptian Literature.* 3 Vols. Berkeley: University of California, 1973-80.

Lindbeck, George A. *The Nature of Doctrine: Religion and Theology in a Postliberal Age.* Philadelphia: The Westminster, 1984.

Lipinski, E. "Epiphanie de Baal-Haddu RS 24.245." *Ugarit-Forschungen* 3 (1971) 81-92.

Liver, Jacob. "The 'Sons of Zadok the Priest' in the Dead Sea Sect." *Revue de Qumran* 21 (1967) 3-30.

McBride, Jr., S. Dean. "Biblical Literature in its Historical Context: The Old Testament." In *Harper's Bible Commentary,* pp. 14-26. Ed. James L. Mays. San Francisco: Harper and Row, 1988.

_____. *The Deuteronomic Name Theology.* Ph. D. dissertation, Harvard University, 1969.

_____. "Jeremiah and the 'Men of ᶜAnatot.'" Paper presented to the Colloqium for Old Testament Research, Colgate-Rochester Divinity School, 23 August 1973.

_____. "The 'Law of the Temple' and the Pentateuchal Tora." Paper presented to the Chicago Society of Biblical Research, April 1981.

_____. "Polity of the Covenant People: The Book of Deuteronomy," *Interpretation* 41 (1987) 229-55.

_____. "The Polity of Ezekiel 40-48." Invited paper presented to the annual meeting of the Society of Biblical Literature, December 1983.

McCarter, P. Kyle. *I Samuel.* The Anchor Bible 8. Garden City: Doubleday, 1980.

McCown, Chester Charlton. "The ᶜAraq el-Emir and the Tobiads." *The Biblical Archaeologist* 20 (1957) 63-76.

Marsh, John. "The Book of Numbers." *Interpreter's Bible,* Vol. 2, pp. 137-310. Ed. George A. Buttrick. Nashville: Abingdon, 1953.

May, Herbert. "Ezekiel." *Interpreter's Bible,* Vol 6, pp. 41-340. Edited by George A. Buttrick. Nashville: Abingdon, 1956.

Mazar, Benjamin. "The Tobiads." *Israel Exploration Journal* 7 (1957) 137-45; 229-38.

Mendenhall, G. E. "Law and Covenant in Israel and the Ancient Near East." *The Biblical Archaeologist* 17 (1954) 26-76.

Mettinger, Tryggve N. D. *The Dethronement of Sabaoth: Studies in the Shem and Kabod Theologies.* Tr. Frederick H. Cryer. Coniectanea Biblica Old Testament Series 18. Lund: C. W. K. Gleerup, 1982.

Meyer, Eduard. *Die Entstehung des Judenthums.* Halle: Max Niemeyer, 1896.

Meyers, Carol L. *The Tabernacle Menorah.* American Schools of Oriental Research Dissertation Series 2. Missoula: Scholars, 1976.

_____. "The Temple" and "temples," In *Harper's Bible Dictionary,* pp. 1021-32. Edited by Paul J. Achtemeier.

Meyers, Eric. "The Persian Period and the Judean Restoration: From Zerubbabel to Nehemiah." In *Ancient Israelite Religion,* pp. 509-21. Ed. Patrick Miller, Paul Hanson, and S. Dean McBride, Jr. Philadelphia: Fortress, 1987.

Milgrom, Jacob. *Studies in Levitical Terminology,* Vol.1: *The Encroacher and the Levite; The Term 'Aboda.* University of California Publications, Near Eastern Studies 14. Berkeley: University of California, 1970.

Milik, J'ozef Tadeusz. "Nouvelles Inscriptions Sémitiques et Grecques du Pays de Moab." *Liber Annus* 9 (1958-59) 330-58.

Millard, A. R. and Bordreuil, P. "A Statue from Syria with Assyrian and Aramaic Inscriptions." *Biblical Archaeologist* 45 (1982) 135-41.

Miller, J. Maxwell and Hayes, John H. *A History of Ancient Israel and Judah.* Philadelphia: Westminster, 1986.

The Mishnah. Tr. Herbert Danby. London: Oxford University, 1967.

The Mishnah: A New Translation. Tr. Jacob Neusner. New Haven: Yale University, 1988.

Moor, Johannes de. *The Seasonal Pattern in the Ugaritic Myth of Ba^clu According to the Version of Ilmilku.* Alter Orient und Altes Testament 16. Neukirchen-Vluyn: Neukirchener, 1971.

Morenz, Siegfried. *Egyptian Religion.* Tr. Ann E. Keep. Ithaca: Cornell University, 1973.

Müller, Carl, ed. *Geographi Graeci Minores.* 2 Vols. Paris: Ambrosio Firmin Didot, 1861-82.

Na'aman, Nadar. "Hezekiah's Fortified Cities and the LMLK Stamps." *Bulletin of the American Schools of Oriental Research* 261 (1986) 3-21.

Neiman, David. "*PGR*: A Canaanite Cult-Object in the Old Testament." *Journal of Biblical Literature* 67 (1948) 55-60.

Nelson, Harold H. "The Egyptian Temple, with Particular Reference to the Theban Temples of the Empire Period." In *The Biblical Archaeologist Reader*, Vol. 1, pp. 147-58. Ed. G. Ernest Wright and David Noel Freedman.

Niditch, Susan. "Ezekiel 40-48 in a Visionary Context." *Catholic Biblical Quarterly* 48 (1986) 208-24.

Noth, Martin. *The History of Israel.* Tr. P. R. Ackroyd. London: Adam and Charles Black, ²1960.

_____. "Studien zu den historisches-geographischen Dokumenten des Josuabuches," *Zeitschrift des Deutschen Palästina-Vereins* 58 (1935) 185-255.

O'Brien, Julia M. *Priest and Levite in Malachi.* Society of Biblical Literature Dissertation Series 121. Atlanta: Scholars, 1990.

Oded, Bustenay. "Judah and the Exile." In *Israelite and Judean History*, pp. 435-88. Ed. John H. Hayes and J. Maxwell Miller. Philadelphia: Westminster, 1977.

Odell, Margaret. "Be Ashamed When I Forgive You: The Restoration of Honor in Ezekiel." Paper presented to the annual meeting of the Society of Biblical Literature, November 1990.

Olmstead, Albert Ten Eyck. *History of the Persian Empire.* Chicago: University of Chicago, 1948 [reprint Phoenix Books, 1959].

_____. "Tattenai, Governor of 'Across the River.'" *Journal of Near Eastern Studies* 3 (1944) 46.

Olyan, Saul M. "Ben Sira's Relationship to the Priesthood." *Harvard Theological Review* 80 (1987) 261-86.

Oppenheim, A. Leo. "The Mesopotamian Temple." In *The Biblical Archaeologist Reader*, Vol. 1, pp. 147-58. Ed. G. Ernest Wright and David Noel Freedman.

Paul, Shalom M. *Studies in the Book of the Covenant in the Light of Cuneiform and Biblical Law.* Supplements to Vetus Testamentum 18. Leiden: E. J. Brill, 1970.

Petit, Thierry. "L'évolution sémantique des termes hébreux et araméens *pḥh* et *sgn* et accadiens *pāḫatu* et *šaknu.*" *Journal of Biblical Literature* 107 (1988) 53-67.

Pritchard, James B., ed. *The Harper's Atlas of the Bible.* New York: Harper and Row, 1987.

Procksch, D. Otto. "Fürst und Priester bei Hesekiel." *Zeitschrift für alttestimentliche Wissenschaft* 58 (1940-41) 99-133.

Rabinowitz, Isaac. "Aramaic Inscriptions of the Fifth Century B.C.E. from a North-Arab Shrine in Egypt." *Journal of Near Eastern Studies* 15 (1956) 1-9.

Rad, Gerhard von. *Deuteronomy.* Tr. Dorothea Barton. Philadelphia: Westminster, 1966.

_____. *Studies In Deuteronomy.* Tr. David Stalker. London: SCM, 1953.

Rainey, Anson Frank. "The Satrapy 'Beyond the River.'" *The Australian Journal of Biblical Archaeology* 1 (1969) 51-78.

Rivkin, Ellis. "The Story of Korah's Rebellion: Key to the Formation of the Pentateuch." In *Society of Biblical Literature 1988 Seminar Papers*, pp. 574-81. Society of Biblical Literature Seminar Papers Series 27. Atlanta: Scholars, 1988.

Rowley, Harold Henry. "The Book of Ezekiel in Modern Study." *Bulletin of the John Rylands Library* 36 (1953) 146-90.

_____. "Zadok and Nehushtan." *Journal of Biblical Literature* 58 [1939]: 113-41.

Sæbø, Magne. "Grenzbeschreibung und Landideal im Alten Testament Mit besonderer Berücksichtigung der *min-ᶜad*-Formel." *Zeitschrift des Deutschen Palästina-Vereins* 90 (1974) 14-37.

Sauer, James. "Transjordan in the Bronze and Iron Ages: A Critique of Glueck's Analysis." *Bulletin of the American Schools of Oriental Research* 263 (1986) 1-26.

Schiffman, Lawrence H. "Priests." In *Harper's Bible Dictionary*, pp. 821-23. Edited by Paul J. Achtemeier.

Schmidt, Erich H. *The Treasury of Persepolis and other Discoveries in the Homeland of the Achaemenians.* Chicago Oriental Institute Communications 21. Chicago: University of Chicago, 1939.

Scott, R. B. Y. "Isaiah, 1-39." *Interpreter's Bible*, Vol 5, pp. 151-380. Ed. George A. Buttrick. Nashville: Abingdon, 1956.

Seitz, Gottfried. *Redaktionsgeschichtliche Studien zum Deuteronomium.* Stuttgart: W. Kohlhammer, 1971.

Septuaginta. Ed. Alfred Rahlfs. Stuttgart: Deutsche Bibelgesellschaft, 1979.

Smend, Rudolf. *Der Prophet Ezechiel.* Kurzgefasstes exegetisches Handbuch. Leipzig: S. Hirzel, 1880.

Smith, Jonathan Z. *Map Is Not Territory: Studies in the History of Religions.* Studies in Judaism in Late Antiquity 23. Leiden: E. J. Brill, 1978.

Smith, Mark. "The Near Eastern Background of Solar Language for Yahweh." *Journal of Biblical Literature* 109 (1990) 29-39.

Smith, Morton. "II Isaiah and the Persians." *Journal of the American Oriental Society* 83 (1963) 415-21.

Snaith, Norman Henry. *Leviticus and Numbers.* New Century Bible. Greenwood: Attic, 1971.

Speiser, Ephraim Avigdor. "Background and Function of the Biblical nāśî." *Catholic Biblical Quarterly* 25 (1963) 111-17

Sperber, Alexander. *The Bible in Aramaic*, Vol. 3: *The Latter Prophets According to Targum Jonathan.* Leiden: E. J. Brill, 1962.

Sperling, David. "Israel's Religion in the Ancient Near East." In *Jewish Spirituality*, Volume 1: *From the Bible through the Middle Ages*, pp. 5-31. Edited by Arthur Green.

192   The Law of the Temple

Spiegelberg, Wilhelm. *Die sogenannte demotische Chronik des Pap. 215 der Bibliotheque Nationale zu Paris, nebst den auf der Ruckseite des Papyrus stehenden Texten.* Demotische Studien 7. Leipzig, 1914.

Stern, Ephraim. *Material Culture of the Land of the Bible in the Persian Period 538-332 B.C.* Warminster, England: Aris and Phillips, 1982.

_____. "The Persian Empire and the Political and Social History of Palestine in the Persian Period." In *The Cambridge History of Judaism*, Vol. 1, pp. 70-87.

The Geography of Strabo. 8 Vols. Tr. Horace Leonard Jones. Loeb Classical Library. Cambridge: Harvard University, 1942.

Talmon, Shemaryahu. "The Cult and Calendar Reform of Jeroboam I." In *King, Cult and Calendar in Ancient Israel*, pp. 68-78. Jerusalem: Magnes, 1986.

Talmon, Shemaryahu; Fishbane, Michael. "The Structuring of Biblical Books: Studies in the Book of Ezekiel." *Annual of the Swedish Theological Institute in Jerusalem* 10 (1976) 127-53.

Targum of Ezekiel. Tr. Samson Levey. The Aramaic Bible 13. Wilmington: Michael Glazier, 1987.

Tkacik, Arnold. "Ezekiel." In *Jerome Biblical Commentary*, pp. 345-65. Ed. Raymond Brown, Joseph Fitzmeyer, and Roland Murphy. Englewood Cliffs: Prentice-Hall, 1968.

Teixidor, Javier. *The Pagan God: Popular Religion in the Greco-Roman Near East.* Princeton: Princeton University, 1977.

Terrien, Samuel. *The Elusive Presence.* Religious Perspectives 26. San Francisco: Harper and Row, 1978.

Torrey, Charles Cutler. *Pseudo-Ezekiel and the Original Prophecy.* New Haven: Yale University, 1930 [reprint, The Library of Biblical Studies. New York: Ktav, 1970].

Tuell, Steven. "The Temple Vision of Ezekiel 40-48: A Program for Restoration?" *Proceedings of the Eastern Great Lakes Biblical Society* 2 (1982) 96-103.

Tushingham, A. Douglas. "A Royal Israelite Seal (?) and the Royal Jar Handle Stamps." *Bulletin of the American Schools of Oriental Research* 200 (1970) 71-78 and 201 (1971) 23-35.

Vaux, Roland de. *The Bible and the Ancient Near East.* Tr. Damian McHugh. London: Darton, Longman and Todd, 1972.

Virolleaud, Charles, ed. *Le Palais Royal d'Ugarit.* Mission de Ras Shamra 11. Vol. 5: *Textes en Cunéiformes Alphabétiques des Archives Sud, Sud-ouest et du Petit Palais.* Paris: Imprimerie Nationale, 1965.

_____. *Ugaritica 5.* Mission de Ras Shamra 16. Paris: Imprimerie National, 1968.

Weinfeld, Moshe. "The Covenant of Grant in the Old Testament and in the Ancient Near East." *Journal of the American Oriental Society* 90 (1970) 184-203.

_____. *Deuteronomy and the Deuteronomic School.* Oxford: Clarendon, 1972.

Weissbach, Franz Heinrich. *Die Keilinschriften der Achämeniden.* Vorderäsiatische Bibliothek 3. Leipzig: J. C. Hindrichs, 1911.

Welch, Adam. *The Code of Deuteronomy: A New Theory of Its Origin.* London: James Clarke, 1924.

Wellhausen, Julius. *Prolegomena to the History of Ancient Israel.* Edinburgh: Black, 1885 [reprint New York: Meridian Books, 1957].

Westermann, Claus. *Basic Forms of Prophetic Speech.* Tr. Hugh Clayton White. Philadelphia: Westminster, 1967.

Wevers, John W. *Ezekiel.* New Century Bible. Greenwood: Attic, 1969.

Widengren, Geo. "The Persian Period." In *Israelite and Judean History,* pp. 489-538. Ed. John H. Hayes and J. Maxwell Miller.

Wildberger, Hans. *Jesaja.* 3 Vols. Biblische Kommentar Altes Testament 10. Neukirchen-Vluyn: Neukirchener, 1982.

Williams, Ronald. *Hebrew Syntax: An Outline.* Toronto: University of Toronto, [2]1976.

Wilson, Robert R. "Ezekiel." In *Harper's Bible Commentary,* pp. 652-694. Ed. James L. Mays.

_____. *Prophecy and Society in Ancient Israel.* Philadelphia: Fortress, 1980.

_____. "Prophecy in Crisis: The Call of Ezekiel." *Interpretation*
38 (1984) 117-30.

Wright, David P. "Deuteronomy 21:1-9 as a Rite of Elimination."
Catholic Biblical Quarterly 49 (1987) 387-403.

Wright, G. Ernest. "Deuteronomy." In *The Interpreter's Bible*, Vol. 2,
pp. 311-540. Ed. George A. Buttrick. Nashville: Abingdon, 1953.

_____. "The Levites in Deuteronomy." *Vetus Testamentum* 4
(1954) 325-30.

_____. "The Temple in Palestine-Syria." In *The Biblical
Archaeologist Reader*, Vol. 1, pp. 169-84. Edited by G. Ernest
Wright and David Noel Freedman.

Zimmerli, Walther. *Ezekiel*. 2 Vols. Tr. Ronald E. Clements (Vol. 1);
James E. Martin (Vol. 2). Heremeneia. Philadelphia: Fortress,
1979-83.

_____. "Ezekiel." In *Interpreter's Dictionary of the Bible:
Supplementary Volume*, pp. 314-17. Ed. Keith Crim. Nashville:
Abingdon, 1976.

_____. "The Message of Ezekiel." Tr. Mrs. Lewis Wilkins and
James Martin. *Interpretation* 23 (1969) 131-57.